MARKETING FEAR IN AMERICA'S PUBLIC SCHOOLS

The Real War on Literacy

MARKETING FEAR IN AMERICA'S PUBLIC SCHOOLS

The Real War on Literacy

Edited by

Leslie Poynor
University of Connecticut

Paula M. Wolfe
University of Wisconsin–Madison

LEA LAWRENCE ERLBAUM ASSOCIATES, PUBLISHERS
2005 Mahwah, New Jersey   London

Lawrence Erlbaum Associates, Inc., Publishers
10 Industrial Avenue
Mahwah, New Jersey 07430

Cover design by Kathryn Houghtaling Lacey

Library of Congress Cataloging-in-Publication Data

Marketing fear in America's public schools / edited by Leslie Poynor and Paula Wolfe.
   p. cm.
  Includes bibliographical references and index.
  ISBN 0-8058-4703-0 (cloth : alk. paper) — ISBN 0-8058-4704-9 (pbk. : alk. paper)
  1. Education and state—United States. 2. Politics and education—United States.
3. Conservatism—United States. 4. Mass media and education—United States.
I. Poynor, Leslie. II. Wolfe, Paula M.

LC89.M225 2004
379.73—dc22
                                           2004050672
                                                 CIP

Books published by Lawrence Erlbaum Associates are printed on acid-free paper,
and their bindings are chosen for strength and durability.

Printed in the United States of America
10 9 8 7 6 5 4 3 2 1

Contents

Preface

The chapters in this book can be described in the four following ways:

1. Chapters on resistance to the conservative agenda;
2. Chapters describing national and/or federal agendas and actions that directly or indirectly contribute to the privatization and corporate control of public education;
3. Chapters linking federal policy to the disappearance of or promotion of particular philosophical and pedagogical approaches to learning;
4. Chapters describing the role of the media in perpetuating the agendas of the corporate and political right.

We begin and end this book with chapters on resistance to the agendas of the corporate and political right. In chapter two, Carole Edelsky provocatively outlines both the problem of and the resistance to the marketing of fear being perpetuated by the corporate and political right. She uncovers how teachers known for their critical, holistic practice are dealing with the current context—a context that she characterizes as the "new McCarthyism." She illuminates how as with the original McCarthyism, this new version too includes witch hunts, blacklists, secrecy, spying, strong curbs on dissent, the loss of constitutionally designed checks and balances, and the key roles played by and favoring corporate interests. Edelsky interviews teachers who see themselves and are seen by others as critical holistic teachers to ask them variations on this question: How have they accommodated, resisted, ignored, and given in to these assaults on their professional autonomy and on education for democracy? This chapter serves as both an introduction and overview of how the climate of fear is created and how it is being resisted.

Once Edelsky has set the stage for us we move into the first section of the book, which begins to examining the players in this game of fear. This section provides a comprehensive look at how recent corporate and government interests have used fear in their efforts to dismantle public education through their initial attacks and subsequent control over pedagogy and testing. Each chapter makes the case that this fear is being used to enact an agenda that disempowers teachers, schools, parents and children.

In this section, Bess Altwerger offers a who's who list of players and a time line of when and how they have been working together to take control of public education away from local constituents and to place it in the hands of corporations. Her provocative chronology provides a historical and political framework for understanding the chapters that follow. Many of these factions/organizations are discussed in depth in the next two sections of the book.

Following on the heels of Altwerger's chapter, Sharon Matthews continues the examination of who the players are and who the players are *not*. In particular, she describes how the power to define and describe reading was handed over from reading experts to special educators highlighting the congruence between special education, the medical model of research, and the political and economic agenda of the players. Then, in chapter five, neurologist Steven Strauss describes the misuse of the medical model of research by the NICHD to support federal policy and the privatization movement. In particular he unravels how this model is misunderstood, misused, and misguided when applied to reading education. Strauss discusses the real motive behind such a model of science—to create a sense of objectivity and reliability that can be used to promote overtly political agendas—and he describes the stress, anxiety, and physical illness that children and families feel as a result of those political agendas.

Once we learn who the major players are, in section two we turn to how their influence has determined philosophical and pedagogical practices in the classroom. In chapter six, Joanne Yatvin describes how the members of the National Reading Panel were able to make 40 years of scientific research and educational practice disappear. In the opposite direction, Connie Weaver and Ellen Brinkley write about the resurgence of phonics as a pedagogical strategy through support from the Religious Right. Weaver and Brinkley describe how the Religious Right has marketed fear by plying on parents' worries that their children's public school experience will lead them away from God. They describe the feat tactics the Religious Right has used with parents and teachers and explain how those tactics and messages disempower public school educators. The authors also suggest helpful strategies to help diminish parents' worries and to defuse the Religious Right's education agenda.

The final chapter in this section is Kyle Shanton and Teresa Valenzuela's disturbing look at the scripted program, Success for All (SFA). Shanton and Valenzuela draw on the stories of a parent, child, and teacher to expose the very real, clandestine politics and intimidation efforts that have been used by the SFA enterprise. The authors show how the program's creator, Robert Slavin, has used political means to promote the current federal agenda and lay claim to the control of teachers' practice of literacy education. Through narrative inquiry, those impacted by the program: teachers, students, and parents now have the opportunity to tell their stories, which otherwise have been silenced from public dialogue. This chapter exposes the war waged on parents, children, and teachers who have attempted to construct teaching and learning as the practice of freedom with a SFA school. It unmistakably reveals the politics of intimidation to sustain this war.

The chapters in section three function to broaden the focus of the book from dealing with issues within the community of "literacy" and illustrate the wide-ranging effects of creating fear and disempowering teachers. These two chapters do not focus strictly on literacy, but rather take a wider lens on the media's role in promoting the conservative and corporate agenda.

In chapter nine, Eric Haas describes the sophisticated Web sites, books, surveys, research papers, and opinion papers of conservative think tanks that are fashioned in a media-friendly manner to ensure the wide dissemination of the conservative agenda. Further, this chapter focuses on how the think tank's low cost sources of "expert" or "expert-sounding" information work to promote a common acceptance of a particular education agenda and to promote policies that create an atmosphere of fear of reprisals in local school constituents through the national media's complicit use and promotion of conservative think tank ideologies and agendas.

Likewise, Chris Faltis and Cathy Coulter's chapter examines the media's role in perpetuating antibilingual and anti-immigrant sentiment through disinformation. Faltis and Coulter discuss the recent successes by wealthy and powerful interests to dismantle bilingual education through well-planned and organized dissemination of questionable information about the value of teaching and learning in languages other than English. They present an in-depth analysis, relying on primary data from newspapers and other sources, which argues that the media disinformation campaign regarding bilingual education was successful because it was supported by concurrent negative campaigns regarding issues of immigration. Both campaigns relied on creating fear toward immigrants and minorities.

Finally, we bring the book full circle by ending with another story of resistance. In the chapter by Rick Meyer and his colleagues, we learn about how teacher educators engaged in acts of resistance through nonviolent civil disobedience during G. Reid Lyon's visit to New Mexico. Lastly, the concluding chapter describes the existing local, state, and national organizations engaged in resisting, fighting, and changing the educational policies driven by the corporate and political right. These organizations offer strategies for teachers and teacher educators to resist federal mandates. These strategies range from blatant protests to subversive practices that can help educators resist the marketing of fear. Because all of these organizations are online, this entire chapter is also accessible at the following Web site: http://www.erlbaum.com/poynor. It is our hope that our readers will investigate these organizations for themselves.

FINAL THOUGHTS

We intend this book to be a message of hope. Although we make the case that there is a decidedly ugly motive behind "No Child Left Behind," we also believe that to triumph, one must understand what is truly happening. However, we are not asking our readers to accept our word regarding the motives of the current educational "reforms." Rather, we ask you to look at the actions rather than the words. In the chapters contained in this book we offer a series of provocative and eye-opening examinations of the real world consequences of the seemingly positive statements like, "increased accountability." We hope that you will judge the words, "no child left behind" not by what they say but by their effects on the real lives of children and teachers. We envision this book to be a voice for an alternative to compliance with unreasonable mandates. At the least it is our hope that this book can be a small voice of truth in the overwhelming onslaught of corporate and media distortions about education.

ACKNOWLEDGMENTS

This book began as a response to Bess Altweger's Key Note Address to the Whole Day of Whole Language at 2001 Annual Meeting of National Council of Teachers of English. We (Paula Wolfe and Leslie Poynor) are indebted to Bess for her inspiring speech and cornerstone chapter in this volume as well as to all of our contributing authors who willingly and cheerfully made their revisions in a timely and professional manner. We are also grateful for the prompt and insightful reviews by Gerald Coles (full-time writer) Prisca Martens, Towson University; Debra Goodman, Hofstra University; and Mary Harmon, Saginaw Valley State University, whose comments only served to strengthen this book. And finally, we are thankful for our editor Naomi Silverman, whose unwavering support and expertise in editing made this book possible. We dedicate this book to our friends and family who have never wavered in their support of our efforts and to all public school children in America.

—Leslie Poynor
Paula Wolfe

CHAPTER ONE

Introduction

Paula Wolfe
Leslie Poynor

People respond to fear, not love.

—Richard Nixon

As reading professors, it is not surprising that our vision for this book began with our concern over the national trend toward standardizing reading curriculum. We knew, as former teachers, that no one program or curriculum can ever serve the needs of diverse and particular students. But as we came to learn and experience more of the tactics and policies of state and federal government officials regarding reading instruction the book began to take on a different face. We experienced disdain, insults, even outright intimidation when we tried to criticize current research and policy in our own state of New Mexico. We started to hear more and more teachers unwilling to voice negative opinions about scripted reading programs and standardized tests. "I'm afraid to say anything," they would claim. Why, we wondered, the heavy-handed tactics? Why the intimidation? Why the forecasts of doom if the federal agenda is not implemented?

In this introductory chapter on education research and policy we take you into the hidden agenda of the corporate and political right in the United States. We look at how and why public opinion and educational policy are manipulated beginning with an examination of fear as a marketing tool to divert the thinking public and then we investigate the underlying agenda.

SELLING "SCIENTIFICALLY BASED
READING INSTRUCTION" AND
THE NO CHILD LEFT BEHIND ACT

Several recent books and articles do an excellent job of disputing the current claims being made by the No Child Left Behind act and its supporting documents, such as the National Reading Panel (NRP) report (see Allington, 2002; Coles, 2003; Garan, 2001). This book serves a different purpose. This book is not about disputing claims or disputing scientifically based reading instruction (although we certainly dispute both). Rather we are concerned with exploring how these claims have been "sold" to the public and the purposes behind this selling.

Two decades ago the report, *A Nation At Risk* (1983) argued that America's global economic performance is not only a result of trade or monetary policy but is directly impacted by the so-called poor "standardized test performance of children aged five to eighteen" (Bracey, 2002, p. 7). It further claimed that schools were failing, in fact failing miserably, to educate the future workforce. As Bracey (2002) points out, when the economy was booming, no one stopped to offer thanks to the schools. Rather, the pervasive view in the general public seemed to be that schools were still failing although there were thoughtful analyses and real evidence to dispute this.

Currently more U.S. high school graduates are attending colleges and universities than in any previous decade (Allington, 2002; Berliner & Biddle, 1995). SAT scores have actually risen over the last decade (Coles, 2003). NAEP data shows fourth grade reading achievement has been going up over the last few years (Allington, 2002). In fact, in the early 1990s reading performance of American fourth graders ranked second in the world (Elley, 1992). And yet, the public perception still seems to be that there is a crisis in our schools that puts our "nation at risk."

Why is this belief so persistent? The answer is complex, of course, but in this book we argue that a major factor is marketing. How can anyone be convinced of the need for school reform efforts if schools are actually doing okay? How can a scripted reading program and standardized tests be sold? First people need to believe that all other programs are failing. They must be forced to understand the issue in only one way, regardless of the facts. The question then becomes, how exactly does this happen?

Manipulating Public Opinion

We begin our investigation with the publication of the Nation at Risk document. Although the document has been widely disputed (Bracey, 2002) it did its job—to decry the failure of U.S. public schools and convince most of the general public that it represented the "truth." How is it possible to do this, and furthermore, to keep people from knowing they are being manipulated?

As Altwerger (chap. 3, this volume), Matthews (chap. 4, this volume), and Yatvin (chap. 6, this volume) show, the easiest way to do this is for those in control to set forth what they want the public to believe and then to go about presenting evidence to support these beliefs. President G. W. Bush's reading czar, G. Reid Lyon, now head of the National Institute of Child Health and Development (NICHD), has been a leader in amassing "scientific proof" that supports a skills-oriented view of reading. Initially in 1998, the NICHD, co-funded a report, "Preventing Reading Difficulties in Young Children" (Snow, Burns, & Griffin) that they hoped would provide them with such evidence. However, when the report was finished it argued instead that teachers should have the freedom to determine what skills students needed to be taught and in what order. So, following quickly on the heels of this report, NICHD sponsored the "National Reading Panel" at the "request" of Congress. It is perhaps not surprising that all but one of the Panel's members had expressed an overt belief in skills-oriented teaching (Yatvin, this volume). Yatvin, as the only dissenting voice on the National Reading Panel, shows in her chapter that the panel, without her consent, agreed to review only one perspective of the reading process based on the skills approach. All research from other perspectives, she shows, simply "disappeared." Perhaps it is not surprising then that Lyon's own biases were confirmed by this report.

But, one might argue, "What about Science! The NRP report was based on science, how can you dispute that?" We certainly do not deny the value (albeit, in our opinion, limited value) of well-designed and well-executed quasi-experimental studies. However, we do argue, along with Strauss (chap. 5, this volume) that the NRP's report does not rely on well designed models but on mischaracterizations of the medical model of scientific research. It is also important to understand that in most instances the NRP report that was shared with the general public was, as Strauss documents, actually based on the "Executive Summary" not the full report. The Executive Summary both misrepresented the findings of the NRP and exaggerated the data from the studies it had used in its meta-analysis (Camilli, Vargas, & Yarecko, 2003).

Immediately after the report's release, the media picked up on the executive summary and gave it wide national reporting—reporting that served to fan the flames of public fears about our "failing" public schools. Glassner (2000) tells us that when fear is used as a marketing tool it is often based on media reports of overstated and misrepresented statistics. One media source will cite from another (Goodman, 1998) and so misrepresentations are reported so often that they become the public "truth."

For example, Faltis and Coulter (chap. 10, this volume) lay out exactly how a public truth is created by providing concrete examples of how media reports are manipulated to support a particular political agenda.

Let's also take look at one example from the NRP. Although the NRP made strong claims for the effectiveness of phonemic awareness (PA) training, the studies they used did not seem to support this. So how did this claim get supported? The members of the panel were able to support their claim by overstating the value of PA while dismissing anything that did not fit with this skills-oriented view of reading. Coles (2003) explored one key study in the PA section of the NRP and argued that instead of finding that PA was effective it, in fact, had little transferability to word reading and spelling:

> At the end of the school year, the researcher found that the training group did significantly better on phonemic awareness tests. However, they also found "no significant differences between the [skills training and as-needed teaching] groups on the tests that matter the most, those of word reading and spelling." This finding the report does not mention. The researchers observed that "the significantly superior scores achieved by the training group in this study on tasks of phonemic awareness suggest that this group should also achieve higher scores on the reading tasks, but his was not in fact the case." These conclusions too are not quoted in the report. (p. 58)

This is certainly not an isolated example. In this book we argue, and provide documentation, that much of the NRP's representations of the data is highly suspect. Evidence seems to have been manipulated and ignored to suit the agenda of the Panel. These distortions were then widely reported across the nation (Allington, 2002).

Assigning Blame

The public has been manipulated to believe that the NRP findings are the only truth, but it also has to be convinced that anyone who does not accept this "truth" is someone to be feared. Who are the people to fear in this scenario? Mainly, they are learner-centered and whole language researchers and teachers, parents, teachers, and policy makers who do not support a skills-only and standardized testing approach to reading instruction, and colleges of education. Edelsky (this volume) lays out how this witch hunt, this New McCarthyism casts some educational researchers as dangerous, self-serving traitors. She offers powerful examples of teachers and researchers who have been publicly ridiculed and "blacklisted." Faltis and Coulter (this volume) outline how the media participated in silencing bilingual education researchers in the debate in California. Shanton and

Valenzuela (chap. 8, this volume) provide powerful narratives of how silencing and intimidation operate to maintain one school's dependence on a scripted program, Success for All. Teachers have been and are being threatened and removed from their jobs. University faculty are being blacklisted. And in a recent speech to the Coalition for Evidenced Based Policy, G. Reid Lyon made the shocking statement that if he had one piece of legislation he could pass it would be to "blow up colleges of education" (Lyon, 2002).

Why the hostility and intimidation? Why the silencing and threats? If one intends to stop the public from questioning the true motives behind the focus on skills-based instruction, then one must demonize the enemy. If people are made to feel afraid or ignorant of what is deemed wrong and unacceptable by those in power, then most will accept what they are told is "right" and "true" and shun the "enemy."

WHY MANIPULATE PUBLIC OPINION?

The argument in this book is that the short answer is money. And, the long answer is money, both the money that corporations stand to make off their scripted, supposedly scientifically-based, prepackaged programs and the money schools stand to lose in terms of decreased federal funding if they do not use such programs. Education is the last major public institution in the United States that is not primarily in the hands of corporate control. Public education represents a multibillion dollar opportunity to private enterprise. By creating the myth of failure of teachers and colleges of education, the political, conservative, and corporate right can then, of course, institute privatization (Bracey, 2002).

By instituting highly scripted programs, the need for qualified, thinking teachers is eliminated. By replacing qualified teachers with alternatively licensed teachers the teacher unions can be dismantled. Colleges of education are no longer needed to train alternative licensure candidates. Rather, short courses can be offered by private universities. In this way, some "teachers" only receive 3 weeks of training before they are placed in classrooms! In order to "assist" these minimally trained teachers, school districts are and will adopt highly scripted programs that ask little more from the "teacher" than reading from a script produced by a publishing company. This produces teachers who are no longer highly educated, prepared, thinking professionals, but rather like assembly line workers who are "policed" by administrators. When the schools then "fail" for-profit alternative schools will come to the rescue.

If I Only Had a Brain

The Scarecrow in *The Wizard of Oz* really believed he needed a brain. It turned out that he did not; he had what he needed all along. But how was he convinced that he had to see the Wizard? The *need* for the Wizard had to be created in his mind. Corporations have long known that need based on fear is an effective marketing tool. How, for example, can people be convinced that they need antibacterial soaps if first a fear of germs is not created? Or how can women be convinced to use pharmaceuticals to prevent osteoporosis? In 1998, Drs. Arminee Kazanjan, Carolyn Green, and Ken Bassett, from the University of British Columbia argued that drug companies are using fear as a tool to convince women that medications are the only way to preserve bone health during menopause, although there is much evidence to the contrary. They argue that the increased marketing regarding women's health issues, including bone health, are driven by economic interests rather than by scientific evidence. By projecting a possible negative future outcome, companies create need where no real need exists.

This is a strategy that the conservative, religious, and political right has learned well from the marketplace. Fear, as a marketing tool, diverts the public's attention away from the actions of the agenda to privatize public education for the benefit of a few corporations.

How is this happening? The rhetoric of concern for children such as, "no child left behind," "higher scores," and "international competition" is one tactic. On the surface these all seem like good ideas—but what is the real agenda? Who really benefits? By claiming that the current school system is failing, the federal government can effectively take over local control of schools by instituting high stakes testing in the name of accountability for receiving federal funding. The government sets standards that cannot be met. The blame for "failure" is then placed on either the students who are expelled from school (as in the case of 522 students expelled from Birmingham City Schools just prior to the administration of a standardized test), or the teachers who are driven out of the profession. For example, in a recent study of high stakes testing in Texas, Flores and Clarke (2003) write:

> Preservice and inservice teachers acknowledge that assessment is an important part of the teaching-learning cycle; however, they feel that high-stakes tests result in a test-driven curriculum . . . focusing on high-stakes testing results in incidental outcomes such as a narrowing of the curriculum, teaching to the test, and teacher flight from public schools as well as from the profession in general. (Findings and Discussion, para. 4)

The rhetoric of concern for children in supposedly failing schools has a powerful impact on how the general public sees teachers. Wayne Johnson, president of the California Teachers Association, argues that what has been created is, "a passionate distrust of the people in our profession, a distrust that more than borders on contempt" (Johnson, 2002, p. 4). There is so much ill feeling toward teachers, who resist the imposed mandates and who are again and again represented as not doing their jobs that many of these teachers have given up fighting the mandates. Some teachers are fearful of retribution for discussing their unhappiness; others feel things have gotten so bad that they no longer care (p. 9).

Why is the general public so likely to believe the fear mongering? "From a psychological point of view extreme fear and outrage are often projections" (Glassner, 2000, p. xxvi). At some level, Glassner argues, the real problems—poverty, inequitable division of resources—are understood. These problems, however, seem too big to deal with, and no corporations would have the public dwell on them for too long. So, it is easier to shift the blame—say it is schools (rather than inequitable funding strategies, for example) that are failing. And thus, a need is created that can only be filled by corporate America.

WHO IS BEHIND THE CURTAIN?

Haas (chap. 9, this volume) and Brinkley and Weaver (chap. 7, this volume) present compelling arguments that the conservative and religious right are powerful influences behind the G. W. Bush administration's education agenda. These authors clearly show who is pulling the strings and that these string pullers have powerful allies. There is ample evidence that the full force of the federal government is being used to support corporate agendas. As Coles (2003) argues, "The Bush approach provides education-on-the-cheap while enhancing the profits of publishers like McGraw-Hill, the major producer of packaged programs" (p. 119).

The federal government, through the Reading First portion of the No Child Left Behind Act, has made sure that scripted programs get into schools. They are not simply trusting that local states and local school districts implement these programs. In the *New York Times* Schemo (2002, January 9) quotes former assistant secretary of education Susan Neuman as saying,

> The Department of Education will send education officials around the country guides that will "carefully content analyze all core reading programs to see whether or not they are scientifically based," on the National Reading Panel's findings. Poor school districts that do not use a standardized reading curriculum "would have to provide evidence they [their materials] work," she said, adding, "I suggest they purchase a core reading program."

It seems clear however, that not all scripted programs are created equal. Some corporate programs get supported and some do not. For example, G. Reid Lyon recently turned down New York City's Reading First grant application because the phonics program they had chosen did not have, as he claims, sufficient "scientific" backing.

Open Court is one of the programs that came highly recommended by the Reading First review board (based on what appears to be questionable statistical evidence). Open Court is a highly scripted reading program that is produced by publishing giant McGraw-Hill. It is perhaps not surprising that McGraw-Hill has had a direct impact on the push for scripted programs nationwide and that Harold McGraw III, chairman and chief executive of the company, was a board member of the Barbara Bush Foundation for Family Literacy. In 2002, McGraw-Hill gave Secretary of Education Rod Paige the $25,000 Prize in Education (Coles, 2003). McGraw-Hill was also the only educational publisher who saw its profits rise during the recent economic downturn of 2000 (Garan, 2001).

It might seem impossible to resist the considerable power of corporations and the federal government. But, as with corporate marketing, it is true that one can only be sold to if one believes there is a need to buy. We believe that information can be a powerful tool in resisting the manipulations of marketing. Meyers and his coauthors (this volume) show us both how dangerous information is to the fear mongers and how we can use information to resist "buying" what we are being sold. We hope that this book can provide at least some of that information.

REFERENCES

A Nation at Risk: The imperative for educational reform. (1983, April). A report to the Nation and the Secretary of Education. United States Department of Education by the National Commission on Excellence in Education.

Allington, R. (Ed.). (2002). *Big brother and the National Reading Curriculum: How ideology trumped evidence*. Portsmouth, NH: Heinemann.

Berliner, D., & Biddle, B. (1995). *The manufactured crisis*. Reading, MA: Addison Wesley Longman.

Bracey, G. (2002). *The war against America's public schools: Privatizing schools, commercializing education*. Boston, MA: Allyn & Bacon.

Coles, G. (2003). *Reading the naked truth: Literacy, legislation and lies*. Portsmouth, NH: Heinemann.

Camilli, G., Vargas, S., & Yurecko, M. (2003, May 8). Teaching children to read: The fragile link between science and federal policy. *Education Policy Analysis Archives, 11*(15). Retrieved August 2003, from http://epaa.asu.edu/epaa/vlln15/

Elley, W. B. (1992). *How in the world do students read? IEA study of reading literacy*. The Hague, Netherlands: International Association for the Evaluation of Educational Achievement.

Ennico, C. (2002). Marketing via the "Fear Factor." *Entrepreneur.com*. Retrieved August 12, 2002, from http://www.entrepreneur.com/Your_Business/YB_SegArticle/0,4621,302409, 00.html.

Flores, B. B., & Clark, E. R. (2003). Texas voices speak out about high-stakes testing: Preservice teachers, teachers, and students. *Current Issues in Education*, 6(3). Retrieved March 3, 2003, from http://cie.ed.asu.edu/volume6/number3/

Garan, E. (2001). *Resisting reading mandates: How to triumph with the truth*. Portsmouth, NH: Heinemann.

Glassner, B. (2000). *The culture of fear: Why Americans are afraid of the wrong things*. New York: Basic Books.

Goodman, K. (1998). *In defense of good teaching: What teachers need to know about the "Reading Wars."* York, ME: Stenhouse.

Johnson, W. (2002, April). Make no mistake about it. *California Educator*, 6(7), 4.

Kazanjan, A., Green, C., & Bassett, K. (1998, September). *Normal bone mass, aging bodies, marketing of fear: Bone mineral density screening of well women*. Presented at the 93rd Annual Meeting of the American Sociological Association, San Francisco, CA.

Lyon, G. R. (2002, November). Remarks made at the conference, "Rigorous evidence: The key to progress in education?" Washington, DC: Sponsored by the Council for Excellence in Government. Retrieved March 3, 2003, from http://www.excelgov.org/displayContent. asp?Keyword_prppcEvidence

Schemo, D. J. (2002, January 9). Education bill urges new emphasis on phonics as method for teaching reading. *New York Times*.

Snow, C., Burns, M. S., & Griffin, P. (Eds.). (1998). Preventing reading difficulties in young children. Commission on the Prevention of Reading Difficulties in Young Children. National Research Council: National Academy of Sciences. Washington, DC.

CHAPTER TWO

Relatively Speaking:
McCarthyism and Teacher-Resisters

Carole Edelsky

If only I could begin like this: it is the best of times; it is the worst of times. It has such a nice (and familiar)[1] ring to it. However, is it really apt? "Worst" certainly seems like a possibility. But "best"? After looking more closely at the McCarthy era and after interviewing 20 critical holistic teachers around the United States it seems more accurate to pull back on the absolutes and say that for education in the United States, things are more relative—both better and worse than I had thought. Worse conditions nationally; better conditions locally; worse in terms of organized resistance; better in terms of varieties of resistance.

STARTING WITH "WORSE" (IT GETS BETTER)

In the 1990s, educational policies and politically commissioned reports linked standards, high stakes testing, accountability, and a separate-skills view of reading. Supported by public opinion (fanned by corporate media), these policies and reports created a climate in education that bore a frightening resemblance to McCarthyism. Some of the markers were: blacklists (of consultants, terminology, bibliographical references) that affected certain kinds of professional employment and research; loyalty oaths; threats and intimidation; and incursions on civil liberties. After the

---

[1]The resemblance is to the opening lines of Charles Dickens' *A Tale of Two Cities*.

horrific attacks on September 11, these and other repressive features escaped the confines of education and made their appearance on the broader national scene, creating a "New McCarthyism" (Baker, 2002; Rothschild, 2001). This new national climate is now doubling back, lending its own flavor and strength to what erupted in education a decade earlier. What is worse about the current situation in education is that the parallels with McCarthyism are even greater than I had imagined.

The Old McCarthyism

McCarthyism was the "most widespread and longest lasting wave of political repression in American history" (Schrecker, 1998, p. x). In the name of protecting the United States against Communism in the late 1940s through the mid-1950s, politicians, bureaucrats, and zealous anti-Communists joined forces and "hounded an entire generation of radicals and their associates, destroying lives [and] careers" using "the power of the state to turn dissent into disloyalty and, in the process, drastically narrowed the spectrum of acceptable political debate" (p. x). It was a crusade that, although taking its name from U.S. Senator Joseph McCarthy of Wisconsin, actually preceded McCarthy's entrance into politics and extended past his death. According to historian Ellen Schrecker, it is part of a centuries old tradition of countersubversion, wherein the perception is that an alien external force is destroying the society from within and must be rooted out. Countersubversion fits well with other traditions in American history—nativist antiforeign sentiment cloaked in super patriotism and business-sponsored anti-union activity. Thus workers' movements and movements for racial equality were attacked as foreign in the 19th century and red-baited as Communist (and therefore as a threat to national security) in the 20th century.

What separates the McCarthy era from the rest of this history is the breadth and intensity of that particular countersubversive crusade. And the credit for that intensification must be awarded to the federal government. In response to the Cold War, the Communist victory in China, and the outbreak of the Korean War, the federal government adopted an anti-Communist agenda, putting its weight and power behind carrying out and legitimizing that agenda. It was the taking on of that crusade by the federal government, not just by a fanatic fringe, that led to hearings, prosecutions, FBI investigations, and court decisions that not only punished individuals but also created a mentality which reached throughout the country (Schrecker, 1998).

McCarthy was a relatively obscure senator (already under attack in Wisconsin for illegal campaign practices) when, on a speaking tour in 1950, he announced that he had in his possession a list (now known to be non-existent) of 205 Communists in the State Department. The number changed to 57 the next day, then 81 ten days later when he returned to Washington. Other anti-Communist zealots had accused the Truman administration of being "soft on Communism" but no one with his credentials had ever used specific numbers. It was those numbers that attracted the media and helped create the tragic circus that followed.

McCarthyism cost the United States dearly. There was the human wreckage—suicides, two executions, prison sentences for those convicted of having unpopular political ideas, harassment by local patriotic citizens. People who, on principle, refused to cooperate with anti-Communist investigations lost their jobs. Thousands identified—correctly or not—as Communists or impugned as merely associating with Communists were purged from large institutions, especially those in left-led unions or those who worked with ideas. Not only "glamorous" Hollywood screen writers but also rank and file elementary and high school teachers and professors lost their jobs and were put on actual or informal, oral blacklists so they would not be able to get another teaching job. McCarthyism inflicted psychological damage as well. Those who were witch-hunted for activities that had been legal at the time and that represented democratic rights were devastated. Respected scholars never regained their reputations once their names had become controversial. Children of those brought before the House Un-American Activities Committee (HUAC) were bullied and ostracized as "Commie Kids." Paranoia became pervasive; people censored themselves, retreating into what Supreme Court Justice William O. Douglas called "a black silence" (Schrecker, 1998).

Despite the huge influx of intellectual talent from World War II–torn Europe prior to and during that same period, McCarthyism crippled intellectual and political life in the United States. It was largely responsible for reforms not implemented, unions not organized, books not published, films not produced, readings not assigned and classroom discussions avoided, and questions not asked—lost opportunities made especially ironic because just a few years earlier the American political landscape had been more varied than it had ever been. McCarthyism ended that diversity—"from race relations to mass media, it narrowed the range of acceptable activity and debate" (Schrecker, 1998, p. 370). Gone was a discussion of class or collective struggle. Gone were certain terms: "industrial capitalism" became industrialism; "boss" lost its negative connotations. Gone from textbooks were certain figures (before Langston Hughes could publish *Famous Negro Music Makers* he had to remove all mention of Paul Robeson or risk having the book banned from school libraries) (Schrecker, 1998).

By the early 1960s, McCarthyism had receded as a driving force. Its most flamboyant warrior was gone from the scene, dead from alcoholism in 1957 and publicly discredited 3 years earlier. The Army–McCarthy hearings, McCarthy's attempt to expose Communists in the Pentagon, were seen by many as going too far. Carried live by the new medium of television, the hearings were indeed an exposé, but not of Communists; they exposed McCarthy's alcohol-laced bullying. (The plea by the Army's counsel, Joseph Welch, for McCarthy to stop his egregious behavior at those hearings became famous: "Have you no sense of decency, sir?") The U.S. Senate censured McCarthy in late 1954 for his "contemptuous behavior." At that time, Senator Herbert Lehman remarked, "We have condemned the individual but we have not repudiated the 'ism' " (Schrecker, 1998, p. 265).

But others were resisting that "ism." Fair-minded Republicans in the Eisenhower administration were beginning to oppose the heavy-handed squelching of dissent. Some brave employers rehired a few of those fired. News media began to report opposing viewpoints. Importantly, the economy was expanding. The fanatic anti-Communist network which continued to share McCarthy's dishonesty, opportunism, and disregard for civil liberties still operated (e.g., through the offices of J. Edgar Hoover), and the Cold War between the United States and Communist regimes would drive U.S. foreign policy for decades to come, but by the early 1960s the crusade *qua* crusade against individuals had lost its punch.

Nevertheless, McCarthyism left a terrible legacy: It "showed how effectively political repression could operate within a democratic society" (Schrecker, 1998, p. 411). That era revealed how few barriers the U.S. Constitution actually offers against using the machinery of government to demonize and then destroy a thus-demonized movement.

That Was Then; This Is Almost Now

By the mid-1990s, that legacy became more obvious as the scene in education began to exhibit features that were chillingly familiar to what had happened under McCarthyism. There were ballot propositions aimed against immigrants, the demonization of a minority view in education (whole language), a "manufactured crisis" about public education (Berliner & Biddle, 1995), increasing restrictions on literacy instruction. The standards movement, high stakes testing and voucher campaigns, presented cynically as equalizers, were dividing people. The same authoritarian populist (Stuart Hall, cited by Apple, 2002) sentiments were available to tap into: xenophobia, nativism, racism, superpatriotism, anti-Communism, anticosmopolitanism, and anti-intellectualism. Some of the same well-connected players were working together: corporations (including corporate media) eager for new ventures; Christian fundamentalists (it was in 1954, the height of the McCarthy era, that the words "under God" were added to the Pledge of Allegiance to separate godless Communists from loyal U.S. patriots; "War, Terrorism," 2001); and right wing supporters in all branches of government. The same tactics for demonizing were apparent: lies and disinformation (about whole language, bilingual education, students' reading, and math achievement); smear campaigns and scapegoating (against specified teachers and researchers associated with whole language or named teachers and principals who opposed the tactics promoted by the business Right such as top-down, rigid standards and high stakes tests); intimidation (of parents and students who refused to participate in high stakes testing, of teachers and principals who dragged their feet to resist dismantling their literature-based reading programs); secrecy (about the content, authorship, and processing of high stakes tests). Most importantly, the federal government began to consistently push a right wing agenda for education under the cover of the need to maintain global supremacy (occasionally explicitly tied to national security).

It is this last similarity between then and almost-now that made me say at the outset "worse than I thought." I had not understood, until I began to look more closely at the McCarthy era, that it was the federal government's shift from merely supporting to actually adopting an anti-Communist agenda that enabled all the other evils of the old McCarthyism. A similar sinister shift in the 1990s reappeared when the federal government used its power for the first time to decide professional debates in reading, bringing with it other features of a new McCarthyism in education. It seemed at the time, however, that this new McCarthyism was confined to education. And then came September 11.

And This is Really Now: The New McCarthyism

Within hours, while people were reeling from shock and grief, lobbyists for the airline industry began pressing for federal aid (its own employees were not to be included in the bailout) (Wayne & Moss, 2001). Indeed, just days after the bombings the *Wall Street Journal* urged President Bush to use the crisis to achieve the entire conservative agenda: tax cuts for the wealthy, oil drilling in the Arctic National Wildlife Refuge, fast track legislation, the appointment of conservative judges (Streisand, 2001). The tragedy provided the right wing with a perfect scenario: an alien threat (terrorists) to national security, shared anguish and loss, a press only too anxious to proclaim loyalty and to abandon its obligation to investigate (Solomon, 2001), general ignorance about U.S. policies and actions in the Third World, ever-simmering American authoritarian populism now brought to a boiling point, and an agenda the Right had been pushing for decades. In its broadest outlines, that agenda is about ensuring the best conditions around the world for corporate capital: privatizing public institutions; low costs for labor; few expenses for protecting the workplace and the larger environment; low tax burdens; access to markets; freedom to move, close, build, and so forth; wide acceptance of market values and beliefs; and "stability" (an absence of dissent achieved by surveillance and other forms of intimidation).

Within months after September 11, the Right was able to push proposals for returning billions in previously paid taxes to major corporations and to seriously erode civil liberties through the U.S.A. Patriot Act. The U.S.A. Patriot Act, its passage itself an erosion because it was "smuggled in" by suspending the usual procedures for congressional legislation (Schneider, 2002), allows the Secretary of State to designate any group as a "terrorist organization" (there is no appeal); grants the government new powers to spy on its citizens; weakens Constitutional checks and balances by giving new powers of detention and surveillance to the executive branch while depriving the judicial branch of oversight to ensure those powers are not being abused (e.g., it allows the FBI to search booksellers' records regarding which customers bought which books [Rothschild, 2001]); allows noncitizens in the United States legally to be detained indefinitely based only on the Attorney General's "certification"; permits Americans engaged in any form of protest to be charged with domestic terrorism if any violence occurs (no matter who started it) (Eisenberg, 2002).

The secrecy that had already become a hallmark of the Bush administration intensified after September 11. Attorney General Ashcroft urged federal agencies not to comply with requests made under the Freedom of Information Act (Rosen, 2002) and President Bush issued an executive order that turned the Presidential Records Act upside down (previously, the White House had to show a compelling reason to withhold papers that had already been scheduled for release; now, researchers have to show a compelling need for the information) (Baker, 2002).

Right-inspired harassment and intimidation for dissenting views increased. Students attending the Ohio State University's June, 2002 commencement were warned they would be arrested if they showed any "signs of dissent" when President Bush spoke (FAIR Action Alert, 2002). Two FBI and Secret Service agents came to inspect the "anti-American activity" displayed in an art gallery in Houston; newspapers pulled political cartoons and cancelled the comic strip Boondocks for antiwar content; columnists were fired for criticizing any aspect of Bush's activity even after their editors had approved those columns; a student was expelled for wearing a T-shirt criticizing the "so-called land of the free" for its "racism, sexism, and homophobia" (Rothschild, 2001). Fifty thousand copies of Michael Moore's book *Stupid White Men* were not released for several months while its publisher, HarperCollins, tried to decide "if it was too offensive" (Moore, 2002). Signing a letter suddenly became news when the local NPR station in Phoenix announced that a professor at the University of Arizona law school was "among those who signed a letter against military tribunals" (NPR, 2001). The William Bennett–founded Americans for Victory Over Terrorism (AVOT) began its own smear campaign, singling out the editor of *Harpers Magazine* for daring to suggest that the meanings of the word *terrorism* might be "elastic" (Berkowitz, 2002). And in a report (Neal & Martin, 2001) from the American Council of Trustees and Alumni (ACTA), founded by Lynne Cheney entitled "Defending civilization: How our universities are failing America and what can be done about it," 117 academics were painted as a fifth column for uttering such statements as "we have to learn to use courage for peace instead of war." The report, which at first named names but then was revised to only include identifications (e.g., "a student at the University of Michigan," "a professor of English at Rutgers") made national news and was to be sent to 3000 trustees (Scigliano, 2001).

As if intimidation were not enough, a noncitizen could now be deported for simply belonging to a group that dissented (guilt by association) (Cole, 2001). On Attorney General Ashcroft's orders, Arab males were to be rounded up and questioned. As of December, 2001, over 1200 noncitizens were being held in secret detention as material witnesses with neither their names, charges, nor locations revealed and with no access to lawyers ("War, Terrorism," 2001). Those noncitizens suspected of actual connections to terrorism were to be tried, in secrecy, by military tribunals. And a new Justice Department program called TIPS (Terrorism Information and Presentation System), was to have been launched in Fall 2002, encouraging millions of Americans to spy on their fellow Americans and to feed that information into a centralized database ("Informant Fever," 2002). Public criticism forced the administration to scale back TIPS but the program did not disappear. By late 2002, it had morphed into something called Total Information Awareness (TIA), designed to allow the government easy access to oceans of data, integrated through TIA, concerning whomever a bureaucrat wished to investigate.

Who passed such laws? No one. With the exception of the U.S.A. Patriot Act for which normal legislative procedures were suspended, none of this was legislated. Rather, executive orders, judicial memos, agency edicts, conservative foundations, and private individuals were the authors of this activity. As with the old McCarthyism that was the result of a "concerted campaign" (Schrecker, 1998, p. xiii), these actions too have been orchestrated within an ideological context in which national security trumps all other values and becomes the cover for all excesses. Moreover, they have occurred within a rhetorical context in which the powerful, while stifling dissent, for example, through the intimidation of an ACTA list or the firing of a tenured Muslim professor for his political commitments (Shapiro, 2002), can brazenly present themselves as under assault by "leftist thought police" (Krugman, 2002).

This new national context gives new meaning to conditions in education both before and after the attacks. It is important now to reassess the "insults" thrown at education prior to September 11, to see them as the government-driven, McCarthyism-like repression that they were. Blacklists in California that prevented state funds from being used for professional development that mentioned invented spelling, cueing systems, whole language, comprehension-centered reading instruction or Sustained Silent Reading and that blackballed consultants whose bibliographies cited Ken or Yetta Goodman among others; the secrecy surrounding high stakes tests; the disinformation emanating from the National Institutes for Child Health and Development and the reports of the National Reading Panel (Garan, 2002; Strauss, 2002); the demonization of whole language; a government-imposed "victory" for phonics; and the corporate media-created "Reading Wars" should now be seen retroactively in the light of that tradition of McCarthyism.

Since September 11, the antiterrorist crusade has become an umbrella over many domains, including education. Bearing an obvious resemblance to McCarthyism's anti-Communist crusade, it circulates now as a national discourse, colors what is happening in many societal domains including education, and it threatens to put another layer of McCarthyism-like activity on what had already been underway in education since the 1990s. Thus, a government agency's investigation of a reading professor's syllabus; Laura Bush's favorably reported designation of teachers as "soldiers of democracy" (Fagan, 2002); the tight tying of the American flag to government mandated reading instruction at a rally where Secretary Rod Paige occasionally slid from talking about reading into talking about terrorism, with the implication, therefore, that opposing the Bush mandate concerning reading amounted to being an enemy of the state (Meyer, 2002); the Massachusetts Department of Education's threat to withhold funds from a conference if testing critic Alfie Kohn spoke at the conference (Greenberger, 2001); the ousting in Maine of a student teacher for teaching his students about Islam (Rothschild & Evans, 2002); the federal government's audacity in legislating a definition of scientific research—all this is tinted (tainted) by the national discourse of this antiterrorist crusade. (Closed tribunals, after all, can rub off on open courts of various ilk.)

As I said at the outset, "worse than I thought." How, then, can the educational scene also be better?

BETTER THAN I THOUGHT

I conducted interviews with 20 critical holistic teachers from Arizona, California, Massachusetts, New Jersey, Oregon, Pennsylvania, Texas, and Wisconsin.[2] I wanted to know about their practice in the current context. What pressures did they experience? What compromises were they making? Did they resist or dissent and if they did how did they get away with it?

What was "better than I thought" became quickly apparent. Although each teacher described a school or district that bore the marks of the national scene, each also reported areas of breathing space. Although combining the 20 reports into one creates the impression of a disaster, noting the differences among local contexts offers some hope.

A Compilation of Disasters

First, teachers were weighed down by pressures from:

- new testing mandates ("instead of doing what's best for kids, we're doing what's best for test scores");
- mandated curricula ("some of it is actually just good ideas gone bad") and demands for formulaic "lessons," schedules, and interactions requiring teachers to try to push all students through the same material at the same pace, reflecting not only a profound distrust of teachers but a complete discrediting of professional knowledge;
- misuse of time (hours spent creating lesson plans and wall charts showing how classroom work matched minute details of state standards; an entire school year's worth of faculty meetings spent on test issues; "a chance for wonderful teachers to be talking about curriculum—like the intersection of genetics and ethics—and instead we're figuring out rubrics scoreable on a 6-point scale");
- inappropriate oversight by literacy "police."

Second, the teachers were disturbed by changes in their working climate:

- increased isolation as team planning disappeared in the face of preplanned programs;

---

[2]Because some of the teachers wanted to remain anonymous for fear of reprisals, I agreed not to identify anyone by name or school. The 20 included elementary, middle school, and high school teachers, reading specialists, special education teachers, and one district administrator.

- increased dependency on the part of many of their colleagues as these other teachers became addicted to preplanned and scripted programs (giving new meaning to "hooked on phonics");
- lowered morale as teachers saw the undervaluing of their work reflected in underfunding (insufficient funds for building repair and basic materials) as well as demeaning, deprofessionalizing district-required "professional development";
- increased incidence of "crazy-making" situations wherein districts did not notice or even applauded contradictions (e.g., promoting both scripted programs and writers' workshops; approving a school's mission to promote multilingualism and multiculturalism but imposing test requirements that forced a focus on English only; co-opting progressive ideas and slogans ["every child can learn" became an excuse for standardization, writing workshop was turned into prescriptive formulae, "student work" came to mean performance on tests, "treating teachers as professionals" was now translated into training for Success For All and Open Court]);
- decreased joy ("what's gone is the fun of it, the joy").

Third, teachers were distressed by changes in their own personal "emotional climate":

- fear of being accused of racism for criticizing standardized tests ("they'll say my objections to these tests mean I don't expect as much from Black kids");
- guilt and anxiety over test scores ("the system has found ways to make scores intensely personal," pitting one teacher against another, "disaggregating data to such an extent they can say Teacher X did not teach African-American boys detail Y of the metric system"; tying scores to bonuses, funding, and takeovers so that a particular teacher could be blamed for letting all his or her colleagues down);
- shame for censoring themselves about September 11 and for not fighting back sufficiently when attacked professionally;
- heartbreak over seeing their English learners "crushed" by low test scores and helplessness in response to knowing "what this does to new teachers."

What's Better (At Last!) Is Local Differences

Despite the previously mentioned litany, there was also locally specific leeway. A few of these 20 educators did not feel under such pressure themselves because theirs was not one of the "tested" grades. More crucial in terms of making the case for "better," particular local districts or schools provided different mandates and different degrees of stringency in enforcing them. Sometimes, a grant from a large foundation offered exemptions from some of the pressure. A few teachers reported exceptionally fine school-adopted programs in fine arts or science or after school programs that provided the kind of rich educational experience students were being deprived of by the mandated curricula. Not all districts made bilingual programs go through terrible contortions. Not all states exerted the same kinds of pressure for test scores (promotion and graduation stakes affected school life more negatively than "merely" publishing scores). In many schools, inconsistency among administrators opened up some space for sensible, substantive curriculum if teachers were willing to claim it. Teachers from Pennsylvania, Oregon, and Arizona said they saw an important part of their job to be deflecting pressure from students (freeing them up to learn "deeply") and making space for good practice for other teachers (giving other teachers "permission" to be professionals and helping them with strategies to "keep their overseers off their backs").

Some of the room to maneuver was due, in some cases, to these teachers' history as whole language teachers. They had chosen to work at schools where their perspective was respected and so now those settings offered them a modicum of protection. They had spent years working with parents and so they were somewhat cushioned by parental support. They had influenced their schools to accept workshop approaches to literacy and now school-level appreciation for reading and writing workshops provided some leeway. Importantly, these teachers' well-developed and articulable theoretical understandings helped them in both conversations and confrontations.

But just as often the leeway could be credited to bureaucracies in crisis. With new state and federal laws and policy mandates and with increasingly meager budgets, administrators often simply had too much to do to be able to monitor all the mandates. School level administrators were so busy all they could manage was a "walk through" of teachers' classrooms, looking for external markings of compliance with a mandated program. Some district office personnel weren't knowledgeable enough to notice that the required forms did not contain the mandated substance.

Better—But Not Great

Locally different breathing spaces are what made me think things were better. But these twenty teachers still found themselves compromising their beliefs. From the passionate opponents of testing who went ahead and gave the high stakes tests ("if I stayed home on testing day, the art teacher would have to give the test and the kids wouldn't get art that day") to kindergarten teachers who gave up choice time, all reported acting contrary to their principles. People spoke of compromises related to:

• new testing demands (creating their own preparation materials, conducting test preparation for almost a quarter of the school year, giving an excessive number of tests);

• new curricular demands (using the mandated—and boring—materials, teaching six-traits writing, giving up recess and play to make time for a rigid "balanced literacy" schedule, sacrificing depth [of long term, engaging inquiry projects] for frenetic breadth [of highly specified standards-based curricula]); and

• civil liberties (agreeing to refrain from asking provocative questions at district meetings, signing oaths of allegiance to district procedures for handling high stakes tests, contributing to shutting down public scrutiny and shutting off public debate by "going along" with demands for secrecy).

These politically sophisticated teachers did not emphasize McCarthyism in the interviews. It is not that they disagreed with my characterization of the new order, and it was not that they did not know they were experiencing professional and civic repression. But I was asking them to talk about how they were dealing with the current context in their professional lives and so that is what they talked about. Instead of focusing on how the new requirement in one district for signing loyalty oaths was an instance of stifling dissent or on how mandated programs repressed political and pedagogical viewpoints, they discussed how they were subverting the new order, the ways they were finding to "dance around the legislation," how they were attempting to slip out of the "noose that [was] becoming tighter and tighter." Although some knew about teachers threatened with job loss, none thought they would be fired and left without professional and economic options. Overburdened, anxious, and often heavy-hearted about what was happening, these teachers were not hopeless. They were indeed afraid but their fear did not paralyze them. They did censor themselves, but not in every professional setting. Even if conditions had become so oppressive that they had changed jobs (moving to another school or another position within the school or district; no one had left education), they saw such a change as something they had initiated, a choice among options.

The sense of having options (and leeway) pervaded each of the 20 interviews. It came out when I asked teachers where they drew the line. As they reported what they wouldn't compromise on ("I won't cheat to get scores up" although districts apparently gave lots of subtle signs to encourage cheating; "I won't use basals [or Open Court or Success For All]";

"I won't use the writing component of Open Court and let Open Court take over my entire literacy program"; "I won't focus on test-driven garbage for the *entire* year"; "I won't teach six traits writing to first graders"; "I won't stay at a school that's taken over by a corporation"; "I won't turn reading into a skills-driven thing"; " I won't be on a test revision committee and let it appear as though I approve of those tests"; "I won't sign an affidavit swearing I won't cheat [if they can trust me without an affidavit not to hit kids and not to sexually abuse them, they ought to be able to trust me on this]"), they always mentioned options. They could teach somewhere else, do something else in the District, take advantage of their prominence locally and nationally to do other work in education, start a charter school, or retire.

THE RESISTANCE

To repeat, all these experienced knowledgeable, powerful teachers were weighed down by the pressures on them. Still, none were immobilized. And so they did resist, creating opportunities for resistance I had not imagined. (At the beginning of this chapter it was these opportunities for resistance I referred to as one of the "better-than's.")

Some resisted within the bureaucracy. There were grievances filed for a personal attack by a principal and for being "written up" as retribution for dissenting. Two teachers worked on as many district committees as possible in order to influence from within. Many said they tried to influence colleagues at school staff meetings, raising questions, and arguing. A few said they spoke up and asked questions in the larger arena of district-level meetings. All resisted in areas of testing and curriculum. One teacher outright refused to give the District-made test because it was "one test too many."

Teachers subverted mandated test preparation by teaching strategies for test taking but refusing to let the test content shape their curriculum. Several attempted to demystify tests and test scores for students, showing them how tests were constructed and why low scores did not signal stupidity. Some taught tests as a genre, teaching children how to write multiple choice items with at least one intentionally tricky choice, analyzing the language of tests, and providing background on the history and gatekeeping intent behind standardized assessments and their *non*inevitability ("kids have to know that people invented them; people can get rid of them").

Resistance to curricular mandates ranged from simply ignoring them to devising curricula that interrogated the mandates themselves. One teacher wrote and published a critique of the mandated materials her

school had adopted. Another made presentations at national conferences about the effects of narrow required pedagogies on her teaching. Several teachers continued to sponsor literature circles and writers' workshops, use their own trade books, conduct long term integrated inquiry projects, and ignore directives to use packaged literacy programs. One teacher taught reading in Spanish to non-English-speaking 6-year-olds despite restrictions against teaching in any language but English. Some produced the required forms but inserted more holistic, critical content. Many resisted with good practice—inserting "the richness of books, story, color, and play" into dreary packages because "everything we can sneak in is a victory." One teacher devised ways to interrogate the mandated curriculum. She let students know that while they could not "talk back to their grandmothers or their principal," they could indeed talk back to books. She established regular procedures for asking children if the assigned Open Court story was one that deserved talking back to and she taught students to critique hidden and not so hidden messages from texts. If her aim was for students to become critically literate, what better materials to use than these packaged ones "with obvious agendas about the dominant culture." Currently, she is trying to figure out, *with her students*, how to handle mandated materials ("they're here for awhile so kids need to learn they don't represent The Truth"), how to negotiate with others when the packaged directions are not working (e.g., when a timed segment is going on too long), and how to advocate in public for something else.

Attitude too was a type of resistance. Some teachers said they refused to lower themselves to the state's insultingly low (if highly specified) standards. Several were explicit about being proud of their excellent teaching, refusing to hide it, wanting others to see it—and to see what their students were able to do.

How have these teachers gotten away with their acts of resistance? They believe the answer is twofold, depending on: (1) who *they* are, and (2) who/what their *districts* are. These are teachers with fine local and sometimes national reputations. They are deeply knowledgeable and practiced in articulating that knowledge. They also know how to "speak their [the bureaucrats'] language"; thus, they can fill in forms, write lesson plans, create matrices, and talk state standards—maybe even better than the bureaucrats can. They are confident professionals. Some are also insulated by their status and history ("I'm in a select school, one I chose, with a principal who agrees with me"). A few are nearing retirement age ("this is my last year; what can they do to me?").

And then there was the character of the local school systems. Policymakers have imposed "reforms" with such speed and entanglements that district personnel are often too busy to attend to the details of classroom practice. Several teachers believed their administrators were not only too busy but were too disorganized to check ("no one is looking") or too ignorant to understand that "illicit" literacy practices were going on under their noses. And in some states, the budgetary shortfalls were so great that there was not enough money to buy all the mandated materials or score some of the mandated tests so administrators looked the other way when teachers went against the mandates.

The resistance I have mentioned so far concerns teachers acting individually, often within their classrooms (although some of this seemingly individual activity owes its character to a few teachers' membership in grassroots educational activist groups). Some teachers also reported efforts at advocacy outside the classroom (lobbying legislators, writing letters to the editor, sending information and articles to sympathetic school board members), and testifying at district or legislative hearings (one educator said that it took a year before teachers in her district understood that state hearings were a sham so they no longer were wasting time trying to prevent the enactment of policies that are a "done deal"; they were "doing damage control" instead). Several teachers spoke of their efforts to prod parents into organizing themselves. The showed parents examples of test items from test preparation booklets, discussing their flaws. One teacher sent personal letters "from [her] home to theirs") to inform parents of their rights regarding opting out of tests and obtaining waivers for certain programs.

However, when I asked how they were resisting professional repression, only a few mentioned involvement in any collective resistance. Philadelphia teachers spoke about joining the collective resistance mounted by the Philadelphia Student Union,[3] "the strongest dissenting voice in Philadelphia." One teacher made the case that "this takes a united response. We have to organize. One teacher can't do it alone." One of the teachers I spoke with did indeed organize. In her case, it was against high stakes tests. She developed a coalition that now has affiliates throughout her state. Those affiliates have conducted teach-ins, informed parents of their right to opt out of the state's high stakes test, pressured legislators to hold hearings, and created a website.

But this teacher was in the minority. It was the relative absence of that organized, collective response that made me say at the outset that things

---

[3]The Philadelphia Student Union, founded in 1995 by high school students, works from the premise that no education reform will "work" unless students are an integral part of the reform effort. PSU has worked in coalition with various unions and smaller groups of progressive teachers. They were the primary resisters opposing the privatization campaign—organizing rallies, walk-outs, teach-ins, and other demonstrations.

are worse than I thought with respect to resistance. Worse but certainly understandable. It takes tremendous time and energy to organize, and teachers are overwhelmed by the new demands on their time (let alone their professional integrity), pulled in so many directions they feel "ready to snap."

Still, repression on the scale of the new McCarthyism at the national level, in which the federal government puts its weight behind a crusade that is tied to patriotism, which in turn is tied to national security, which is then used as an excuse for pushing a decades-old right wing agenda that includes education (restricting learning, teaching, and thinking, let alone civil liberties)—such repression requires resistance on a grand scale. Perhaps educators can not organize such resistance. Perhaps parents, students, school janitors, and school bus drivers have to do the organizing with a focus on their own issues. But educators can seek out those organizers, swell their ranks, and find umbrella issues important to all. The old McCarthyism was pushed back into the shadows by many forces, particularly economic and governmental activity. But at least some credit can be given to increasingly vocal opposition and resistance to the forces of fear.

In his 2002 Commencement Address at Vassar College, playwright Tony Kushner urged graduates to organize, to resist complying with those forces of fear whose aim, always, at bottom, is injustice. In this book on marketing fear, it is appropriate to quote Kushner's advice to those graduates, and by extension, to all of us (2002, pp. 17–18).

What are we doing here, Kushner asks. We are here "to organize . . . to be political . . . to be citizen[s] in a pluralistic democracy . . . to be effective, to have agency, to make a claim on power, to spread it around, to rearrange it, to democratize it. . . ." Why? Because we are "the citizen[s] of a flawed but actual democracy. . . . [W]hen we despair, we open the door to evil, and evil is always happy to enter." Look around, Kushner advised. "See what despair and inaction on the part of citizens produces. Act! Organize. . . . The world ends if [we] don't. . . . Will the world end anyway," even if we organize against injustice and repression and (my inclusion: against seemingly disconnected but actually related evils like the Reading Excellence Act, the No Child Left Behind Act, and the U.S.A. Patriot Act)? "Quite possibly. These are monstrous times and there's no telling. Look across the globe—when have you ever seen such a dismaying crew in occupation of every seat of power, a certifiable nutcase here, a tinpot dictator there, a feckless, blood-spattered plutocrat in this office, an unindicted war criminal in that office, miscreants, meshugenas, maniacs, and every one of them has the means of doing the most appalling damage." To battle such a fearsome situation requires hope. "[H]ope isn't a choice, it's a moral obligation, a human obligation, an obligation to the cells in [our] bod[ies]."

And hope, indeed, is what shone through the interviews with these 20 educators. That, too, is better than I thought.

REFERENCES

Apple, M. (2002). Patriotism, pedagogy, and freedom: On the educational meanings of September 11. *Teachers College Record*. Available online at http://www.tcrecord.org/Content.asp?ContentID=10939

Baker, R. (2002). What are they hiding? *The Nation*, 274(7), 11–16.

Berkowitz, B. (2002). Bush & Bennett. *Z Magazine*, 15(6), 17–19.

Berliner, D., & Biddle, B. (1995). *The manufactured crisis*. Reading, MA: Addison-Wesley.

Cole, D. (2001). National Security State. *The Nation*, 273(20), 4–5.

Eisenberg, E. (2002). Briefing on USA Patriot Act. Talk given at meeting of Arizona Institute for Peace Education and Research (AIPER), March 1, 2002, Tempe, AZ.

Fagan, A. (2002). First lady cites teacher need. *The Washington Times*. Available online at http://asp.washtimes.com.printarticle.asp?action=print&ArticleID=20020315-2

Fairness and Accuracy In Reporting (FAIR) Action Alert. (2002, June 17). A changed president—or a new repression? (circulated on e-mail listserve).

Garan, E. (2002). *Resisting reading mandates: How to triumph with the truth*. Portsmouth, NH: Heinemann.

Greenberger, S. (2001, December 14). ACLU sues over MCAS speaker. *Boston Globe* (circulated on e-mail listserve).

Informant fever. (2002, July 22). Editorial. *New York Times*, A18.

Krugman, P. (2002). The smoke machine. *New York Times*. Available online at http://nytimes.com/2002/03/29/opinion/29KRUG.html.

Kushner, T. (2002). A word to graduates: Organize! *The Nation*, 275(1), 115–119.

Meyer, R. (2002). Paige . . . long notes, 4/9/02. (circulated on e-mail listserve).

Moore, M. (2002). STUPID WHITE MEN (Michael Moore's book finally being published). http://www.michaelmoore.com/2002_0205.html

National Public Radio (NPR), KJZZ local news. (2001, December 17).

Neal, A., & Martin, J. (2001). Defending civilization: How our universities are failing America and what can be done about it. Project of the Defense of Civilization Fund, American Council of Trustees and Alumni. (circulated on e-mail listserve).

Rosen, R. (2002, January 6). On the public's right to know/The day Ashcroft censored Freedom of Information. *San Francisco Chronicle*, Editorials. (circulated on e-mail listserve).

Rothschild, M. (2001). The new McCarthyism. *The Progressive*. Available online at http://www.progressive.org/0901/roth0102.html

Rothschild, M., & Evans, C. (2002, March 23). Student teacher canned for teaching Islam. *The Progressive*. (circulated on e-mail listserve).

Schneider, K. (2002). The Patriot Act: Last refuge of a scoundrel. Magazine of the American Library Association, internet column for March 2002. http://lii.org (circulated on e-mail listserve).

Schrecker, E. (1998). *Many are the crimes: McCarthyism in America*. Boston: Little, Brown & Company.

Scigliano, E. (2001). Naming—and un-naming names. *The Nation*, 273(22), 16.

Shapiro, B. (2002, January 8). When a tenured professor loses his job for vocally backing the Palestinian cause, Jeb Bush applauds, Bill O'Reilly boos and academics say it's the worst threat to free speech since Sept. 11. *Salon News*. (circulated on e-mail listserve).

Solomon, N. (2001). Media war without end. *Z Magazine*, 14(12), 5–9.

Strauss, S. (2002, May). *Challenging the NICHD reading research agenda*. Paper presented at the annual meeting of the International Reading Association, San Francisco.

Streisand, B. (2001). Remarks on accepting the 2001 Liberty and Justice Award. Talk given at the 4th annual Rainbow/PUSH coalition Awards dinner. (circulated on e-mail listserve).

War, terrorism, and America's classrooms: Teaching in the aftermath of the September 11th tragedy. (2001). Special Report, *Rethinking Schools, 16*(3), 15.

Wayne, L., & Moss, M. (2001). Bailout showed the weight of a mighty, and fast-acting, lobby. *New York Times*. Available online at http://nytimes.com/2001/10/10/business/10AIR.html?ex=1003756212&ei=1&en=a5e

PART ONE

THE PLAYERS

This section provides a comprehensive look at how recent corporate and government interests have used fear in their efforts to dismantle public education through their initial attacks and subsequent control over pedagogy and testing. Each chapter makes the case that this fear is being used to enact an agenda that disempowers teachers, schools, parents, and children.

CHAPTER THREE

The Push of the Pendulum

Bess Altwerger

In November 1989, the National Council of Teachers of English convened the first Day of Whole Language in Baltimore, Maryland. At that time, whole language theory and practice had begun to emerge from "underground" and enter the mainstream of public education. Organizers, therefore, expected a sizable attendance. But in delivering the opening keynote address "Whole Language Teachers: Empowered Professionals" I was astounded at the size of the audience, which at over 1500, exceeded our highest expectations. The sheer number of attendees at my keynote and other sessions that day inspired hope that we were truly on the brink of making deep and profound changes to traditional education and teaching. In my keynote, I challenged teachers to consider powerful distinctions between activities and learning experiences, control and collaboration, practice and authenticity. And I spoke about my vision of whole language teachers and educators as empowered and critical professionals committed to serving as advocates and activists for their students and our society.

Although many of us understood the democratizing, transformative power of whole language education at that pivotal moment in history, we were yet to comprehend the magnitude of its potential as evidenced by the unprecedented level of opposition subsequently waged against it. Although from its inception, whole language was a pedagogy that challenged mainstream theoretical paradigms and institutionalized instructional practices, we were yet unaware of the threat we evidently posed to those, who in that very year of 1989, had already formed an agenda for seizing control over public education. The National Business Roundtable, an organization representing 200 of the most powerful U.S. corporations had launched their "Education Initiative" in response to George Bush's call for comprehensive school reform. As noted on the timeline presented in Table 3.1, several events prior to 1989 had already set the stage for the undeniable "push of the pendulum" back to the hegemonic educational practices that whole language sought to transform.

Clearly, it was never whole language practices per se that posed the greatest threat to the governmental/corporate agenda. After all, what would a political bureaucrat or corporate executive know of theme cycles, literature circles, and reading–writing workshop? Rather, it was the liberatory ideology realized through these practices, and the potential activism of the teachers implementing them, that constituted the real threat to their agenda. In the January–February 2001 *Education Researcher*, Paula Wolfe and Leslie Poynor argue that "Whole language closely resembled a sociopolitical movement inextricably linked to conflicts over hegemonic control," not some radical swing of a pendulum cycle, but a "theoretical, pedagogical and socio-political reform movement" (Wolfe & Poynor, 2001, p. 15). Regarding whole language, not just as a modern reincarnation of progressive practice, but as a sociopolitical movement is critical to understanding our current circumstances. The backlash against whole language cannot be regarded as an inevitable swing of the education pendulum back to a more traditional paradigm, but a battle for control over American education and its role in American society. As we shall see, the three main pillars of the government/corporate agenda to control education were: establishment of national standards and standardized curriculum, high stakes testing, and punitive accountability. A large scale whole language movement, by virtue of its core sociopolitical principles of education, would constitute the greatest danger to the realization of these government/corporate goals, as indicated here:

The "Danger" of Whole Language

Affirms	Opposes
Authentic, teacher-based assessment	High stakes standardized testing
Collaborative curriculum, critical inquiry	Standardized, national curriculum
Rich and varied multicultural literature	Basal readers, contrived texts
Teaching for individual strengths and needs	One-size-fits-all reading programs
Educational justice and equity	Inequities in school funding practices
Inquiry based, reflective practice	Test-based "accountability"

As one reads the list on the right, it becomes immediately obvious that whole language stood in direct opposition to every aspect of the government/corporate agenda that has ultimately been imposed across the country through intimidation, mandate, and law. Although many whole language teachers never truly appreciated the political and ideological dimensions of their own practice, it was clearly understood by the architects of this agenda. Discrediting whole language would be a necessary prerequisite to achieving the public support required for implementing reactionary educational policy. To that end, a massive media campaign was launched to attack whole language on the basis of its position toward phonics and to firmly frame the struggle as one of methodology rather than ideology. It is crucial to recognize, however, that phonics is not, and never was, anything more than a convenient and powerful tool used to win public opinion and beat back the gains made in empowering teachers and democratizing schools.

One reason why the phonics card could be used so effectively is that the whole language movement had not adequately educated the public as to its democratic principles, nor had it forged critical alliances with other progressive forces within our communities. Our position on phonics instruction, not our democratic ideology, therefore became the single most salient characteristic of whole language from the point of view of both the general public and many teachers. (For further discussion of this point see Altwerger & Saavedra, 1999.) Discrediting the whole language position on phonics through "proving" the efficacy of intensive, systematic phonics, therefore became tantamount to the discrediting of whole language entirely—and all the progressive practices it had supported. Had the whole language movement been more politically proactive and vocal, the phonics controversy might not have been so successfully exploited.

In the remainder of this chapter, I demonstrate that the campaign to push the pendulum and institute the government/corporate agenda for public schools has a surprisingly long and insidious history. It has hinged on the use of several key strategies (listed next), implemented at key moments over 2 decades:

Strategies Used to "Push the Pendulum"

Government sponsored reports
Nationwide media campaigns
Publications of conservative foundations and think tanks
NICHD control over research
State and federal legislation
Implementation of high stakes testing
Mandated use of commercial reading programs

The following timeline notes the implementation of each of these key strategies. It demonstrates that our current setback in the battle to achieve critical, democratic education has been the result of a carefully orchestrated campaign, involving multiple power sources, and culminating in the implementation of the No Child Left Behind Act—the most ominous, undemocratic intrusion into public education in American history.

The first major event on our timeline marks the beginning of the successful government strategy to use federally sponsored agencies and panels to conduct seemingly scientific reviews of the "research." Through specific guidelines in the RFP and funding criteria, these "research reports" were deliberately framed to substantiate predetermined "truths" about the role of phonics in reading. The 1985 publication, "Becoming a Nation of Readers" was developed by the highly reputable, government funded Center for the Study of Reading at the University of Illinois. Although the Center had previously established a clear research focus on comprehension and cognitive processes in reading, and had contributed hundreds of reports on these subjects, it was their publication of this one government sponsored document that once again placed the issue of phonics in the national limelight. "Becoming a Nation of Readers" did not refute the need for a focus on meaning and literature in early reading instruction, but it firmly supported a predominant role for phonics (Commission on Reading, 1985). The media attention that this report's endorsement of phonics received overshadowed the entire volume of comprehension research that the Center had previously disseminated. Despite its somewhat "balanced" position, "Becoming a Nation of Readers" served as a catalyst and rationale for future government research reports on phonics. In the foreword of the next bonanza for the government's phonics campaign, "Beginning to Read" (Adams, 1990), P. David Pearson describes how the government capitalized on Becoming a Nation of Readers for its subsequent request for proposals leading to Adams' report:

> In 1986, when those of us at the Center for the Study of Reading were competing for the U.S. Department of Education's Reading Research and Education Center, we could not help but notice the prominence of phonics and other issues in early reading in the Request for Proposals distributed by the Office of Educational Research and Improvement (OERI). We knew that we could not ignore these issues in our proposal. We also knew that in addressing them we would focus the phonics furor on the center. Our solution, which became part of our proposal to OERI, was to agree to take on a major report that would thoroughly review all aspects of phonics and early reading instruction in a straightforward, evenhanded way . . . we were surprised that OERI would ask its center for reading research to undertake such a review. In two previous funding cycles the focus of the federal government's funding for reading had a deliberate bias toward comprehension research. . . .

TABLE 3.1
The Push of the Pendulum
Timeline

1985	Publication of Becoming a Nation of Readers ("phonics first and fast" Pearson).
1986	RFP for U.S. Dept of Education's Reading Research and Education Center (Emphasizes phonics and beginning reading research).
1987	NICHD Initiative to "develop and apply early identification methods to pinpoint those children during kindergarten and the first grade who are at risk for reading failure" (Lyon, 1999) leading to studies in 12 sites.
1989	Business Roundtable issues Education Agenda.
1990	Publication of 'Beginning to Read' by Marilyn Adams, Center for the Study of Reading, University of Illinois. (Emphasizes explicit and early instruction in phonemic awareness and phonics).
1991	Reid Lyon assumes directorship of reading research at NICHD of NIH.
1995	NAEP Report of 1994 results (decline of California ranking).
	Heritage Foundation publishes "See Dick Flunk" blasting whole language and lauding direct instruction in phonics.
1997	Reading Excellence Act drafted by Goodling's Committee (formulated by Douglas Carnine and Hans Meeder).
1997	Director of the NICHD directed by the U.S. Congress to convene a National Reading Panel to determine the most effective approaches for teaching children to read.
1997	Publication of first version of Foorman research (Revised version, Foorman, Francis, Fletcher, Schatschneider, & Mehta, 1998).
1997	Release of Grossen research synthesis of NICHD's "30 years of research: What we know about how children learn to read" (Grossen, 1997). Commissioned by the Center for the Future of Learning and Teaching and the Pacific Bell Foundation.
1998	Release of "consensus report," "Preventing reading difficulties in young children" by the National Research Council of the National Academy of Sciences (Commissioned by the U.S. Depts. of Education and Health and Human Services).
1998	Learning First Alliance issues "Every Child Reading: An Action Plan" Learning First Alliance Board of Directors.
1999	Congress creates the "21st Century Workforce Commission" to develop workforce with 21st century literacy skills, headed by Hans Meeder.
1999	AFT distributes "Teaching Reading IS Rocket Science" to all colleges of education. Written by Louisa Moats, supported by NICHD grant (Moats, 1999).
1999	National Reading Panel report "Teaching Children to Read" published by NICHD.
2000	Passage of Reading Excellence Act.
2001	Rod Paige named Secretary of Education (former superintendent of Houston Public Schools, McGraw-Hill award recipient).
2001	Bush's education advisory team formed with Reid Lyon as "Reading Czar."
2001	Abell Foundation issues report calling for end of teacher education and certification.
2002	Passage of Bush's Education Bill: "No Child Left Behind."

Ironically, in the end, it was Becoming a Nation of Readers, with its clear support of "phonics first and fast" that spawned the legislation . . . commissioning this report on phonics. (Pearson, 1990, p. v)

Critiques of Adams' government sponsored book noted the obvious bias in favor of experimental research based on subskills models of reading, despite the proliferation of qualitative and descriptive early literacy research over the previous decades. Huge gains in our understanding of literacy development, grounded in an anthropological, ethnographic model of research, had been virtually ignored by this publication, which established phonemic awareness and phonics knowledge as principle factors in early reading achievement. This exclusion of nonexperimental studies was to become the hallmark of government sponsored reviews of reading research and a highly successful way to promote phonics and denigrate whole language.

In 1987, the NICHD, one of the National Institutes of Health that focuses specifically on child health and human development, received government funding establishing a new research initiative to "develop and apply early identification methods to pinpoint those children during kindergarten and the first grade who are at risk for reading failure" (Lyon, 1999). The magnitude of this event cannot be underestimated. It located reading "failure" in the realm of health and medicine, and established it in the public's consciousness (with the support of the media), as a national epidemic that must be cured through scientific medical research. Furthermore, funneling research funding through the NICHD ensured government control over the direction of reading research, while maintaining a facade of scientific neutrality. And with the NICHD selection of research sites (12 resulting from this initiative), the federal funds could more easily bypass Colleges of Education, in favor of medical departments and research centers that embraced an experimental, medical model of research. The power of this strategy would not be fully realized until Reid Lyon, a virtual unknown in the field of reading and staunch supporter of experimental research and intensive, systematic phonics instruction, assumed directorship of reading research at the NICHD in 1991, the year following the publication of Adams' book.

Perhaps the most significant event on our timeline occurred in 1989, the same year as the Baltimore whole language conference, when the Business Roundtable accepted the challenge of President George Bush (the first) to make a commitment to reform elementary and secondary education:

The Roundtable agreed that schools were preparing too few students to meet world standards in core academic subjects . . . the Roundtable CEO's therefore made a 10 year commitment—not just to improve individual schools but to reform the entire system of public education. (The Business Roundtable, May 1995)

This agenda to reform the entire public school system, called the "Business Roundtable Education Initiative," was an endorsement of, and plan for implementing the National Education Goals developed by Bush and the state governors.

There are at least two reasons that the Business Roundtable would be anxious to play a significant role in the control of public schools. First and foremost is the preservation of their competitiveness in the global economy, a goal that can only be achieved through the production of a "21st century workforce." "As organizations representing American business and employing some 34 million people, we are concerned that the graduates of America's schools are not prepared to meet the challenges posed by global economic competition" (Augustine, Lupberger, & Orr, 1997). The Business Leader's Guide to Setting Academic Standards states it more bluntly: "More and more, we see that competition in the international marketplace is in reality a 'battle of the classrooms' " (Augustine, 1997, p. 2). Although their publications never explicitly endorse any particular approach to instruction (or mention phonics), the types of knowledge, skills, and dispositions desired by business and demanded by the world economy presupposes an industrial model of standardization that stands in direct opposition to the critical literacy and transactional model of learning underlying whole language. And what is their stated strategy for implementing this model of education? "Many steps must be taken to achieve success, but we agree that three are particularly important, and we commit our organizations to substantive action in these areas: First, helping educators and policy makers set tough standards, applicable to every student in every school; second, assessing student and school-system performance against those standards; and third, using that information to improve schools and create accountability, including rewards for success and consequences for failure" (Augustine et al., 1997). And in a thinly veiled threat to states that don't follow their prescription for school reform, they state "we will align our business practices to foster meaningful student achievement. . . . We will take a state's commitment to achieving high academic standards into consideration in business location decisions" (Augustine et al., 1997). The three pillars of the corporate strategy for public school reform—standards, assessment, and accountability—would be enacted by threat of economic retribution.

The second explanation for the Business Roundtable's interest in control over education pertains to the potential profitability of standardization and assessment, especially in the area of reading. One needs only to review the roster of the Business Roundtable to notice the membership of Harold

McGraw III, CEO of The McGraw-Hill Companies. A longtime competitor in the commercial reading program arena, McGraw-Hill and other basal reading publishing companies had begun to lose their place in the reading instruction market as a consequence of the growing whole language movement, which favored authentic trade books and generative curriculum. Some companies took the approach of marketing their programs as "whole language basals," attempting to join the movement rather than fight it. Although this had the adverse effect of commercializing and distorting whole language, it didn't totally destroy it. But now, with powerful political and economic forces instituting national standards (and standardization), testing and accountability, education would be fertile ground for lucrative contracts with school systems for commercial programs and standardized assessment. As publisher of two phonics based commercial reading programs, Open Court and SRA Reading Mastery, as well as the CTBS test, McGraw-Hill was in a particularly advantageous position to enjoy skyrocketing profits. Additionally, as Steven Metcalf points out in his 2002 feature article in *The Nation*, there was one further advantage enjoyed by McGraw-Hill. "While critics of the Bush administration's energy policies have pointed repeatedly to its intimacy with the oil and gas industry . . . few education critics have noted the Administration's cozy relationship with McGraw-Hill. At its heart lies the three-generation social mingling between the McGraw and Bush families. The McGraws are old Bush friends, dating back to the 1930's" (Metcalf, 2002). He goes on to note that Harold McGraw sat on the board of Barbara Bush's literacy foundation, McGraw received the highest literacy award from President Bush in the early 1990s and that Secretary of Education Rod Paige, then Superintendent of Houston schools, was awarded the McGraw Foundation's highest educator's award. Furthermore, "Harold McGraw was selected as a member of President George W. Bush's transition advisory team, along with McGraw-Hill Board member Edward Rust Jr., the CEO of State Farm and active member of the Business Roundtable on educational issues" (Metcalf, 2002, p. 2). This scandalous relationship between government and business, and later with the NICHD (through research endorsing Open Court as a "scientifically valid" reading program) has netted McGraw-Hill astronomical profits with assurance of more to come with the enactment of No Child Left Behind. It is widely acknowledged that with the legislation's emphasis on "scientifically-based" research (a code term for scripted phonics-based instruction), statewide adoption of McGraw-Hill's two programs all but guarantee proposal acceptance.

With the Business Roundtable initiative underway and the NICHD now firmly in position to steer the course of reading research, the government/corporate agenda had moved closer toward realization. Although the strategy to use federally funded reports, such as Adams' book, had resulted in a heightened level of controversy within the academic community, this had gone largely unnoticed by the general public and most teachers. But that was soon to change. In 1995 the Department of Education issued "NAEP 1994 Reading: A First Look" (Williams, 1995; with a complete revised version released later in 1996) reporting the results of the 1994 National Assessment of Educational Progress test data. Although nationally, NAEP reading scores had not significantly changed over the previous decade, the state of California had experienced a marked drop in its ranking from 1992 to 1994 in comparison to other states. This became an enormous opportunity to claim that lower California reading scores was a direct result of the literature-based reading instruction that had been initiated in that state through the 1987 English-Language Arts Framework. The media engaged in an immediate feeding frenzy, reporting to the public that literature-based instruction, which it equated with whole language, was a failure in the state of California and threatened other states with a similar literacy crisis. The bias of the media was immediately apparent, given that the following conditions present in the state of California could have easily been blamed for any actual drop in the literacy rate in California.

California: The Real Story

California ranked at the bottom of the country in:

Per-pupil spending

Class size

Certified teachers

School library quality

Public library quality

California ranked high in:

Percentage of students living below the poverty line

Teachers without degrees in education

Percentage of students speaking English as a second language

No mandatory kindergarten

Any one of these factors could have been presented by the media as the root cause of California's decline in the state rankings. The fact that California's libraries were ranked near the bottom while books per student correlated with NAEP scores (Krashen, 1996) could have occupied media attention. Ignored completely was the fact that Maine, which scored at the top of the state rankings, had more enthusiastically embraced whole language practices than California. According to an analysis of the 1994 NAEP data by Kenneth Goodman (Goodman, 1998), Maine outscored California in the use of trade books over basals, time spent on silent reading, and self-selected reading. And yet whole language became the target of a media blitz, both in California and nationally, marking the initiation of one of the most successful strategies used to push of the pendulum: media campaigns. It would be used again in full force later in 1997 immediately before congressional consideration of the Reading Excellent Act, submitted by Senator Goodling, chairman of the House Committee on Education and the Workforce, and designed by Douglas Carnine (DISTAR author) and Hans Meeder. At that time the public was flooded with reports of a literacy crisis and the failure of whole language by virtually every news outlet, from *Newsweek* and *Time* magazines, to major newspapers to spots on Prime Time and 60 Minutes. The strange coincidence of timing and perspective across all media, lent seriousness and legitimacy to the claims about the literacy "crisis" and failure of whole language, and prepared the public for the first use of legislation to control reading instruction. This, of course, was no coincidence.

According to journalist Robert McChesney, in a report published by the organization FAIR (Fairness and Accuracy in Reporting), only nine "first tier" corporate giants owned virtually all of the country's media outlets at that time. For example, News Corporation owned Fox News, the *London Times* and the *New York Post*. Time Warner owned CNN, TNT and 24 magazines. This explains how there could be such media-wide consensus on the virtues of phonics, the condemnation of whole language and a virtual blackout of alternative perspectives. McChesney (1997) further reveals that:

> each of the nine first tier media giants has joint ventures with, on average, two thirds of the other eight first tier media giants. . . . By any standard of democracy, such a concentration of media power is troubling if not unacceptable. (p. XX)

These media giants work incestuously for the "corporate good" much like, if not synonymously, with the national or state Business Roundtables. (In fact, the *Baltimore Sun* is a member of the Maryland Business Roundtable as are many local media in their own states.) One could argue that our first amendment right is clearly compromised when we have the right to speak but not to be heard. Indeed, the voices of whole language and other progressive educators remained loud and strong, but they were only rarely heard by the public.

The year of 1997 also marked the public emergence of conservative foundations and think tanks in the campaign to push the pendulum to the right. The Heritage Foundation, among the most powerful, politically influential, and conservative of such foundations, began to publish special Policy Review reports on reading. The most widely distributed of these, available through special reprints, was called "See Dick Flunk" (Palmaffy, 1997). This publication proclaimed phonics as the answer to all reading ills, blamed whole language for the failure of California readers and the literacy crisis in general, and blamed the entire reading profession for rejecting NICHD's solid scientific findings about the benefit of phonics and the proven success of DISTAR. It resurrected past heroes such as Rudolf Flesch and Jeanne Chall, and introduced their conservative readers to the new heroes—Bonita Grossen, Keith Stanovich, Barbara Foorman, and of course, Reid Lyon—the star researcher/cheerleader for the government/corporate agenda.

Touted as indisputable evidence for systematic and explicit phonics instruction by both the Heritage Foundation and NICHD, was another federal and corporate (Pacific Bell) funded report also released in 1997 by Bonita Grossen, titled "Thirty years of research: What we now know about how children learn to read." Although, according to Reid Lyon, the NICHD's early literacy initiative did not begin until 1987, Grossen claims that the NIH had accumulated 30 years worth of data supporting the need for intensive, systematic phonics instruction. Despite the fact that Allington and Woodside-Jiron (1997) and Gerald Coles (2000) among others, would argue convincingly that there was scant evidence from the research studies (including the much publicized study by Foorman, Francis, Fletcher, & Schatschneider, 1998) cited by Grossen to support her instructional implications, the report nevertheless asserts the following principles of effective reading instruction:

- Begin teaching phonemic awareness directly at an early age.
- Teach each sound-spelling relationship systematically.
- Teach frequent, highly regular sound-spelling relationships systematically.
- Show children exactly how to sound out words.
- Use connected, decodable text for children to practice the sound-spelling relationships they learn.
- Use interesting stories to develop language comprehension (but use of these stories as reading material is ruled out during early stages of reading acquisition).
- Balance, but do not mix (comprehension and decoding instruction should be separate).

With this report under attack for its exaggerated and unsubstantiated recommendations, the U.S. Department of Education and the U.S. Department of Health and Human Services took steps to sponsor yet another report, this time under the auspices of the National Academy of Sciences.

The committee it formed headed by Catherine Snow, a noted language development researcher, issued their report "Preventing Reading Difficulties in Young Children" in 1998, and was hailed as a consensus report that would end the "reading wars." The committee issued a set of recommendations that seemed to balance the significance of explicit phonemic awareness and phonics instruction with an early focus on comprehension, invented spelling, independent reading reflecting individual interests, assisted or supported reading of more difficult texts, and outside reading. Apparently, these recommendations did not go far enough for those commissioning the report in endorsing explicit systematic phonemic awareness and phonics instruction. Therefore, before the NRC report was even released, the U.S. Congress convened the National Reading Panel, whose members were appointed by the NICHD itself under the leadership of Reid Lyon. In discussing this pivotal event, Richard Allington (2002) refers to an article by Catherine Snow, Chair of the NRC (Snow, 2001), in which she notes that Reid Lyon and Duane Alexander (Director of the NICD) regarded the NRC report as too "ambiguous" in its consensus findings and lax in its criteria for scientifically trustworthy research. Allington (2002) offers this assessment:

> In other words, the NRC committee didn't actually endorse explicit, systematic phonics as the "scientifically based" plan. So it would it was time to try another tactic. (p. 40)

Before the National Reading Panel published their findings in 2000, two other influential, widely distributed documents would urge every level of the educational establishment—school administrators, teachers, teacher education institutions, and teacher educators—to redesign and rethink reading instruction. The first of these documents, Every Child Reading: An Action Plan, was published by the "Learning First Alliance" in 1998. This national coalition of organizations, such as the American Association of Colleges for Teacher Education (AACTE), National Association of State Boards of Education (NASBE) and the American Federation of Teachers (AFT), offered their interpretation of the NRC Report. I myself was handed the Learning First Alliance by the dean of my college, who had received it, along with his colleagues across the country as "definitive" proof that whole language and other progressive pedagogies had been officially abandoned by the educational establishment, in favor of a more scientifically based perspective. Although the document unequivocally supports explicit, systematic phonics, a closer reading reveals the endorsement of a "balanced approach," which integrated methods deriving from a number of philosophies. Basing its position on the NRC report, the Learning First Alliance proclaimed the end of the "reading wars," thereby perpetuating the myth that the assault on whole language was a consequence, not of a carefully orchestrated and choreographed campaign on the part of the government/corporate conglomerate, but of academic squabbling among reading researchers and theorists. The document seemed to be saying "can't we now just all get along and teach everything—no matter how contradictory?"

This absurd position of eclecticism would have a strong influence on reading curricula and teacher education programs in the direction of "balance" between phonics and meaning, literature and decodable texts, and the abandonment of any cohesive theoretical and philosophical framework. But a more damaging document was yet to be issued. In 1999 the AFT in an unfortunate statement about reading instruction, published the document "Teaching Reading IS Rocket Science" written by the NICHD loyalist Louisa Moats. The largest teachers' union in the country would endorse an extremist position formulated by Louisa Moats and presented as a grossly underjustified set of recommendations for teacher preparation based on her creative interpretation of research findings. These recommendations, shown here, would fuel the campaign already brewing to eliminate academic freedom and steer the course of teacher education:

TABLE 3.2
Teaching Reading IS Rocket Science (By Louisa Moats for AFT)

Recommendations for teacher preparation and certification:
Research should guide the profession
   Eliminate popular misconceptions such as:
   • Competent teachers do not use published reading programs.
   • Avoiding published reading programs empowers teachers.
   • Reading a lot is the best way to overcome a reading problem.
   • Children should be taught to guess words on the basis of meaning and syntax.
   • Skills must always be taught in the context of literature.
   Establish core standards, curriculum, and entry level assessments for new teachers.
   • Align teacher education curricula, standards for students, and licensing requirements for teachers.
   • Create professional development institutes for professors and master teachers.
   • Press the developers of textbooks and instructional materials to improve their products ("only reading programs that incorporate practices and materials validated by research should be adopted for general use") (Moats, 1999, p. 25).

This set of recommendations published by the AFT, are of major significance because they represent a virtual blueprint for the subsequent assault on teacher education (now in full swing as a result of NCLB legislation), and because they mark the wholesale betrayal of teachers by the union leadership. Through its complicity in the government/corporate effort to control public schools, the AFT bureaucrats seriously erode the professionalism of our country's teachers and teacher educators.

The new millennium began with a momentous year for the government/corporate agenda. The year of 2000 marked the publication of the National Reading Panel Report and congressional approval of the Reading Excellence Act. The Reading Excellence Act, preceded by a fanfare of media hype, was the first of two acts of Congress that have encoded into law a state definition of reading, reading instruction and scientific research. The legislation limited federal funding for reading only to those programs based on "reliable, replicable research," a phrase that referred to the experimental, "medical model" studies included in the National Reading Panel meta-analysis of reading research. The Reading Excellence Act became the most successful use, to that point, of legislating federal control over reading instruction.

The report of the National Reading Panel provided impetus for the legislation of 2000 as well as the disastrous No Child Left Behind bill passed later in 2002. With a significant sleight of hand in the preparation of a somewhat inaccurate summary report and glossy publicity booklet (Armbruster, Lehr, & Osborn, 2001), the report yielded the long awaited return on the investment in government commissioned reports. Although it has met with widespread criticism from within the panel itself (Yatvin, 2002), as well as the larger reading research community (Allington, 2002; Coles, 2001, 2003; Cunningham, 2001; Garan, 2001; Krashen, 2001), it has continued to thrive as the centerpiece of the propaganda campaign to win public support for federal and corporate control of public schools and teacher education. Through free and widespread distribution of "Put Reading First," the glossy publication coproduced by The National Institute for Literacy, the NICHD, and the U.S. Department of Education, the public is given a spruced up version of the panel's actual findings discussed in the full report. A selection of the claims made about phonics communicated to parents and educators through "Put Reading First" are found in Table 3.3. Many of these claims are either generalized and exaggerated versions of the actual findings of the NRP or interpretations that go far beyond them. Some of the actual findings of the NRP report are somewhat surprising in their limited support for a regimen of systematic and explicit phonemic awareness and phonics instruction. These are either summarized, paraphrased or directly quoted in Table 3.4.

The systematic manipulation of research and public opinion achieved through government sponsored panels and reports, nationwide media campaigns, foundation publications, and the NICHD controlled research agenda, finally culminated in congressional approval of George Bush's No Child Left Behind legislation in 2002—the last item on our timeline. It followed the appointment of Rod Paige, former superintendent of Houston

TABLE 3.3
Claims in "Put Reading First"

Systematic and explicit phonics instruction significantly improves kindergarten and first-grade children's word recognition and spelling.

Systematic phonics instruction produces the greatest impact on children's reading achievement when it begins in kindergarten or first grade.

Both kindergarten and first-grade children who receive systematic phonics instruction are better at reading and spelling words than kindergarten and first-grade children who do not receive systematic instruction.

Systematic and explicit phonics instruction significantly improves children's reading comprehension.

Systematic phonics instruction results in better growth in children's ability to comprehend what they read than non-systematic or no phonics instruction.

Systematic and explicit phonics instruction is effective for children from various social and economic levels.

Systematic and explicit phonics instruction is most effective when introduced early.

Systematic and explicit phonics instruction provides practice with letter-sound relationships in a predetermined sequence. Children learn to use these relationships to decode words that contain them.

Non-systematic programs of phonics instruction

Literature-based programs that emphasize reading and writing activities. Phonics instruction is embedded in these activities, but letter-sound relationships are taught incidentally, usually based on key letters that appear in student reading materials.

Basal reading programs that focus on whole-word or meaning-based activities. These programs pay only limited attention to letter-sound relationships and provide little or no instruction in how to blend letters to pronounce words.

Sight-word programs that begin by teaching children a sight-word reading vocabulary of from 50 to 100 words. Only after they learn to read these words do children receive instruction in the alphabetic principle.

Further, adding phonics workbooks or phonics activities to these programs of instruction has not been effective. Such "add-ons" confuse rather than help children to read.

(Armbruster, Lehr, & Osborn, 2001)

Public Schools (and McGraw-Hill award winner) as secretary of education, and Reid Lyon as presidential advisor on reading in 2001. It was also preceded in the same year by yet another foundation report, this time published by the Abell Foundation virtually calling for the end to teacher certification and university-based teacher education programs (Abell Foundation, 2001). NCLB, and in particular, Reading First and Early Reading First sections legalize a virtual federal takeover of public education and achieves the goals of the Business Roundtable to institute national standards (and standardization), assessment and accountability. NCLB legislates yearly standardized state reading tests (yielding the individual scores businesses desired), threatens financial consequences for schools that do not meet standards, and specifies every aspect of reading education eligible for funding—from "scientifically based" curriculum, to "scientifically based" professional de-

TABLE 3.4
The NRP Report . . . The Truth and Nothing But The Truth

Phonemic Awareness:
Over the period of one school year, only 5–18 hours of phonemic awareness instruction
is recommended.

Phonics:
"There were insufficient data to draw any conclusions about the effects of phonics instruction with normally developing readers above 1st grade" (pp. 2–116).
Systematic phonics instruction [including embedded approaches] produced better results
than no systematic phonics at all. There were no significant differences found among
the five approaches studied.
There was no evidence found that phonics transferred to conventional spelling or reading comprehension of authentic texts using real words and longer passages. (Invented
or developmental spellings of kindergartners and first graders were accepted in positive findings.)
There were no findings reported on the effectiveness of decodable texts.

Independent reading (SSR):
Literally hundreds of studies suggest that "the best readers read the most and the poor
readers read the least . . . the more that children read, the better their fluency, vocabulary, and comprehension" (pp. 3–21). (But these were not included in the report.)

Comprehension: Vocabulary
"Vocabulary should be taught both directly and indirectly . . . repetition and multiple ex-
posures are important." . . . Learning in rich contexts, incidental learning and use of
computer technology all enhance the acquisition (pp. 4–27).

Comprehension: Text Comprehension
There are seven different instructional approaches found effective, including comprehension monitoring, cooperative learning, use of graphic and semantic organizers, question answering, question generation, story structure, summarization.
"Quality literature helps students to build a sense of story and to develop vocabulary
and comprehension" (pp. 2–97).

Scripted Commercial Programs
Some commercial programs "are scripted in such a way that teacher judgment is largely
eliminated. Although scripts may standardize instruction, they may reduce teachers' interest in the teaching process" (pp. 2–96).

---

velopment, to "scientifically based" reading programs. Whole language
and critical, democratic education makes way for the creation of a 21st
century workforce: functionally and technologically literate, compliant,
competent enough to do the job, but not creative or critical enough to
question the overall corporate agenda. Positions requiring true analytical
and intellectual rigor will be filled by children of the elite and ruling class
who attend private schools that do not require federal funds, and are
therefore exempt from these federal regulations. Publishers of phonics-
based commercial reading programs have struck gold by being sanctioned

as reflecting "scientific" research. And companies like McGraw-Hill that publish standardized reading tests have hit the mother lode through required yearly testing.

We have come to the end of our timeline, but not the end of our journey. Teachers, parents and students all across the United States and in every community are expressing their anger and concern over one-size-fits-all "dumbed-down" curriculum and high stakes testing. States like Maine are publicly criticizing NCLB and have considered refusing to comply with federal policy. Professional organizations, such as NCTE, are publishing statements and passing resolutions condemning NCLB and the federal intrusion into schools and teacher education programs. In some communities, parents, teachers, and students are taking to the streets in front of state departments of education to protest current policies. Cars can be seen in the streets of Los Angeles to Washington, D.C. sporting bumper stickers proclaiming "My child is more than a test score." Although the government/corporate agenda for education may appear to have been realized, the battle for critical, democratic, and equitable schools is far from over. We have learned a long and painful lesson from the last 20 years that the battle for a just and equitable society starts with the battle over the classroom, and the future of our children depends on us.

REFERENCES

Abell Foundation. (2001, October). Teacher certification reconsidered. *Abell Report*. Baltimore, MD.

Adams, M. (1990). *Beginning to read: Thinking and learning about print*. Cambridge, MA: MIT Press.

Allington, R. L. (Ed.). (2002). *Big brother and the national reading curriculum*. Portsmouth, NH: Heinemann.

Allington, R. L., & Woodside-Jiron, H. (1997). *Adequacy of a program of research and of a "research synthesis" in shaping educational policy*. Albany, NY: National Center on English Learning and Achievement. Report Series 1.15.

Altwerger, B., & Saavedra, E. (1999). Foreword. In C. Edelsky, *Making justice our project*. Urbana, IL: NCTE.

Armbruster, B. B., Lehr, F., & Osborn, J. (2001). *Put reading first: The research building blocks for teaching children to read*. Partnership for Reading, a collaborative effort of the National Institute for Literacy, the National Institute of Child Health and Human Development, and the U.S. Department of Education.

Augustine, N. (1997, July). *The business leader's guide to setting academic standards*. The Business Roundtable. Available online at www.brtable.org

Augustine, N., Lupberger, E., & Orr, J. F. (1997, July). *A common agenda for improving American education*. The Business Roundtable. Available online at www.brtable.org.

Business Roundtable. (1995). *Continuing the commitment: Essential components of a successful educational system*. Available online at www.brtable.org

Coles, G. (2000). *Misreading reading: The bad science that hurts children*. Portsmouth, NH: Heinemann.

Coles, G. (2001). Reading taught to the tune of the "scientific" hickory stick. *Phi Delta Kappan, 83*(3), 205–211.

Coles, G. (2003). *Reading the naked truth: Literacy, legislation and lies*. Portsmouth, NH: Heinemann.

Commission on Reading, National Academy of Education. (1985). *Becoming a nation of readers*. Washington, DC: National Institute of Education.

Cunningham, J. (2001). The national reading panel report. *Reading Research Quarterly, 36*(3), 326–335.

Foorman, B. R., Francis, D. J., Fletcher, J. M., & Schatschneider, C. (1998). The role of instruction in learning to read: Preventing reading failure in at-risk children. *Journal of Educational Psychology, 92*, 37–55.

Garan, E. M. (2001). What does the report of the National Reading Panel really tell us about teaching phonics. *Language Arts, 79*(1), 61–70.

Goodman, K. S. (1998). Who's afraid of whole language: Politics, paradigms, pedagogy, and the press. In K. S. Goodman, (Ed.), *In defense of good teaching: What teachers need to know about the "reading wars."* Portsmouth, NH: Heinemann.

Grossen, B. (1997). *30 years of research: What we now know about how children learn to read (A synthesis of research on reading from the National Institute of Child Health and Development commissioned by the Center for the Future of Teaching and Learning with funding support from the Pacific Bell Foundation)*. Santa Cruz, CA: Center for the Future of Teaching and Learning.

Krashen, S. (1996). *Every person a reader: An alternative to the California task force report on reading*. Culver City, CA: Language Education Associates.

Krashen, S. (2001, October). More smoke and mirrors: A critique of the national reading panel (NRP) report on "fluency." *Phi Delta Kappan, 83*(2), 119–123.

Learning First Alliance. (1998). *Every child reading: An action plan*. Washington, DC: Lyon.

Lyon, R. (1999, October 6). *Education research: Is what we don't know hurting our children?* Statement for the House Science Committee, Subcommittee on Basic Research. U.S. House of Representatives.

McChesney, R. (1997, November/December). The global media giants: The nine firms that dominate the world. *Extra*. Fairness and Accuracy in Reporting.

Metcalf, S. (2002, January 28). Reading between the lines. *The Nation*.

Moats, L. (1999). *Teaching reading IS rocket science: What expert teachers of reading should know and be able to do*. Washington, DC: The American Federation of Teachers.

National Reading Panel. (2000). *Teaching children to read, an evidence-based assessment of the scientific research literature on reading and its implications for reading instruction*. Washington, DC: National Institute of Child Health and Human Development.

Palmaffy, T. (1997, November/December). See Dick flunk. *Policy Review*. The Heritage Foundation.

Pearson, P. D. (1990). Foreword: How I came to know about Beginning to read. In M. Adams (Ed.), *Beginning to read: Thinking and learning about print*. Cambridge, MA: MIT Press.

Snow, C. E. (2001). Preventing reading difficulties in young children: Precursors and fallout. In T. Loveless (Ed.), *The great curriculum debate* (pp. 229–246). Washington, DC: Brookings.

Snow, C. E., Burns, M. S., & Griffin, P. (Eds.). (1998). *Preventing reading difficulties in young children*. Washington, DC: National Academy Press.

U.S. Department of Education, O.E.S.E. (2002). *No Child Left Behind: A desktop reference*. Available online at http://www.ed.gov/offices/OESE/reference.pdf

Williams, P. (1995). *NAEP 1994 reading: A first look*. Washington, DC: Educational Testing Service for National Center for Educational Research and Improvement, U.S. Department of Education.

Wolfe, P., & Poynor, L. (2001). Politics and the pendulum: An alternative understanding of the case of whole language as educational innovation. *Educational Researcher, 30*(1), 15–20.

Yatvin, J. (2002, January). Babes in the woods: The wanderings of the National Reading Panel. *Phi Delta Kappan, 83*(5), 364–369.

CHAPTER FOUR

Who Gets to Play?
How and Why Reading Researchers
Were Left Out of the
No Child Left Behind Act

Sharon Matthews

The reauthorization of the Elementary and Secondary Education Act, now entitled No Child Left Behind (NCLB), ushered in comprehensive legislation aimed at significantly altering the way our nation's children are taught to read. Although the focus of concern centers on our children, and rightly so, a closer look at workings behind the public view is essential to an understanding of how this legislation was crafted and implemented in ways that will ultimately lead to the failure of many of our children. Just outside of the public eye, and somewhat removed from the media spotlight, specific groups of people profit in multiple ways from this legislative agenda. Who are these groups and in what ways do they profit? Myriad answers apply to this question. However, research into the proponents of the "scientifically based" reading instruction movement in particular yields interesting patterns.

Educators and parents should be informed as to who gives voice to the current agenda, as well as who is silenced in that process. The lack of professional respect and courtesy displayed by these groups is alarming and deserves a spotlight in the conversation that must take place if there is to be hope that our children's needs will be addressed above personal considerations of wealth, notoriety, and power. The public should be made aware of who profits from reading legislation requiring schools to purchase materials deemed appropriate by the federal government. The commonalities between who is given voice and who profits financially must be closely examined in order to discern why decisions affecting the lives of our children are being made. Finally, an understanding of how instruction for all students will be structured under this new plan offers a fascinating look at how reading teachers' and researchers' insights and professional knowledge are ignored in favor of a view of the child as deficient and the reading process as isolated and disconnected.

THE GIVING AND TAKING OF VOICE

While our children face the adversities of NCLB, another group must also contend with the political and personal repercussions of this piece of legislation. Beyond the troublesome mandates requiring yearly standardized testing and the dubious distinction of scientifically based reading strategies as the only appropriate means by which to educate our students, lies another layer of politics—a separate agenda that requires deeper investigation. Professional educators who wish to disagree with current pedagogical mandates are being silenced. Their voices are not heard on either federal or state levels as they attempt to criticize the existing reading agenda.

As President Bush and his loyal cohort herald the arrival of sweeping reform, a sizable number of educators at every level of the education community call out for an opportunity to be heard. As reading researchers and concerned classroom teachers attempt to establish debate over NCLB and Reading First legislation, they continually find they have no platform from which to speak. This lack of agency is evidenced at all levels, but is readily apparent with regard to reading research. The majority of education professionals testifying before the House Committee on Education and the Workforce have been staunch supporters of the Bush plan. Among the most visible is Reid Lyon, chair of the Child Development and Behavior Branch of the National Institute for Child Health and Development (NICHD).

Lyon has enjoyed a long-standing relationship with George W. Bush that has enabled him, through this association, to authoritatively proclaim himself as qualified to define reading instruction that will address the needs of all students. Interestingly enough, Lyon earned his PhD from the University of New Mexico in psychology and developmental disabilities. Although touted as "the reading guru" (Davis, 2001) by President Bush as well as frequently being referred to as a reading researcher, a search of ERIC documents reveals that Dr. Lyon has written and published only two articles that could be considered within the reading field. Those publications were entitled *Why reading is not a natural process*, and *Toward a definition of dyslexia*. He co-authored four articles that specifically mention reading, although three of the four are concerned with reading disability. Those titles include: *Differentiating between difficult-to reme-diate and readily remediated poor readers: More evidence against the IQ-Achievement discrepancy definition of reading disability* (fourth author); and, *Subtypes of reading disability: variability around a phonological core* (fifth author of nine). *Critical conceptual and methodological considerations in reading intervention research*; and, *Wanted: Teachers with knowledge of language* were co-authored with Louisa Moats. Lyon's work focuses on a narrow conceptualization of the reading process, and is clearly predicated on scientifically based methodologies. And yet, his own work is seriously suspect and prone to threats of validity. Critiquing the concept of learning disabilities, Coles (1987) found that Lyon's methodology, and therefore, his hypotheses and conclusions, were highly questionable. Questions about arbitrary sorting of test scores that could have landed a child in one subgroup as easily as in another, the ambiguous meaning of the "neuropsychological" tests, the weak association of neuropsychological test profiles and types of LD did not temper this or similar interpretations of other subtypes in the study (p. 236).

Lyon's conceptualization of scientifically based reading research, as well as a narrow assessment of "disabled readers" is now being superimposed on all children as evidenced by Reading First and NCLB legislation that requires all students be subjected to discrete instruction that bears a striking resemblance to that imposed on children placed in special education programs.

Lyon is concerned that his beliefs are not reflected in the education of preservice teachers, and by colleges of education in general. This point was made abundantly clear at a policy forum conducted by the Coalition for Evidence-Based Policy in November 2002, when he stated:

> How do kids learn to read? What goes wrong when they don't? How do we prevent it? That should be the content that teachers and others in education actually acquire. Do they acquire it? No. You know, if there was any piece of legislation that I could pass, it would be to blow up colleges of education. I know that's not politically correct. Those are some of the most resistant, recalcitrant places you will ever get to. And I'm not sure it's going to get a heck of a lot better, because again philosophy and belief drive how their folks are taught and how their folks come to teach others. (p. 84)

These seditious statements reveal how little professional regard Lyon holds for his colleagues with whom he ontologically disagrees. Rather than appeal for dialogue, he blatantly calls for the destruction of the same entity that granted him access to the education community. Would the same rhetoric have been so well received if it had come from someone outside of the scientifically based camp? The answer is an unequivocal no.

Louisa Moats, another prominent member of the NICHD, has enjoyed the opportunity to testify before Congress concerning her stance on how children learn to read. Her work (Moats, 2000) as a reading researcher is clearly defined by the belief that children must be instructed in isolated, sequential segments. Her vehement dislike of holistic instruction is evident in the following passage:

Whole language persists today for several reasons. A pervasive lack of rigor in university education departments has allowed much nonsense to infect reading-research symposia, courses for teachers, and journals. Many reading programs have come to covertly embody whole-language principles. Additionally, many state standards and curricular frameworks still reflect whole-language ideas. Rooting out whole language from reading classrooms calls for effort on eight separate fronts:

1. Every state should have language-arts content standards and curricular frameworks for each grade from kindergarten through third grade that are explicitly based on solid reading-research findings.
2. State assessments should be calibrated to show the effects of reading instruction as delineated in well-written state standards.
3. State accountability systems should emphasize the attainment of grade-appropriate reading, spelling, and writing skills by third grade.
4. States should adopt rigorous licensing exams for new and veteran teachers alike.
5. Alternative teacher-preparation programs should be encouraged.
6. Traditional teacher-preparation programs of education should focus on training and retention of effective teachers.
7. State-guided textbook adoptions should focus on the alignment of the material with research evidence about what works best, and publishers should be required to show for whom their product works and under what conditions.
8. Journalists and policymakers need to examine closely instructional programs and packages offered in the name of "balanced" reading. (Moats, 2000)

These comments clearly reveal a lack of willingness to debate opinions based on reliable research and professional knowledge. Moats' words are inflammatory and contribute little in the way of the academic rigor she seems so quick to disparage.

A disturbing aspect of NCLB is the concerted effort by politicians and researchers who agree with the mandates to quiet all who would attempt to establish dialogue. Blanket determinations of acceptable research ignore the rich account of the reading process as studied by reading researchers dedicated to studying how young readers transact with, and make meaning from text. Because these researchers understand reading processes in ways fundamentally opposed to the part-to-whole stance, their attempts to debate the efficacy of sweeping mandates are met with disdain. The obstacles established for opponents of scientifically based reading instruction are formidable. One important distinction requires further discussion. The continual use of the words *reading researchers* is not meant to be redundant, but to bring to the forefront that reading researchers have had little to no chance to affect the decision-making process. Garan (2002), one of the first reading educators to criticize the work of the National Reading Panel, described the professional background of the members appointed by the NICHD. She noted,

> Oddly enough, the majority of the fourteen-member panel had never been directly involved in actually teaching children to read but came from an unusual assortment of occupations. These included a certified public accountant, a physics professor, a neuro-scientist, an assistant director of the National Science Foundation, a director of urban education, and seven cognitive psychologist/scientists. Only two panel members had close links to the actual teaching of reading. (p. 3)

An important correlation here is that these members were appointed by the NICHD. Their lack of theoretical and pedagogical knowledge presupposed their compliance to narrowly define reading, which ultimately led to a willingness to rely on quantitative data to reveal insights they were unable to glean from thick descriptions provided in qualitative studies. Prominent reading researchers were systematically silenced by these appointments, as they have been throughout the entire process, beginning with the appointment of the National Reading Panel.

In reality, the existing climate of suppression was foreshadowed by proponents of current mandates. Snow, Burns, and Griffin (1998) stated in the introduction to their edited volume:

> The study reported in this volume was undertaken with the assumption that empirical work in the field of reading had advanced sufficiently to allow substantial agreed-upon results and conclusions that could form a basis for breaching the differences among the warring parties. The process of doing the study revealed the correctness of the assumption that this has been an appropriate time to undertake a synthesis of the research on early reading development. The knowledge base is now large enough that the controversies that have dominated discussions of reading development and reading instruction have given way to a widely honored *pax lectura*, the conditions of which include a shared focus on the needs and rights of all children to learn to read. (pp. v–vi)

The announcement regarding correctness of assumptions erroneously leads readers to believe that some sort of informed truce was achieved. In fact, this work merely hints at the professional consideration that was afforded to participants in the discussion of how children learn to read. By declaring a truce that never existed, the campaign of repression was successfully planted years before evidence of true intentions became evident.

Although silenced and often ridiculed for their beliefs, professionals unable to contend with these mandates refuse to sit quietly and passively accept this fate on behalf of our nation's children. Concerted efforts to quash alternative stances indicate fear on the part of those who are unable or unwilling to accept that dissenting voices exist. However, educators who understand the reading process differently are actively seeking to have their voices heard. Numerous articles (Meyer, 2002; Strauss, 2003; Yatvin, 2002) and books (Allington, 2003; Coles, 2000, 2003; Garan, 2002) decry the legislative process that has sanctioned the mistreatment of education professionals and ignored the educational needs of our children.

PROFITING FROM THE AGENDA

Although many advocates of scientifically based reading instruction have experienced financial or professional gain as a result of their connections to NCLB, corporate America has benefited as well. The McGraw-Hill Publishing Company has profited tremendously from an association between the McGraw and Bush families. Not only was Harold McGraw III a member of Barbara Bush's Foundation, he also participated in a meeting at the White House attended by Fortune 500 CEOs from which *The Nation* reported the following:

> One, Harold McGraw, the publishing scion and current chairman of McGraw-Hill, summed up: "It's a great day for education, because we now have substantial alignment among all the key constituents—the public, the education community, business and political leaders—that results matter." (Metcalf, 2002)

NCLB mandates for scientifically based reading instruction have significantly increased the profits of the company based solely on the sales of basal series for elementary students and testing products sold to schools. These connections did not come about by chance. After completion of the National Reading Panel report, a summary report was prepared for dissemination of the panel's findings. Coincidentally, the summary report was written in part by a public relations firm, Widemeyer Baker, which is also employed by McGraw-Hill (Strauss, 2003). This report was widely distributed to policymakers and the media. Based on this commentary, McGraw-Hill was able to link the various series it produces directly back to specific wording suggested as appropriate for the reading education of young children (i.e., research based, scientifically based, replicable, reliable). Profits in the education division rose twelve percent in the fourth quarter of 2002 and though the company reported a loss of $2.8 million in 2001, they recently reported a 2002 fourth quarter profit of $134.9 million (Diaz, 2003).

These relationships, and the profits that are realized as a result of legislative support, extend to another group of business leaders, the Business Roundtable. Harold McGraw III is a member of that group. The intentions of the Business Roundtable were critiqued by Altwerger and Strauss (2002):

> To understand the recent dramatic shift in reading pedagogy, one must not underestimate the agenda of the Business Roundtable, since this organization has more than sufficient resources, power, and influence to sway policymakers, whether or not its goals have the support of teachers and educators. The Business Roundtable's main objective is not quality education but the preservation of the competitiveness of corporate America in the global economy. (p. 258)

McGraw-Hill basal series have given several direct-instruction authors another chance to put their pedagogical beliefs into practice. Open Court, co-authored by Marilyn Jager Adams is among the few programs deemed appropriate to provide scientifically based reading instruction. It is currently "only one of two reading programs that California school systems are allowed to buy with state funds" (Coles, 2003, p. 77). Adams' connections run far deeper than Open Court. She also contributed to the work of the National Reading Panel and co-authored a phonemic awareness program with Barbara Foorman (Garan, 2002).

Also an NICHD funded researcher, Barbara Foorman, reviewed the phonics section for the National Reading Panel. Her work with the NRP is a clear exploitation of the occasion to review her own work:

> [O]f the 38 articles included in the NRP's meta-analysis, Foorman was the lead or secondary author of four. In other words, she contributed more than 10 of the articles reviewed by the NRP and was a reviewer of her own work. (Strauss, 2003, p. 438)

Foorman's ethical decisions regarding her research have been called into question in previous instances as well. Coles (2000) devoted a chapter of *Misreading Reading* to a discussion of a 1998 study of which Foorman was lead author. Coles contends:

> From the time of this first announcement [February 1997 release of *Preventing Reading Difficulties in Young Children*] until a month after the publication of the National Academy of Science report (approximately fourteen months) *no one* who might have been potentially critical of the research was allowed to read a prepublication manuscript on the Foorman study. Responding to all requests for a copy, the researchers declared the study "embargoed" until publication. Although media articles were allowed to report the study's supposed findings, Foorman and her colleagues rejected all criticism as premature because the report and its actual facts had not been released. Despite all this secrecy, the researchers themselves had no qualms about including, prior to publication, their study's "facts" for the National Academy of Science committee's review of reading research and allowing these yet-published "facts" to become part of a major report of a national, prestigious scientific organization. (p. 41)

Clearly, a vital concern centers on how this researcher appears to have manipulated two situations in favor of avoiding criticism by colleagues in the field. An unwillingness to release a manuscript that has already been publicly cited highlights a consistent pattern of denial that opposing stances exist and that vigorous debate would serve our children well.

Proponents of systematic phonics instruction consistently work to restrict critique of their stance on reading. The Committee on Education and the Workforce, as a governmental entity, has encouraged these actions by providing a platform for researchers who are advocates of explicit instruction without providing access to reading researchers who espouse holistic theory. A search of the committee's website reveals that no prominent reading researcher who opposes an explicit, systematic view of reading has appeared to provide testimony. Evidence previously noted indicates that a prohibition of viewpoints critical of the current agenda exists to silence reading professionals.

SHIFTING READING PRACTICE

As a result of the NRP, the subsequent summary report, NCLB and Reading First legislation, the agenda of the NICHD, and the consequent prominence of publishing companies, a forced shift in reading pedagogy is occurring in the United States. Buoyed by constant validation, advocates of explicit instruction criticize reading researchers and educators in numerous ways. One of the most interesting critiques though not specifically directed at holistic educators alone, but at anyone attempting to meet the needs of students, occurred during Susan Neuman's visit to the University of the Pacific:

If implemented the right way, [NCLB] will put an end to creative and experimental teaching methods in the nation's classrooms. "It will stifle, and hopefully it will kill (them)," said Neuman, U.S. assistant secretary of education. "Our children are not laboratory rats." (Balta, 2002)

Neuman's statements are indeed troubling, but actually only hint at the offensive that is thriving due to the current legislative agenda. However, her comment that children are not laboratory rats could be perceived as a direct contradiction of the scientifically based faction's principle that only treatment and control groups are reflective of appropriate research. Without a doubt, teachers as creative individuals who actively seek to meet individual as well as group needs are not welcome according to the assistant secretary of education. Unfortunately, she is not alone in that belief.

What is a forced shift in reading practice? Neuman's comments give a hint to the focus of the agenda, but the entire campaign is more comprehensive. Teachers are central to the implementation of NCLB, but therein lies the concern. As professionals, teachers implement methods based on their theoretical groundings. They strive on a daily basis to provide instruction based on individual needs. Scripted lessons, however contradict their work by forcing all children to receive instruction in one particular way and at one particular time. Professional teachers do not need to follow tightly scripted lessons, which are the focus of direct instruction materials provided by publishers. Regrettably, these textbooks now comprise the only acceptable programs for adoption according to federal law.

In addition to scripted, sequential lessons that must be executed directly as written, reading practice is being shifted simply by ignoring the fact that knowledgeable reading professionals exist in schools and universities. The vast majority of NRP members, as well as influential governmental officials like Reid Lyon, are not reading educators or researchers, but instead professionals whose daily work focuses on learning disability in children. Allington (2003) argues:

If we are going to go with evidence, let's start with the evidence on the "success" of school programs for students identified as learning disabled . . . [M]aybe we should ask just why anyone should adopt the direct-instruction phonics interventions that have been part and parcel of failed learning disabilities interventions for the past thirty years. The failure of direct instruction to teach learning disabled children to read seems to be related simply to bad instructional design. . . . But putting the special education direct-instruction gurus in charge of reforming American reading instruction—even Orwell wouldn't have imagined such an outcome. (p. 275)

Most special education teachers and researchers maintain a view of reading instruction that closely matches that of sponsors of scientifically based instruction. Special education pedagogy more closely resembles a medical model in that instruction is prescribed in small units in the hope of curing the student's problem so that he may be returned to the general learning community. Consequently, a medical model of instruction is now being implemented against all students in our schools. The number of special educators serving at the federal and state levels far exceeds that of reading professionals (Ohanian, 2003). The application of such a model is of grave concern to Apple (1990). He asserts,

> By using official categories and constructs such as those defined by and growing out of existing institutional practices—examples might be studies of the "slow learner," "discipline problems," and "remediation," curriculum researchers may be lending the rhetorical prestige of science to what may be questionable practices of an educational bureaucracy (citing Douglas, op. cit., pp. 70–1) and a stratified economic system. That is, there is no rigorous attempt at examining *institutional culpability*. (p. 134)

The public, and a majority of educators, are unaware of the takeover of reading instruction by the special education community. Although the knowledge possessed by special educators is valuable to the institution of the public school, the knowledge base was never intended for the entire school population. Otherwise, there would be no need for the community to exist at all. Reading educators' knowledge and practice should be paramount to reform, a proactive element, rather than a silenced and reactive component of the process.

CONCLUSION

The systematic silencing of professional voices, both reading educators and researchers has been the focus of this chapter. The campaign against all who would oppose direct instruction is a concerted effort that is validated on many levels. Rampant disregard for professional courtesy, as indicated by disturbing quotes highlights the urgency with which this effort to effect reading education has proceeded.

A small group of direct instruction researchers and authors as well as business leaders have gained notoriety and power as a result of various associations with governmental officials. The current political climate has endorsed their stance without recognizing the value of all knowledge and ways of knowing. These people profit by having their agenda lauded at the expense of noted reading researchers, by gaining a platform to extend the scope of their work, and by financial reward.

Although not allowed a public voice in the debate over reading reform, reading researchers and educators will not cease to struggle on behalf of the millions of children who will be affected by this legislation. They re-fuse to have their theoretical knowledge base and research dismissed as ir-relevant. Our children deserve a vigorous debate that provides a platform for every person to discuss how the needs of all children rather than the desires of a few adults might be addressed.

REFERENCES

Allington, R. L. (2003). *Big brother and the national reading curriculum: How ideology trumped evidence*. Portsmouth, NH: Heinemann.

Altwerger, B., & Strauss, S. L. (2002). The business behind testing. *Language Arts, 79*(3), 256–263.

Apple, M. W. (1990). *Ideology and curriculum*. New York: Routledge.

Balta, V. (2002, October 25). Assistant secretary: No waivers of No Child Left Behind Act. *The Record*. Available online at www.recordnet.com/daily/news/articles/102502

Coalition for Evidence-Based Policy. (2002, November 18). *Rigorous evidence: The key to progress in education?* Available online at www.excelgov.org.

Coles, G. (1987). *The learning mystique: A critical look at learning disabilities*. New York: Fawcett Columbine.

Coles, G. (2000). *Misreading reading: The bad science that hurts children*. Portsmouth, NH: Heinemann.

Coles, G. (2003). *Reading the naked truth: Literacy, legislation, and lies*. Portsmouth, NH: Heinemann.

Committee on Education and the Workforce. House of Representatives, U.S. Congress. Avail-able online at www.edworkforce.house.gov.

Davis, B. (2001, April 23). Phonics maven is at center of Bush's education push. *Wall Street Journal*, p. A24.

Diaz, C. B. (2003, January 28). McGraw-Hill posts profit, textbooks help. *Reuters*. Available online at www.reuters.com

Garan, E. M. (2002). *Resisting reading mandates: How to triumph with the truth*. Ports-mouth, NH: Heinemann.

Metcalf, S. (2002, January 10). Reading between the lines. *The Nation*. Available online at www.thenation.com.

Meyer, R. J. (2002). Captives of the script: Killing us softly with phonics. *Language Arts, 79*(6), 452–461.

Moats, L. C. (2000). Whole language lives on: The illusion of "balanced" instruction. Thomas B. Fordham Foundation. Available online at www.edexcellence.net/library/wholelang.

Ohanian, S. (2003). Information from www.susanohanian.org.

Snow, C. E., Burns, M. S., & Griffin, P. (Eds.). (1998). *Preventing reading difficulties in young children*. Washington, DC: National Academy Press.

Strauss, S. L. (2003). Challenging the NICHD reading research agenda. *Phi Delta Kappan, 84*(6), 438–442.

Yatvin, J. (2002). Babes in the woods: The wanderings of the National Reading Panel. *Phi Delta Kappan, 83*(5), 364–352.

CHAPTER FIVE

Warning: Current Federal Education Policy May Be Hazardous to Your Health

Steven L. Strauss

THE MISNAMED "MEDICAL MODEL" OF READING RESEARCH

In the year 2000, the National Reading Panel, operating under the auspices of the National Institute of Child Health and Human Development, a member institute of the National Institutes of Health, itself funded through the U.S. Department of Health and Human Services, issued its report on evidence-based instructional methods in reading. This report, or at least the summary version of it, is frequently cited as the scientific justification for the current administration's No Child Left Behind Act, which takes the Clinton–Gore Reading Excellence Act one step further, in not only legislating direct phonics instruction in U.S. classrooms, but in proposing punitive measures against students, teachers, and schools who do not comply with the mandates.

In the report's introduction, the panel states that its evaluation of the instructional research on reading was in accordance with the usual standards of medical research:

> The evidence-based methodological standards adopted by the Panel are essentially those normally used in research studies of the efficacy of interventions in psychological and medical research. These include behaviorally based interventions, medications, or medical procedures proposed for use

in the fostering of robust health and psychological development and the prevention or treatment of disease. (National Reading Panel Report, 2000, p. 5)

Pursuing this medical standards theme, a recent forum sponsored by the Coalition for Evidence-Based Policy heard representatives of the current federal administration compare evidence-based research in education to that in medicine. The Council for Excellence in Government, in a discussion of the forum, and of a report prepared jointly by the Coalition for Evidence-Based Policy and the U.S. Department of Education, declared that,

> In contrast to education, randomized trials in medicine and welfare policy have produced remarkable advances.
> Randomized trials in medicine, employment and welfare policy, and other fields are considered the 'gold standard' for evaluating the effectiveness of interventions. In medicine, randomized trials have produced extraordinary advances in human health, for example, helping to bring about a decrease in coronary heart disease and stroke by more than 50 percent over the past half-century. The report notes that medicine also provides important examples of how even the most careful nonrandomized studies—such as those investigating Hormone Replacement Therapy—can sometimes produce erroneous conclusions and lead to practices that are ineffective or harmful.

But the claim that the new focus in education research is following the lead of medical science is both false and misleading. It is false because nothing about the NRP's work, or the work of the U.S. Department of Education, reveals any sensitivity to the full spectrum of questions that are routinely and obligatorily asked in evaluations of medical interventions, most importantly, questions that are not only about the benefits of intervention, but are about the *risks* as well. The claim of adhering to a medical model is misleading because the public is inclined to consider medical science the paragon of humanistically-motivated science, trusting that government endorsed positions imply both efficacy and safety, neither one of which has been demonstrated by the NRP or the Department of Education, their pronouncements notwithstanding.

It should be clearly noted that the NRP report explicitly acknowledges that it only looked at "research studies of the efficacy of interventions." Likewise, the Council for Excellence in Education noted that the medical model of current government education policy is based only on studies of "the effectiveness of interventions." But efficacy is merely one of several necessary criteria that together characterize an investigation of a proposed intervention as medical in nature. Alone, and isolated from safety studies and other considerations, it cannot rise to this level of characterization. Pouring hydrochloric acid on a skin wart is extremely effective in eliminating the wart. But what would we think of our government if it sanctioned this highly effective method of wart elimination without advising us of the potentially tragic consequences?

Thus, the government's case for having provided a medical model of interventions applicable to reading and education is substantially inadequate, and on this basis alone should be rejected. Equally damaging to its case is that the coercive pedagogical practices embodied in No Child Left Behind violate the ethical spirit of medical intervention. Hearing government representatives talk about applying presumably humane, yet rigorous, medical standards to education in the same breath that they talk about punitive grade retention, withdrawal of funding, and school closures is, at best, mind boggling. But all of this becomes perfectly consistent when we grasp that medical standards have nothing to do with the substance of the government's reform, only with its Madison Avenue appearance.

HOW MEDICAL SCIENCE REALLY WORKS

Research of new medications proceeds according to a very strict protocol, which the government itself is only too aware of. The protocol consists of a series of investigative phases, in which, from phase I to phase IV, medicines are evaluated for pharmacokinetics and pharmacodynamics; beneficial effects and the doses necessary to achieve them; toxic effects and the doses necessary to achieve them; and, finally, post-marketing benefits and toxicities, based on sample sizes now larger than the ones used in the first three phases.

Phase IV is particularly important because it can reveal cases in which carefully designed randomized controlled trials of medicines are simply too narrow in scope to detect serious untoward reactions. This occurred, for example, with the antiseizure medicine felbamate and the cholesterol-lowering agent baycol, where phases I through III demonstrated acceptable efficacy and safety, only to lead to fatal cases of aplastic anemia and other serious problems once released to the public.

It simply does not matter how beneficial or effective a medicine is if it carries a risk of toxicity that is beyond an agreed on level of acceptability— it will not be approved or widely utilized. There will be warnings on the package inserts about the potential risks and side effects. And, there will certainly be mention made of how the medicine is not for everyone.

Furthermore, even if a treatment intervention is shown to be demonstrably effective in alleviating a certain condition, with relatively low risk, this does not automatically make it a standard of care for that condition. The various medical academies and specialties grade the degree of recommendation for using a certain treatment intervention as either a standard of care, practice guideline, practice option, or practice advisory. A standard of care is based on the firmest and most compelling investigative studies of the safety and efficacy of a specific treatment protocol for a particular pathologic condition. A practice guideline is based on a more moderate degree of clinical certainty. A practice option is based on less certain clinical evidence. And a practice advisory recognizes some clinically favorable evidence.

And even in the case of a standard of care, the best of all the conditions, a physician is still not legally obligated to treat the patient according to that standard. The physician has the right to explain to the patient and the patient's family why, in his or her opinion, what is considered the standard of care may not be appropriate for that individual. The patient can agree or disagree with the physician, and is generally encouraged to seek out second opinions in such difficult cases. The only liability for the physician is in not informing the patient of all the available options, even the ones that are not considered standard.

Conversely, the patient always retains the right to refuse treatment, even if it is considered the standard of care, and even if the physician believes it is the appropriate treatment. No patient is legally required to submit to any kind of treatment. And a patient can opt for an available treatment, even if it is not considered the standard.

The U.S. Department of Education, together with the NICHD, and through the willing collusion of Democratic and Republican politicians, is misleading the public in stating that research on "what works" in education is following the medical model, because not even the medical treatment that works the best for some condition, and is considered the standard of care, is legally forced on anyone, and especially not under the threat of loss of social options. It is inconceivable that a law could exist that would demand, with appropriate threats, that a surgeon operate on a patient when neither the surgeon nor the patient wants the procedure done, or that an internist prescribe a certain medication when neither the internist nor the patient wants to risk a potential side effect. But this, in essence, is the government's spin on the medical model. Rather than following medical guidelines, the government is distorting them wholesale.

If the government were consistent in its claim of following the medical model, it would issue recommendations about both efficacy and safety, and leave the final decisions about "interventions" in the hands of teachers, parents, and students. Sadly, the government has not even mentioned the safety issue, let alone studied it. If it were truly following a medical model of interventions, the government would not punish anyone for making a decision it did not like by withdrawing, or threatening to withdraw, the necessary funding.

This more democratic system would in reality make teachers more accountable, although now more accountable to students and parents, not to government bureaucrats. Teachers would have to knowledgeably explain and defend their choice of teaching methods, rather than saying: "I'm just following government orders." But this is a responsibility embraced without hesitation by the professional teacher, as it is analogously by physicians, none of whom would ever defend their choice of treatment on grounds of simply "following orders."

The subjects of isolated "what works" experiments are rats, not human beings. In contrast, the real world of medical interventions, as it applies to people, involves far more than research on what works. Indeed, it involves far more than research on side effects and toxicities. The fundamental controlling factor in taking research on medical intervention to the patient is the democratic right of the patient to refuse treatment. Medical intervention proceeds only after informed consent is obtained, which means that, in the end, treatment decisions are made by the patient, or the patient's surrogate, after having been fully informed by the physician of the available options, including known benefits and risks. This is the ultimate standard of care in medical practice, and it is impossible for a model of intervention to be a *medical* model if it does not incorporate this fundamental principle.

PHONICS TOXICITY AND OTHER SIDE EFFECTS

A democratically convened, open public forum on how medical standards might apply to issues in education would welcome challenging questions as a way to lead to answers that, in the end, help our children become healthier and happier members of society. In the current setting, these questions should include the following:

1. Who in the government can show us in what way research on phonics and phonemic awareness has proceeded through phases that examine both efficacy and safety?
2. Who can show us the rigorously-obtained scientific evidence that coercive pedagogy, such as high-stakes testing and accountability, leads to the desired results of improved reading levels, and that it does so without an unacceptable level of toxicity?
3. Where are the package inserts in the boxes of commercial phonics programs listing warnings about their inappropriate use, and that they should not be thought of as a substitute for a minimum daily dose of real reading?

To those who might argue that such questions do not apply to reading research, I would argue that they must apply if one insists on using a medical model. Such questions are so standard in medical science that to violate them would be unthinkable.

Are there side effects of too much phonics? The research clearly shows what happens to readers who are toxic on it. They read slowly and laboriously, and, ultimately, do not read for meaning (Goodman, Burke, & Watson, 1996)—if they are not turned off to reading altogether.

What about the side effects of high-stakes testing and accountability? Writing for the National Association of School Psychologists, Anderson, Whipple, and Jimerson (2002) expressed concerns over grade retention, one of the high stakes, noting that,

> Surveys of children's ratings of twenty stressful life events in the 1980s showed that, by the time they were in 6th grade, children feared retention most after the loss of a parent and going blind. When this study was replicated in 2001, 6th grade students rated grade retention as the single most stressful life event, higher than the loss of a parent or going blind. This finding is likely influenced by the pressures imposed by standards-based testing programs that often rely on test scores to determine promotion and graduation. (para. 8)

The authors also pointed out that grade retention is "one of the most powerful predictors of high school dropout, with retained students 2 to 11 times more likely to drop out of high school than promoted students" (para. 7).

The Journal of the American Medical Association published the views of a number of prominent child and adolescent psychiatrists about increased levels of stress and family dysfunction in association with the new testing climate (JAMA, May 23/30, 2001). So even those who make it through the system may be emotionally damaged in the process.

Stress in children is known to be a risk factor for headaches, asthma, depression, and many other problems. Grade retention, like U.S. illiteracy itself, is a risk factor for drug abuse and crime (Anderson, Whipple, & Jimerson, 2002). Can we be sure that the increasingly stressful climate associated with testing will not cause more school violence?

Preliminary assessments of children's reactions to high-stakes testing have not shown that it motivates them to learn. Rather, it leads to all sorts of emotional and psychological distress. For example, Wheelock, Bebell, and Haney's (2002) interpretation of children's drawings about their experiences with high-stakes tests suggests significant problems with anxiety, anger, hostility, boredom, sadness, and loss of motivation. If this were the documented outcome in a specific case of parenting, we would have no problem calling it child abuse and emotional maltreatment.

PROBLEMS WITH THE NRP'S META-ANALYSIS

A medical model of interventions, as we have seen, includes efficacy studies, safety studies, practice parameters, and informed consent. Merely investigating "what works" does not constitute a medical model. Such a narrow approach isolates treatment efficacy, and takes it out of its crucial, human context. Efficacy, by itself, is irrelevant if the corresponding risk is too high (the safety issue), if the evidence in its favor is not strong (the practice parameter issue), or if the patient simply refuses the recommended treatment (the informed consent issue).

Unfortunately, the only thing about the NRP study of instructional interventions in reading that is reminiscent of medical research is that it used a meta-analysis to pool together efficacy data from a number of studies. Missing is any acknowledgment of the safety issue, not to mention practice parameters and informed consent. And the method of meta-analysis is hardly unique to medicine.

In order to increase sample sizes, meta-analyses have become an increasingly popular research tool in medicine. But the technique can be applied to any collection of studies, even ones that are of sordid clinical utility, such as how much electricity a torture victim can bear without being killed in the process. Interestingly, there are meta-analyses that have claimed negative outcomes for other key components of the federal government's education agenda, such those reported by Anderson, Whipple, and Jimerson (2002), who "conclude that the cumulative evidence does not support the use of grade retention as an intervention for academic achievement or socio-emotional adjustment problems."

Such studies, of course, did not enter into the government's arguments for No Child Left Behind. It is quite clear that those responsible for No Child Left Behind, and for the NRP report, followed the unscientific practice of choosing just those studies that supported predetermined conclusions, ultimately, a predetermined political agenda. This is the unfortunate fate of science performed in the service of a state with an ulterior political motive. Isolate phonics from everything else we know about reading, and still call it reading; isolate efficacy studies from everything else we know about medical interventions and still call it a medical model.

Even the meta-analysis carried out by the NRP in the name of medical research is of dubious medico-scientific quality. The medical literature on standards for doing a meta-analysis emphasizes a fully blinded approach, in which reviewers have no clue as to who the authors are of the various studies reviewed, what journals the studies appeared in, and so on (Egger et al., 1999). But the NRP meta-analysis violated this fundamental principle of medical research by employing an author of more than ten percent of the works reviewed for its phonics section as the sole reviewer of that section (Garan, 2001; Strauss, 2003).

Representatives of the National Institute of Child Health and Human Development have claimed virtually every aspect of reading and reading research to be a medical phenomenon. This is the case for its definition of reading and reading disability (Shaywitz, 1996), for the technology used to study reading (Rumsey, 1996), and for the methodology used to assess interventions (National Reading Panel Report, 2000). It is also true for the newly proposed "What Works Commission," a federal watchdog agency, supposedly modeled along the lines of the Food and Drug Administration, that will maintain surveillance over materials used in reading classrooms (Traub, 2002).

But James Cunningham has insightfully pointed out, in his review of the NRP report, that the medical metaphor for reading and education is fundamentally misguided:

> This argument is based on a metaphor of reading instruction being like the curing of psychological and physical diseases. The Panel's unquestioned assumption of this metaphor has the regrettable effect of reducing schooling in general, and reading education in particular, to a series of low- or noninteracting interventions. What if healthy human development is a better metaphor for schooling and the teaching of reading, pre-K through Grade 5 and beyond, than is the metaphor of treatments for specific mental or medical ailments? (2001, p. 330)

Apt as Cunningham's remarks are, they are only relevant to an understanding of the work of the NRP, or similar government front groups, as long as that work really does follow a medical model. But in ignoring the question of risks of treatment, and in violating a fundamental principle that ensures the integrity of a meta-analysis, and in a number of other matters that we have discussed, the NRP's work is only a pitiful caricature of a medical model of research, one which maligns the integrity of the medical field itself.

Still, Cunningham's point is well-taken. The notion that education is just the identification and curing of diseases of learning does not speak to the majority of children who are normal and healthy in their development. It might place otherwise irrelevant imperfections, the stuff of human character, under the magnifying glass, and assign them to inappropriate treatment protocols. But taking the promotion of "healthy human development" as the goal of education encourages teachers and educators to focus first and foremost on each student's potential for personal and interpersonal happiness, regardless of imperfections.

In fact, medicine itself, like Cunningham's education, is primarily concerned with optimizing an individual's capacity for fulfillment in life, and not with the curing of disease. Most diseases, in fact, are incurable. This in no way detracts from the importance of searching for cures to diseases. Nor does it detract from the proper role of a physician in the physician–patient relationship—physicians treat medical problems, without necessarily eliminating them, because not treating them leads to symptoms that detract from a patient's quality of life.

THE MEDICAL METAPHOR: TROJAN HORSE FOR AN ATTACK ON DEMOCRACY

The invocation of a medical metaphor by the NRP and the Department of Education is nothing more than a marketing ploy used by the government to sell its reading and education agenda to the public. This is the outer form that their argument must take, because the real, behind-the-scenes agenda that is the driving force for the current changes in education would likely be unacceptable to the public. This agenda derives from the demands of corporate America.

Corporate America has made it very clear to the government that it indeed has its own literacy crisis, which it wants resolved as quickly as possible (Business Roundtable, 1999). Its current U.S. workforce does not have the digital technology literacy skills needed to maintain U.S. corporate competitiveness over the Europeans and the Asians (Business Roundtable, 1995). Corporate America wants schools to be thought of as "workforce development systems," whose function is to churn out a new breed of "knowledge workers" (Business Roundtable, 1993). To avoid any straying from this agenda, it has demanded that this be the focus of school curricula (under the guise of "standards"), that it be tested repeatedly to monitor progress, and that punishment be meted out to anybody who does not proceed in accordance with these marching orders (Business Roundtable, 2000). The crisis mentality of corporate America is part of the package being sold to the public, but formulated instead as our crisis (Business Roundtable, 1999). Their intense fear of losing out to international competitors is translated and broadcast as the fear we should all have that, without government intrusion into curriculum, methods of instruction, and assessment, our children will not have marketable, employable skills.

Indeed, Reid Lyon, the director of reading research at the NICHD, has promoted the alleged literacy crisis in the United States as "a significant public health problem" (Lyon, 1997, para. 2) and "a serious national problem" (Lyon, 1997, para. 6). His rationale for this includes the association of illiteracy with drug abuse and crime (Lyon, 1997, para. 8). But this is just another medical metaphor sleight-of-hand. Are we supposed to be-

lieve that illiteracy causes drug abuse and crime? And even if it is a contributing factor, then why not focus on treating the causes of illiteracy itself?

Lyon, of course, claims that he is doing just that. Referring specifically
to the alphabetic principle that supposedly governs letter-sound relationships, he stated that:

> Unfortunately, children are not born with this insight, nor does it develop
> naturally without instruction. Hence the existence of illiterate cultures and
> of illiteracy within literate culture. (Lyon, 1997)

The enlightened science of the federal government's spin doctors attributes third world and domestic illiteracy to failure to learn the alphabetic
principle! Poverty and outrageous discrepancies in wealth distribution,
most certainly the fundamental crisis in this whole matter, play no role in
the science of the NICHD.

The hypocrisy of government concern about public health and literacy
showed itself during congressional hearings on the Reading Excellence
Act, the precursor to No Child Left Behind. The Senate version of the bill
was introduced by Senator Paul Coverdell of Georgia, who motivated it as
follows:

> We clearly have a literacy crisis in this Nation when four out of 10 of our
> third-graders can't read. Without basic reading skills, many of these children
> will be shut out of the workforce of the 21st century. According to the 1993
> National Audit Literacy Survey, more than 40 million Americans cannot read
> a phone book, menu or the directions on a medicine bottle. Those who
> can't learn to read are not only less likely to get a good job, they are dispro-
> portionately represented in the ranks of the unemployed and the homeless.
> Consider the fact that 75 percent of unemployed adults, 33 percent of moth-
> ers on welfare, 85 percent of juveniles appearing in court and 60 percent of
> prison inmates are illiterate. (Coverdell, 1998)

But not only are there forty million Americans who allegedly can not read
a phone book, there are also forty million Americans who in fact have ab-
solutely no health insurance coverage. So why don't we hear government
officials clamoring for a Health Excellence Act to guarantee every citizen
high quality, scientifically proven health care coverage?

The answer, of course, is that the health level of the U.S. workforce is
not yet an obstacle to going to work. Therefore, it is not a crisis, although
it ranks twenty-fourth in the world on the World Health Organization's
Disability Adjusted Life Expectancy (DALE) rating (World Health Report,
2000), a measure of healthy life expectancy. In a WHO press release,
WHO's director of its Global Programme on Evidence for Health Policy,
Dr. Christopher Murray, stated that, "[t]he position of the United States is

one of the major surprises of the new rating system. Basically, you die earlier and spend more time disabled if you're an American rather than a
member of most other advanced countries" (WHO, June 4, 2000).

But the allegedly meager level of high-tech literacy skills, in the areas of
digital technology and software and hardware troubleshooting, may be
surpassed by corporate America's overseas competitors, quickly and irre-
versibly, threatening short-term profit levels and long-term profitability.
This is a crisis.

The medical marketing maneuvers of the government reflect an awareness on its part of constraints imposed on politicians and corporate execu-
tives by the current level of consciousness of the American people. It
would be unacceptable to simply say to American teachers, parents, and
students: "We are now going to make you practice phonics in every elementary classroom, and we are going to punish you if you do anything
else, and we will still punish you if you do phonics but don't get the test
scores up. And teachers, we may even threaten you with educational malpractice lawsuits if you don't use scientifically proven methods." But this
is precisely the undemocratic subtext of the government's actions.

Sometimes, however, one of the players in this tragicomedy slips, exposing his impatience with democracy, acknowledging, indeed, that democracy is an obstacle to corporate America's education agenda. This is
the meaning of Reid Lyon's remarks, uttered on November 18, 2002 before attendees at a forum of the Coalition for Evidence-Based Policy, in
which he was speaking as a representative of the NIH, that is to say, as a
government functionary, "If there was any piece of legislation that I could
pass it would be to blow up colleges of education" (para. 6).

This open disdain for democratic principles is merely another expression of the political extremism that has characterized Lyon's views on
education over the years: support for a legal definition of science, for legally
mandated instructional methods, and for the violation of academic freedom
that must follow from this; support for high-stakes testing and accountability, even in the face of predictable adverse social and psychological consequences; and opposition to local control of schools that accompanies the
federal government's strings-attached funding policy.

Standing in the way of the government's plans to carry out the education agenda of corporate America are massive numbers of students, teachers, and parents who have been won over to alternative views of education, including meaning-centered reading programs, supported by more
than 3 decades of scientific research. The government must eliminate this
obstacle if it is to succeed in its goals. Far be it to proceed democratically,
and engage the public in a calm and rational debate over curriculum, class
size, funding, and even assessment and accountability. There is no room
for democratic process—we have a crisis on our hands. And, of course, the

government's position might not prevail if it debated the matter fairly and openly. It finds threats of grade retention and loss of funding, and the casuistry of the medical metaphor, more persuasive.

Thus, the medical metaphor is one piece of a larger puzzle of propaganda, coercion, and "manufacturing consent" (Herman & Chomsky, 2002). It is the piece that promotes a public attitude of trust in the government's agenda. Lyon himself, referring to phonics and phonemic awareness, has stated that the NICHD promotes "the most trustworthy scientific evidence." But the other pieces of the puzzle, such as high-stakes testing and accountability, are just frank intimidation.

WHO BENEFITS FROM ALL OF THIS?

A genuine medical model applied to issues in education would never be as narrow as the one promoted by the federal government. The government, in its subservience to the corporate agenda to create a new workforce with 21st century literacy skills, is concerned only with "what works," and not with the equally important "at what price?"

According to whose medical model is there a provision that if test scores remain abnormal, the patient gets punished? Certainly this is not the model that the average individual would support, nor any physicians or health care professionals that I personally know of. But, absurd as it might seem, we all know that this is precisely the medical model employed by the misnamed health insurance industry, which denies coverage to people with pre-existing conditions, or tries to limit coverage to people with expensive conditions. Fail the bloodtest—lose your health care. Fail the reading test—lose your education.

And, just as the insurance companies' position is not a model for providing quality health care to all people, neither is the government's position a model for providing quality education for all people. The rich will, of course, get all the health care they need, and send their children to their exclusive private schools. These schools are exempt from the federal mandates. The rest of the student population will fight to stay alive in the internecine battle to earn a hunting license to track down a job as a 21st century "knowledge worker." This license will be called a *diploma*.

The diploma-as-hunting license metaphor was made perfectly clear by June E. Streckfus, who, speaking as the executive director of the Maryland Business Roundtable for Education, said that, "the [high school] diploma will have value to businesses statewide. If a business is hiring a young person who has a Maryland diploma, [the employer will know] they will have a high level of basic skill" (Maushard, 1998).

Of course, Streckfus's comment does not explain what will happen to students who do not earn a diploma. But this is actually a very serious question. The medical model of reading is supposed to enhance our capacity to give youngsters the literacy skills they will need to be competitive in the job market (literature buffs need not apply). But the passing scores will be drawn arbitrarily. On what basis will they be drawn? The answer depends on whether anyone benefits from failing scores. Those with a stake in scores being low will apply pressure to have the cut-off marks reflect that interest.

Of course, it seems absurd to imagine that some element of society could have a vested, material interest in scores being low. In medicine, nobody wants to be diagnosed with a "high-stakes" illness, one that cuts off social options. Such high-stakes illnesses include epilepsy, which restricts one's legal ability to drive; orthopedic injuries, which can end the career of an athlete; and even migraine headaches, which can lead to lost time with family and absence from work.

A student does not see himself or herself as benefiting in any way from failing a high-stakes test. Yet there is a group in our society that regards those who fail as ripe for recruitment—the military. And this is no hypothetical conjecture.

On exactly the same day that Lyon uttered his reprehensible comment about blowing up colleges of education, National Public Radio host Tavis Smiley broadcast a program on the little-known military recruitment clause of the No Child Left Behind Act. He asked Bill Carr, director of military personnel for the Department of Defense, to explain the provision's intent:

> It's to allow recruiting to proceed more efficiently. What we found in the past 20 years is that about two-thirds are going to college today of high school graduates as compared to about half 20 years ago. And, as a consequence of that and a little bit lower propensity to serve, we find that the cost per recruit has just about doubled. So if we can get better access, easier access while still respecting the parents' right to preserve the privacy of their students' records, then we're able to save some defense dollars. (para. 7)

Of course, this in no way explains why the Department of Defense's desire to save the taxpayers some money is part of the No Child Left Behind Act. Clarifying the position somewhat, Carr added,

> The school maintains control of the privacy, subject to the parents' wishes. And the military is empowered to request the information (student directories, SLS) and the difference here from the past is that the school is compelled to ask the parents rather than simply not asking them and denying us outright. So it simply requires that schools ask parents and, if they deny to

third parties, we would not receive it. Otherwise we would. And that's
gonna make our recruiting more efficient, perhaps easier on the recruiters
and perhaps less costly for the public. (NPR, 2002, para. 24)

In this response, the military's goal is "perhaps" to save some money, but
more specifically to make "recruiting more efficient." But again, why is it a
part of the No Child Left Behind Act?

Jamie Raskin, professor of constitutional law at American University,
also on the program, commented that "with this provision slipped into the
No Child Left Behind Act, what we've got is part of the creeping loss of individual privacy that's going on throughout American society." Although
parents can object to the school providing their child's name to the military, David Goodman, of *Mother Jones* magazine, and another guest on
the program, noted that "opt-outs are notorious for very low compliance."

When an education bill includes one provision that will doubtlessly
lead to dramatic increases in the number of students retained, and another provision that opens up far easier access to students by military recruiters, it's easy to do the math. According to the National Center for Fair
and Open Testing (Fairtest), "[m]ore than one-quarter of Baltimore's students are being retained this year. Nearly 20,000 of the 70,000 students in
grades 1–8 were held back. Standardized test results were one major crite-
rion." The military lost no time sending its recruitment letters to Maryland.

Now that we are supposed to be involved in an "endless war" against
terrorism, there will be a need for an endless pool of potential recruits.
Those who make it through the workforce development system will become knowledge workers. Those who do not will fight the wars to defend
this system—unless they wind up in prison instead.

ATTACK ON DEMOCRACY—THE REAL DISEASE

The hypocrisy and contradictions of the government's version of a medical model of education research are better appreciated if we see its educational reforms package for what it really is—a political program. Else-
where, I have referred to the current emphasis on intensive phonics as
"neophonics," to emphasize that it is really one component of this larger
political program (Strauss, 2003). The neophonics political program includes federally-mandated phonics instruction, high-stakes testing, and
accountability. It is the neophonics political program as a whole that best
reveals the overall inconsistencies.

As previously noted, for example, although there may be one meta-
analysis that supposedly endorses the use of intensive phonics instruction

in classrooms, there are others that show the social and psychological dangers of high-stakes testing. Also, Lyon claims that "of the ten to fifteen percent of children who will eventually drop out of school, over 75% will report difficulties learning to read." But at the same time he supports the use of high-stakes testing and accountability, which promotes grade retention, and thereby increases the risk of school drop out.

This Orwellian agenda is larger than either one of the major political parties. It is, in fact, fully bipartisan in the overall support it has received, reflecting what the two parties have in common, as opposed to where they may differ. The present loyal opposition under Bush is not even asking the kinds of questions that need to be asked, just as the previous loyal opposition under Clinton did not ask them—as if just posing critical questions is disloyal. But what will we have allowed to happen if practicing democracy is indeed considered disloyal?

It is now more urgent than ever to reemphasize the view that formal education should be the social means of providing children with a set of experiences that maximizes their own capacity for creative self-expression, and for their participation in a democratic society. How alarming it is that defending Cunningham's simple but eloquent notion of education as "healthy human development," probably the only legitimate medical metaphor, has become tantamount to defending democracy itself. Indeed, we will not have a healthy, free, democratic society if we back away from fighting the social disease that parades itself as a medical model of education.

REFERENCES

Anderson, G. E., Whipple, A. D., & Jimerson, S. R. (2002, October). *Grade retention: Achievement and mental health outcomes.* National Association of School Psychologists. Retrieved on December 26, 2002, from http://www.nasponline.org.

Business Roundtable. (1993). *Workforce training and development for U.S. competitiveness.* Retrieved on December 26, 2002, from http://www.brtable.org.

Business Roundtable. (1995). *Continuing the commitment: Essential components of a successful education system.* Retrieved on December 26, 2002, from http://www.brtable.org.

Business Roundtable. (1999). *No turning back: A progress report on the Business Roundtable education initiative.* Retrieved on December 26, 2002, from http://www.brtable.org.

Business Roundtable. (2000). *Essential components of a successful education system.* Retrieved on December 26, 2002, from http://www.brtable.org.

The Council for Excellence in Government. *Rigorous evidence: The key to progress in education?* Retrieved DATE from http://www.excelgov.org.

Coverdell, P. (1998, March). The Reading Excellence Act, Senate Testimony. *Congressional Record,* p. S1293. Retrieved February 20, 2004, from httt://www.thomas.loc.gov.

Cunningham, J. W. (2001). The National Reading Panel Report. *Reading Research Quarterly, 36*(3), 326–335.

Egger, M., Davey-Smith, G., & Phillips, A. (1997). Meta-analysis: Principles and procedures. *British Medical Journal, 315*(7121), 1533–1537.

Garan, E. (2001). *Resisting reading mandates: How to triumph with the truth.* Portsmouth, NH: Heinemann.

Goodman, Y. M., Watson, D. J., & Burke, C. L. (1996). *Reading strategies: Focus on comprehension* (2nd ed.). Katonah, NY: Richard C. Owen.

Herman, E. S., & Chomsky, N. (2002). *Manufacturing consent: The political economy of the mass media.* New York: Pantheon.

Lyon, G. R. (1997, July). Testimony of G. Reid Lyon, Ph.D. on children's literacy before the Committee on Education and the Workforce, U.S. House of Representatives, July 10, 1997, retrieved on December 26, 2002 from. http://www.edworkforce.house.gov.

Maushard, M. (1998, January 31). Business group is force in education. *Baltimore Sun.*

Mitka, M. (2001). Some physicians protest "High Stakes" Tests. *Journal of American Medical Association, 285*(20).

National Institute of Child Health and Human Development. (2000, April). *Report of the National Reading Panel: Teaching children to read, an evidence-based assessment of the scientific research literature on reading and its implications for reading instruction—reports of the subgroups.* NIH Publication No. 00-4754. Washington, DC.

National Public Radio. (2002, November 18). *Analysis: Civil liberties of high school students in regard to military recruitment,* transcript. Retrieved on December 26, 2002, from http://www.readbygrade3.com.

Rumsey, J. M. (1996). Neuroimaging in developmental dyslexia: A review and conceptualization. in G. R. Lyon & J. M. Rumsey (Eds.), *Title*, Page, Publisher.

Shaywitz, S. E. (1996, November). Dyslexia. *Scientific American.*

Strauss, S. L. (2003). Challenging the NICHD reading research agenda. *Phi Delta Kappan,* Vol, Iss, Pages.

Traub, J. (2002, November 10). What works? *New York Times, Education Life Section.*

Wheelock, A., Bebell, D., & Haney, W. (2002). *What can student drawings tell us about high-stakes testing in Massachusetts?* Manuscript, Boston College. Retrieved on DATE from http://www.csteep.bc.edu" www.csteep.bc.edu.

World Health Organization. (2000, June 4). WHO issues new healthy life expectancy rankings: Japan number one in new 'healthy life' system. *World Health Organization, Press Release.* Washington, DC, & Geneva, Switzerland.

World Health Organization. (2000). *The World Health Report 2000, Health systems: Improving performance.* Geneva, Switzerland.

PART TWO

THE INFLUENCE
OF FEDERAL POLICY

In this section the authors examine how the major players have influenced philosophical and pedagogical practices in the classroom. These chapters link federal policy to the disappearance of or promotion of particular philosophical and pedagogical approaches to learning.

CHAPTER SIX

Making Whole Language Disappear: How the National Reading Panel Worked Its Magic

Joanne Yatvin

THE FORBIDDEN WORDS

At the official meetings of the National Reading Panel (NRP) over its 2 year existence, the words "Whole Language" were uttered only twice. Both times I was the one who spoke them, hoping that I might arouse some flicker of interest in the major advance in the teaching of reading over the past 30 years. No one seemed to notice, and the panel's discussions of discrete skills went on just as before. I was wary of pushing too hard, knowing that, on the surface at least, the panel was "whole language free." Over the long haul, it seemed wiser to try to slide some whole language elements into the range of topics the panel had decided to investigate than to stand on a soapbox demanding that whole language receive the full and respectful attention I believed it deserved.

Why was whole language so completely ignored by the NRP, when this panel, convened by Congress, was charged specifically to "assess the effectiveness of various approaches to teaching children to read"? I can only infer members' motives because the few reasons publicly offered were merely excuses, having to do with the paucity of research on whole language elements. What I do know is that the panel was stacked to support the philosophy and research interests of the National Institute of Child Health and Human Development (NICHD), the organization that had selected its members. Largely ignoring nominations from nationally recognized experts and respected organizations, such as the National Council of Teachers of English; NICHD had appointed eight experimental researchers, one physician who had worked closely with the institute in the past, two university administrators without any background in reading, one teacher educator, one middle school teacher, one certified public accountant, and one elementary school principal (me). Thus, the most obvious and credible explanation of the panel's unwillingness to examine whole language is that most members had an ideological allegiance to a skills model of reading, a few had a professional conflict of interest , and the rest had too little knowledge and experience to resist the authority of the majority's expertise.

At its first meeting in April 1998, the NRP set an investigative agenda that left no room for a direct examination of whole language. Prodded by NICHD officials, who asserted that the Panel's job was to build on the work of National Research Council committee that had just issued its report, *Preventing Reading Difficulties in Young Children*; the panel decided, almost without discussion, to base their review of reading research on the same three areas: decoding, comprehension, and fluency. Later, pressed by one panel member whose major research interest was computer technology, the panel agreed to add that topic to its list. After a series of open hearings held around the country, at which participants called for greater national attention to and support for teacher education, the panel added that topic, too, as its fifth area for review.

Although I do not question the place of technology or teacher education in the full vista of reading instruction in America, I saw those areas as peripheral to the panel's particular charge. Members' willingness to include them, while excluding writing, spelling, instructional materials, oral language development, and other basic elements of school literacy programs, was incomprehensible to me, and more than a little frustrating. But rather than oppose the addition of new areas, I decided to try to use them as a wedge for including others I considered more important. At the panel's first two meetings and in e-mail messages[1] exchanged over the

---

[1]Here is just one of several e-mails (names omitted), that I sent to panel members after the first NRP meeting:

>Date: Tue, 26 May 1998 10:57:18 -0800
>To:childread@list.gov.nih
>From:yatvinj@ortrail.k12.or.us (Joanne Yatvin)
>Subject:Panel charge
>
>   I've been too busy setting up the Portland meeting to respond to
>comments on the Listserv (also too busy to read them carefully). I don't
>know if I agree with (Panel member X) about technology or second language, but I do
>know that I think (Panel member Y) is defining our charge too narrowly, thereby keeping
>out what might be valuable contributions to our knowledge. Why are we

next few months, I proposed a broader framework for the review of research that would allow several new topics to be included. Such a framework would not be based on any particular model of reading, but would address the range of teaching approaches used in America's classrooms, including, of course, whole language. In my mind, a broader, nonphilosophical framework would better serve the panel's mission than the one already chosen. I did not see how we could determine the effectiveness of various teaching methods as Congress asked us to do if we did not look at all the widely used classroom approaches. Although two or three panel members agreed with me, the majority remained committed to the areas already selected. In the end, diplomacy and logic failed, and the originally chosen areas were the only ones investigated and the only ones reported on in the Panel's final document.

WIELDING THE MAGIC WAND
OF EXPERIMENTAL SCIENCE

After setting the areas for its review of research and forming subgroups to work on each of them, the Panel turned to the task of specifying criteria for selecting studies and a process for analyzing them. Once again prodded by NICHD officials, the panel decided that a study had to be experimental or quasi-experimental. NICHD's argument for using experimental studies was that educational research had long operated on very low standards by accepting into its body of research literature all kinds of case studies, descriptions of classroom processes, anecdotal reports of effective teaching strategies and analyses of children's thinking. Now was time for the NRP to lead a crusade for the adoption of a "Gold Standard" in educational research, similar to that used in medical research, by relying only on true experiments. Although there were indications from discussion that members did not completely buy this argument, there did not seem to be any way to blend descriptive studies with experimental studies in the large scale comparisons the panel was going to have to do. Therefore, they agreed to omit descriptive studies from their reviews of research.

>bound to three topic divisions that were selected hurriedly and almost
>casually at our first meeting, probably because they were the ones in the
>other report (that I can't think of the name of right now)?
>   It seems to me that if any member of the panel believes there is a
>significant body of research in any area that has an impact on the
>teaching of reading, we should include it in our consideration. "There
>are more things in heaven and earth than are dreamt of in your philosophy,
>Horatio."
>
>Joanne

Once eligible studies were identified, they would be subjected to a meta-analysis. The merit of a meta-analysis is that a large, complex body of studies can be be rendered comparable and comprehensible by transforming the results of each comparison within a study to a single number called an effect size. Meta-analysis produces a simpler, clearer picture of a treatment's effectiveness than one can get by just looking at studies separately and trying to make judgments. At the same time, however, a meta-analysis buries details, distinctions and anomalies, making it more difficult to understand for whom and under what circumstances a treatment worked well and if it also had relatively weak components.

In discussing the requirements of meta-analysis, panel members realized that such a process might not always be feasible for their own reviews. If the particulars of the treatments in the eligible studies differed too much, reviewers would have to use more traditional methods of comparison. In the areas of vocabulary instruction and comprehension strategies, that is exactly what happened, and the subgroups reviewing those studies had to evaluate them qualitatively.

POOF! WHOLE LANGUAGE DISAPPEARS

These decisions, nonideological as they appear, sealed the fate of whole language within the NRP. Under its selection criteria, few whole language studies would be eligible because most of them are descriptive rather than experimental. Whole language researchers and teachers are primarily interested in the complex interactions among students, texts, the classroom situation and the teacher, not in the separate dimensions of a particular method or set of materials. Moreover, those few experimental whole language studies that might make it into the pool for review, would be overwhelmed by the much greater number of studies of skills treatments. In addition, a meta-analysis would tend to conceal any subtle positive effects whole language had on children's reading because an effect in a category of major importance, such as text comprehension, carries no more weight than an effect in minor category, such as decoding nonsense words.

As a way of testing its selection criteria and methodology, the panel decided that each subgroup should begin its review of research by pursuing a single topic of its own choosing. After such a preliminary examination, the whole panel would decide which topics would be investigated next. As might be expected, the subgroups' first choices reflected their members' research interests rather than the prominence of topics in school programs. So "guided oral reading" and "computer technology" got the benefit of panel members' full attention when there were time and energy to spare, whereas "reciprocal teaching" was put on the back burner. Months later, when the Panel stepped back to list all the topics they thought they should investigate under their charge, they realized that the time allocated by Congress[2] was not going to be nearly enough to cover all of them. Through an open vote—incidentally, the only vote taken by the panel throughout its tenure—they selected thirteen topics which, they then believed, was a manageable number for the 18 months of work time left. Among the thirteen were oral language development, home influences on children's reading, print awareness, instructional materials for beginning reading, and assessment instruments, topics that obviously were not part of the five originally chosen areas.

Although the addition of new topics raised my hopes that the panel would at last engage in a broad and unbiased examination of the field of reading research, I should have seen that it was nothing more than an illusion. Allowing subgroups to exercise their preferences for sequencing the topics for review pushed any topics that did not fit in with panel members' philosophical views to the back of the line. More damaging, however, were the inadequate time limits for the panel to complete its work and the insufficiency of technical support from NICHD. These factors made certain that the panel would never get far enough into its list of topics to reach any related to whole language.

A ONE-EARED RABBIT COMES OUT OF THE HAT

At the end of almost 2 years of operation the NRP was obliged to submit a final report to Congress. Time had run out and so had the energies of panel members. In no way could that report, entitled *Teaching Children to Read*, be considered complete. It contained discussions, results, and conclusions on only eight topics: the five selected as first choices and three more the panel managed to cover later on. All its conclusions were based on the review of only 438 studies. Many of the most important questions about reading instruction were never even asked: How does writing contribute to learning to read? Are decodable texts a help to beginning readers? Does using invented spelling help children learn to decode? What motivates children to read on their own? What are the benefits of reading aloud to children? How does prior knowledge, including the knowledge of how types of texts are constructed, affect children's ability to learn to read?

Phrased in simple language, the NRP's conclusions were:

---

[2]Originally, Congress authorized only 9 months for the panel to do its work. At its third meeting in the fall of 1998, the panel told NICHD that a thorough review of research was impossible in that time frame. NICHD delivered that message to Congress, and another year's time was allocated.

- Phonemic awareness works
- Phonics works
- Repeated oral reading with feedback works
- Encouraging children to read more does not appear to work, but there were very few studies in the database
- Vocabulary instruction works
- Comprehensions strategies work
- Computer instruction shows promise even though there were too few studies to draw a conclusion
- Teacher education appears to work although the chain of cause and effect is hard to see

The NRP report also contained a "Minority View," a short section that I felt compelled to write when I realized at last just how narrow and shallow the final report was going to be. I foresaw that, despite the disclaimers the panel had inserted into the body of its document, the report would be taken by Congress and the public as a comprehensive and definitive judgment on school reading instruction. As a matter of both principle and practicality, I had to say loudly and clearly that it was no such thing. I did not expect that my minority view would be widely read or heeded, and, indeed, it has not been. NICHD has done its best to hide its existence by omitting it from the NRP summary booklet and by not mentioning it in any of its voluminous promotional literature. This was easy to accomplish because the summary and the information released to the press were not produced or overseen by the panel, but by a public relations firm that had a longtime working relationship with NICHD.

I must add that NICHD went even farther to keep my views from being heard. During the time that I was writing an article for the educational journal, *Phi Delta Kappan* (2002), I was prevented from logging into the NRP archives where I would have been able to find the exact dates of events and quotes from meeting minutes. NICHD also refused to pay my expenses to speak on a panel at a national educational meeting although it was paying those of another speaker on the same panel. Despite the fact that I have never criticized the findings or the scientific procedures of any of the NRP subgroups, only the narrowness and shallowness of the report as a whole, apparently, NICHD wants no hint of dissent to reach the public ear.

AND FOR OUR NEXT TRICK, WE PRESENT . . .

With its report to Congress in April 2000, the NRP officially ended its tenure. Since then, however, the contents of the report have taken on a life of their own, or, more accurately, three separate lives, each with a potential for lasting impact on American education. One life is a national movement to make the five topics the panel investigated and the skills model they are based on the official curriculum of all school reading programs, and, in so doing, to banish whole language. The second life is a campaign designed to enthrone experimental research as the "gold standard," in education and, conversely, to render descriptive research illegitimate. And the third is a rising effort among independent educators and researchers to reexamine the science, logic, and language of the NRP Report to uncover more accurate and significant results.

. . . DISINFORMATION

Almost universally, the NRP's failure to review a broad range of topics has been interpreted to mean that unmentioned topics, particularly those involved in whole language teaching, were found to be ineffective or were not even worthy of investigation. The subtitle of the NRP Report, which was not authorized by the Panel or even made known to them before publication, was certainly instrumental in creating this impression: "An Evidence-Based Assessment of the Scientific Research Literature on Reading and Its Implications for Reading Instruction." In NICHD press releases, the U.S. Department of Education's guidelines for "Reading First" applications, the National Institute for Literacy's booklet, *Put Reading First*,[3] and various other publications, the NRP's findings have been labeled the "five essential components of reading instruction," although the panel never termed them such, and specifically stated in its report that it considered many other topics to be worthy of inclusion in a school reading program.[4]

---

[3]*Put Reading First* was developed by the Center for the Improvement of Early Reading Achievement (CIERA) and was funded by the National Institute for Literacy (NIFL). It can be obtained by contacting NIFL at ED Pubs, P.O. Box 1398, Jessup, MD 20794-1398 or downloaded from the NIFL Web site at www.nifl.gov. Although the first edition of this document "inadvertently" omitted my name from the list of NRP members, subsequent editions have included it.

[4]In the introduction to its report the NRP (2000) stated:

It should be made clear that the Panel did not consider these questions [*questions about whether or not the topics selected improved children's reading*] and the instructional issues that they represent to be the *only* topics of importance in learning to read. The Panel's silence on other topics should not be interpreted as indicating that other topics have no importance or that improvement in those areas would not lead to greater reading achievement. It was simply the sheer number of studies identified by Panel staff relevant to reading (more than 100,000 published since 1966 and more than 15,000 prior to 1966) that precluded an exhaustive analysis of the research in all areas of potential interest. (*Reports of the Subgroups*, p. 3)

Leading the movement to legitimize the five NRP topics as the foundation of effective reading instruction is the Federal government, its educational spokespeople and its agencies. Through publications, legislation, grant offerings, political appointments, and threatened sanctions to schools, the government has proclaimed that there is only one acceptable way to teach reading. The language and intent of government documents, such as the "No Child Left Behind Act" and its accompanying "Reading First Initiative" are unmistakable. Both call repeatedly for "scientifically based instruction" and the "essential components of reading instruction" and define those terms as the findings of the NRP. In almost the blink of an eye, a biased and incomplete review of reading research has been transformed into the final scientific judgment on all that is needed for successful reading instruction. As might be expected, basal series publishers and proponents of single component programs have jumped onto the bandwagon, claiming that the NRP findings validate the content of their materials. Additionally, attendees at Department of Education academies for parties interested in Reading First grants, report that speakers cited certain commercial materials as being "scientifically based," with the clear implication that if states agreed to recommend such materials to their schools, those states' applications would be looked on favorably.[5]

In the same government publications and speeches whole language is never mentioned. Government officials and hirelings prefer to speak in code. U.S. Assistant Secretary of Education, Susan Neuman in a speech in Stockton California in October 2002 stated that the No Child Left Behind Act would "put an end to creative and experimental teaching methods in the nation's classrooms."[6] Reid Lyon, Chief of the Child Development and Behavior Branch of NICHD, on numerous occasions, has made statements deprecating colleges of education, presumably because they are the guilty ones who have been preparing teachers to teach whole language. In its discussion of phonics instruction, "Put Reading First," which is being distributed to teachers nationwide, asserts that literature-based programs "do not teach phonics explicitly and systematically."[7]

---

[5]See, for example, comments by Michael Pressley who attended one of these academies, in Richard L. Allington, *Big Brother and the National Reading Curriculum*, Heinemann, 2002, p. 77.

[6] This statement was reported by Victor Balta in the Stockton, California *Record,* October 25, 2002.

[7]This statement appears in a highlighted box at the bottom of page 17. It is interesting to note that the authors also make clear that adding phonics to such programs does not make them acceptable. The message seems to be that whole language is no good no matter how you try to supplement it or integrate skills instruction with it.

. . . AND TRANSFORMATION

At the same time the federal government has been instrumental in the campaign to establish experimental research as the only legitimate form of educational science. In the methodological overview section of the summary booklet, the following judgment on educational research appears:

> In what may be its most important action, the Panel then developed and adopted a set of rigorous research methodological standards. These standards guided the screening of the research literature relevant to each topic area addressed by the Panel. This screening process identified a final set of experimental or quasi-experimetnal research studies that were then subjected to detailed analysis. The evidence-based methodological standards adopted by the Panel are essentially those normally used in research studies of the efficacy of interventions in psychological and medical research. These include behaviorally based interventions, medications, or medical procedures proposed for use in the fostering of robust health and psychological development and the prevention or treatment of disease.
>
> It is the view of the Panel that the efficacy of materials and methodologies used in the teaching of reading and in the prevention or treatment of reading disabilities should be tested no less rigorously. However, such standards have not been universally accepted or used in reading education research.[8]

Since the appearance of the NRP Report, this position has been affirmed in numerous statements and actions by the U.S. Department of Education and the National Institute of Child Health and Development. Only experimental and quasi-experimental studies are being funded by these agencies, and the trend has moved into private funding institutions. The applications of states applying for Reading First grants are being carefully scrutinized for the names and credentials of university professors named in partnerships with state departments of education. In some cases, curriculum vitae and course syllabi are being requested in order to give assurance that the professors involved are on the "right side" of educational research.

---

[8]This statement by an unnamed author, appearing in the "Methodological Overview" section of the full NRP report, page 5, has proved to be the launching pad for the government's campaign to name experimental research the only legitimate form of educational research. Although I do not know its origin, I believe it was written by an employee of Widmeyer-Baker, the public relations firm hired by NICHD to put together the NRP subgroups' reports and disseminate them to the public.

CRITICS REVIEW THE SHOW

Amid all this authoritative and well-financed pressure from high places for one type of reading instruction and one type of reading research, a small independent movement is emerging in the educational community in an attempt to restore objectivity, scholarship, and intellectual freedom to the field of reading. Some highly respected educators and researchers have taken a closer look at the NRP Report, thus giving it a third and, perhaps, more reputable life. In his recently published book, *Big Brother and the National Reading Curriculum,* Richard Allington (2002) presents his own view of the inadequacies of the report and includes the views of James Cunningham, Michael Pressley, Elaine Garan, and Steve Krashen, as well as my own critique of the Panel's process. Each author offers a different but telling perspective. Allington focuses on the aims of NICHD, the agency that selected the panel and manipulated it in directions that supported that agency's research agenda. Cunningham faults the Panel for bringing their own particular, and outdated, philosophy of science to what should have been an objective review of all accepted branches of science and, in addition, for violating its own philosophical principles when it was more convenient to do so. Pressley takes the Panel to task for the conceptual narrowness of its investigations that over-simplified the complexity of classroom instruction and compartmentalized the interactiveness of the reading process into a small set of discrete skills. Garan criticizes the scientific processes the panel used and their careless language in representing their findings. She also reanalyzes the phonics data to show that different and more honest results can be extracted from it. Krashen does much the same with the section on encouraging children to read more, emphasizing the number of high quality studies that the Panel did not include in their analysis. My section reiterates the dissatisfaction I expressed in my minority report with the panel's narrow and shallow coverage of topics. It also describes the Panel's waywardness in following the lead of NICHD and its own members' self-interests.

Other educators and researchers have also published critiques of the Panel's report in journals or spoken out about the Report's flaws at professional conferences. I know of two reevaluations of the panel's data that are works in progress. Additionally, Constance Weaver, Elaine Garan, and I have produced a pamphlet[9] aimed at educators at all levels who may be applying for grants or being pressured to make changes in their teaching methods and course content. In this pamphlet, we have attempted to state

---

[9]This pamphlet, "Reading First: Cautions and Recommendations," was published privately by the authors. It can be downloaded from http://www.EdResearch.info and distributed by readers.

the findings of the NRP Report clearly and accurately and contrast them with the exaggerations and misrepresentations appearing in government publications and voiced by proponents of a skills-based reading curriculum dominated by phonics.

Because the people just mentioned are all acting without financial backing, special access to the press, or the political power to shape national, state, or local educational policy, their scope of influence so far has been limited. It will take time and support from influential groups and individuals for their message to be heard. The public and government officials need to know that there is more to science than experimental studies, more to reading instruction than phonics, and more to pedagogy than science.

THE SHOW MUST GO ON

Although the three movements I have described continue on their public trajectories, something even more important is happening beneath the notice of most of us. Educational research moves on. As the NRP reported, there were approximately 100,000 studies on reading available in the electronic data bases in 1998. Certainly, 5 years later there are many more, and, certainly, this number will continue to grow. Whatever one's opinion is of the NRP report, we must recognize that it represents only a limited knowledge base at only one point in time. As reading research progresses, informed by the NRP Report, the perspectives of its critics, and the reevaluation of its contents; we must believe that new findings will emerge to enlarge and deepen our knowledge rather than constrain and rigidify it. Only through unfettered exploration of teaching and learning by a variety of experimental and descriptive means, can researchers, educators, decision makers, and parents bring significant improvement to the teaching of reading.

REFERENCES

Allington, R. L. (2002). *Big brother and the national reading curriculum: How ideology trumped evidence.* Portsmouth, NH: Heinemann.

Armbruster, B. B., Lehr, F., & Osborn, J. (2001). *Put reading first: The research building blocks for teaching children to read.* Jessup, MD: National Institute for Literacy.

National Reading Panel. (2000). *Teaching children to read: An evidence-based assessment of the scientific research literature on reading and its implications for reading instruction: Reports of the subgroups.* Washington, DC: National Institute of Child Health and Development.

Yatvin, J. (2002). Babes in the woods: The wanderings of the National Reading Panel. *Phi Delta Kappan, 83*(5), 364–369.

Yatvin, J., Weaver, C., & Garan, E. (2002). *Reading First: Cautions and recommendations.* (Self-published; available online at http://www.EdResearch.info)

CHAPTER SEVEN

Phonics, Literalism, and Futuristic Fiction: Religious Fundamentalism and Education Policy

Ellen Brinkley
Constance Weaver

Life in a post–9/11 world has changed us all to one degree or another. Friends tell us that the events of 9/11 have been a factor in personal decisions to get married (or divorced), have a child, join a church, or take a new job. We listen to the news and feel vulnerable and anxious when we are told to "stay alert." We need to do *something*, but we struggle to know what. We begin to learn about new enemies and feel a new sense of fear about the future.

In the midst of such global concerns, the "war" about the teaching of reading pales in comparison. But the anxiety felt by teachers and teacher educators is deeply troubling. We resent newly mandated curricula, texts, and tests. We struggle with parents who wonder whether their schools will adequately teach their children to read, and we lose patience with those who worry that the curriculum will promote sinful values and lifestyles. We are angry about the federal government's insistence on teaching phonics as a precursor to reading. We feel at odds with legislators, parents, publishers, pressure groups, and each other. In our lowest moments, we feel trapped and powerless and afraid for the future of good education and our children.

Meanwhile, the public gets an earful of opinions about public education that are being expressed by very public figures. Our local newspaper recently reported on a talk that radio talk-show host Laura Schlessinger gave in the area. She criticized public schools as "indoctrination centers, not education centers" and urged parents in the audience to "put your child in private schools. If you don't have them, form them" (Bonfiglio,

2002). In a similar vein James Dobson, president of Focus on the Family, urged California parents in a radio audience to leave their public schools: "I think it's time to get our kids out," he said in a departure from his previous position that supported public schools, as well as Christian schools and home schooling. His daily radio program is reported to reach 5 million listeners in the United States (Dobson to Californians, 2002). These voices echo that of Robert Simonds, president of Citizens for Excellence in Education, who is not nearly so well known but even more passionate about the stand he takes, as described in his monthly "President's Report":

> Our goal of "RESCUE 2010," started in February, 1998, is to save our 20 million beautiful Christian church children still attending public schools. The best, quickest and most certain way to do that is to rescue them; that is, take them out of our ungodly government indoctrination schools and get them into Christian or home schools as quickly as possible. Our latest figures show a little over three million (since Feb. 1998) have now exited the public schools. Think of the rejoicing in heaven over saving one lost child—how great must it be when the angels welcome three million back into God's planned education. (2001, January)

The struggles and controversies that trouble us are about money and politics and power. And fundamentally, as just suggested, they are often about religion as well. We believe that as educators and citizens, we need to consider the impact of political power and religious fundamentalism[1] on curriculum and teaching practices and on federal education policy. This chapter describes some of the concerns and controversies. It explains the origins and views of those who use fear and politics and religion to try to control the public agenda. And it suggests how we might begin to turn our fears and frustrations into clear-headed, positive action.

PHONICS, LITERALISM, AND GOD

In a public hearing, someone once said that "God believes in the beauty of phonics" (Moffet, 1988, p. 226). Why would anyone make such a claim?

---

[1]Armstrong (2000) defines *fundamentalist* as a term used first by American Protestants in the early decades of the 20th century to "distinguish themselves from the more 'liberal' Protestants, who were, in their opinion, entirely distorting the Christian faith. Fundamentalists wanted to go back to basics and reemphasize the 'fundamentals' of the Christian tradition, which they identified with a literal interpretation of Scripture and the acceptance of certain core doctrines." Armstrong also cites Marty and Appleby (1991), who discuss "fundamentalisms," which are "embattled forms of spirituality that have emerged as a response to a perceived crisis. They are engaged in a conflict with enemies whose secularist policies and beliefs seem inimical to religion itself. Fundamentalists do not regard this battle as a conventional political struggle, but experience it as a cosmic war between the forces of good and evil" (pp. xii–xiii).

Perhaps a hint is provided in the ad for a grammar series in a home school-ing catalogue from one of the major fundamentalist publishers of educa-tional materials: "Grammar is taught with the purpose of making clear to the students the orderly structure of their language, a picture of God's or-derly plan for the world and for their lives" (A Beka Book, 1996). There is some evidence that phonics is viewed in much the same way. For exam-ple, Winters implies that systematic phonics is best, citing 1 Corinthians 14:40, "Let all things be done decently and in order" and Isaiah 28:10, "For precept must be upon precept" (Winters, 1995).

Christian fundamentalists rely on the order and precepts they find in the Bible to guide their thinking and actions. A foundational belief that supports this practice is the idea that the Bible is literally "the word and the Words of God" (Averill, 1990, p. 57; see also Brinkley, 1994, 1995; Holderer, 1995). A fundamentalist Christian's task, therefore, is to unlock the meanings God embodied in the scriptures, a task that requires that ev-ery word must be read correctly. Focusing on phonics seems, logically, to be the best way of "getting" all the words. James Chapman (1986) insists that

> the emphasis upon individual words, has always been of paramount impor-tance to Christian educators, who believe in the verbal inspiration of the Scriptures and in quality education. . . . If one uses the whole-word method, which treats phonetic words as if they were ideographs, one can get away from stability, from standards, from restraint, from traditional pronuncia-tion, from traditional spelling, and from correct and incorrrect forms of speech. (pp. 13, 15)

Thus intensive phonics is more than a way of teaching reading or, alleg-edly, a means of getting the words right: it is a means of preserving stan-dards in education and in life.

The preservation of standards is consistent with fundamentalists' belief in absolutes, stemming from the belief in God as the absolute, supreme being. Fundamentalists also believe in a sharp distinction between the godly and the ungodly, the saved and the lost; and the dichotomy between good and evil, right and wrong. They believe that standards and authority in education are paramount. Because phonics can be laid out neatly in se-quenced lessons (even if children do not necessarily learn letter/sound re-lationships that way), it fits nicely into the worldview that there are stan-dards that must be maintained and taught by appropriate authority figures. Robert Holderer, who taught for many years in fundamentalist schools, explains this viewpoint as follows:

> Likewise, as God established an orderly universe (Genesis) and gave human-ity language as part of that order, traditional "rules only" methods [such] as

phonics, spelling drill, diagramming sentences, and so on are God's law for
teaching the young. Many Fundamentalists believe that integrated strategies
that subsume rules [such] as Whole Language are repugnant to God because
they are "relativistic" and repudiate "rules." (Holderer, 1995, p. 77)

It seems clear, then, that standards, rules, authority, and control are key
issues for religious fundamentalists, who may easily gravitate toward intensive, systematic phonics because it fits their worldview.

Certainly phonics is a real issue for many fundamentalist parents. But
for many, phonics is only part of the issue. A substantial amount of literature and information disseminated by fundamentalist political groups (the
National Right to Read Foundation, Phyllis Schlafly's Eagle Forum, Norma
and Mel Gabler's Educational Research Analysis, the Christian Coalition,
The National Association for Christian Education's activist arm Citizens for
Excellence in Education, Marlin Maddoux's *Point of View* radio talk show,
and others) calls not only for teaching phonics intensively and systematically, but also simultaneously for rejecting whole language teaching methods in the schools. In other words, they insist on teaching beginning reading through intensive phonics because they believe in it, but also because
it's a way of rejecting whole language without having to admit their religious basis for opposing it.

What is it about whole language that they object to? In part, of course,
it's the perceived abandonment of "rules"; the assumed relativistic teaching of phonics in the context of reading and writing rather than prior to
reading; and the underlying psycholinguistic research, to the extent they
are aware of it, that demonstrates clearly that reading is not a process of
identifying every word so much as a process of constructing meaning from
texts (Goodman, 1967; Rosenblatt, 1978; Pearson & Stephens, 1992).
Samuel Blumenfeld, for instance, claims that the whole language concept
of reading is based on the philosophy of deconstructionism, which he explains (via Derrida) as "an attack on the notion of absolute truth and literal
comprehension of a written text" (1992, p. 6). At least the latter part of
this statement is accurate, for psycholinguistic research has demonstrated
beyond reasonable doubt that everyone's reading of any text is determined or affected by his or her own prior knowledge, experiences, and
beliefs. This fact, however, is perceived as anathema to those who believe
that texts, especially the Bible, have one literal meaning for all readers.
Given this belief, the fundamentalists view phonics as the route to accurate word identification, and accurate word identification as the route to
uniform understanding of texts. Never mind that reading does not work
that way.

Whole language is particularly suspect because whole language teachers engage children in literature discussions, wherein students formulate

and discuss their own interpretations of the texts. Religious fundamental-ists are sometimes uncomfortable with this departure from standards and from the authority of one right answer, with the Bible being the quintes-sential authority. Thus the act of giving students choice in what they read, the idea that meaning does not actually reside in texts, the practice of liter-ature discussions, the practice of encouraging critical thinking, and the ba-sic whole language view of learning as constructing concepts rather than memorizing facts—all these are perceived as contrary to a worldview in which there are right and wrong answers to almost everything. Indeed, teachers who encourage independent thinking are by that act alone seen as attempting to discredit biblical absolutes through relativism (Holderer, 1995, p. 78).

No wonder, then, that religious fundamentalists have been eager to in-still intensive, systematic phonics in place of whole language. Whole lan-guage is considered far too dangerous. By some twist or abandonment of logic, whole language is even claimed to be "a devilish means to keep chil-dren illiterate" (Holderer, 1995, p. 78; see also Blumenfeld, 1984, 1996; Spohn, 1995).

Mel White (1994), formerly a ghostwriter for religious fundamentalists, and Wesley E. Miller (1984) have both "documented how Fundamentalist leadership has twisted facts carelessly (although some are deliberate) and has often refused to recant falsehoods when proven wrong" (Holderer, 1995, p. 81). Nowhere has this been more evident than in what is said about phonics and whole language. For example, the "Illiteracy" paper (Sweet, 1989) prepared as a U.S. Senate Republican Policy Committee document is riddled with misinformation; irrelevant statistics from which inaccurate causal-effect relationships are drawn; research from only one perspective, despite contrary research evidence; and false claims that a psycholinguistic view of reading and whole language education are really just the same as a "whole word" approach. When leading whole language advocates have patiently corrected some opponents in these misconcep-tions, they have found that the opponents continue thereafter to make the same misstatements in the public arena (e.g., Kenneth Goodman, per-sonal communication, and Connie Weaver's own experience).

In a discussion of various fundamentalist critics and criticisms of educa-tion, Caddy, Hall, and Marzano (1996) observe that fundamentalists' "ob-jections to educational programs and practices aren't based on their edu-cational merit," but on religious grounds (p. 49). They cite Eric Buehrer, who in *The New Age Masquerade* has argued that certain programs and practices should be objected to on religious rather than practical grounds (p. 49). Such observations give insight into why critics of whole language in particular and education in general (e.g., Cumbey, 1983; Groothuis, 1988; Marrs, 1987) do not necessarily try to be fair or accurate in their scholarship; why they do not necessarily care for logical argument, nor scrutinize their evidence in light of contrary research evidence; why they make claims that are demonstrably contrary to fact; and why they continue to distort information when confronted with inaccuracies. The end is seen as too important to take chances with because, as religious fundamentalists view it, whole language and public education in general may endanger not only children's minds, but their very souls.

FICTION, LITERALISM, AND RELIGION

Religious fundamentalists in the Christian, Jewish, and Muslim faiths pay close attention to the reading of texts and often insist that their children memorize, word for word, significant passages of the Bible, the Torah, or the Koran. Believing that meaning resides in a literal reading of words and sentences and assuming that there is just one way to interpret a text, many fundamentalist readers adopt the stance expressed in a simplistic slogan: "God said it, I believe it, that settles it." This stance makes the stakes for reading very high, because fundamentalists tend to believe that eternity in heaven or hell can depend on an accurate reading of the Word of God.

Religious fundamentalist parents occasionally indicate a preference that their children stick to reading nonfiction texts in the classroom, that is, texts that are ostensibly true. Fiction—that which is literally *not* true— seems to pose a greater risk in the minds of some parents, who fear that their children may perceive literary texts as factually true. When Joan DelFattore (1992) studied censorship cases, she discovered that some adult protestors themselves "did not distinguish between what a fictional character says and what the story is 'officially' promoting, nor did they see any difference between asking *whether* something is true and teaching that it *is* true" (p. 47).

Given such misperceptions, it is no surprise that every year works of literature are challenged more often than books of any other type. In recent years the Harry Potter books by J. K. Rowling have topped the American Library Association's "Banned Books Week" list of texts that have been challenged, primarily by parent protestors. Perhaps the enormous popularity of the Potter series has made it more likely that they would be attacked. Most parents, however, have shared their children's excitement about the series, especially when they noticed their children choosing to read long, hard-cover books when they could be playing video games, watching TV, or cruising the Internet. In a time of new global fears, the Potter books provide safe, vicarious adventure; young heroes with superpowers; and clever surprises that capture the imagination of young readers. They are real "page turners," exactly the kind of books that adults often choose for their own leisure reading.

But Harry, the young hero of the story, is a wizard who attends the Hogwarts School of Witchcraft and Wizardry, and the wizards and witchcraft create a problem for some parents—the same parents, for example, who express fears that celebrating Halloween will make their children more vulnerable to satanic, supernatural powers. Those who disapprove of the Potter books, as well as those who applaud them, often compare the series to C.S. Lewis's *Chronicles of Narnia* and to J. R. R. Tolkien's *Lord of the Rings*. Richard Abanes (2002) contrasts Rowling's use of the supernatural with that of Tolkien and is especially critical of Rowling's use of terminology that closely resembles that found in published texts about the occult. Arbanes fears that some young readers will be seduced into "magick— i.e., real-world occult practices," which he carefully distinguishes from the "magic" that is imaginary and found in most fantasy books and fairy tales. Magick—spelled with a "k"—is much more to be feared, he says, because it "operates in a real way in our real world" and may involve occult practices that "invade fantasy when they are too accurately presented by an author" (p. 37).

Other authors praise the Harry Potter texts, even suggesting that they can serve as a bridge to Christianity. For example, the author of *The Gospel According to Harry Potter: Spirituality in the Stories of the World's Most Famous Seeker* (Neal, 2002) has hosted Harry Potter Bible study groups in her home, and the author of *A Charmed Life: The Spirituality of Potterworld* (Bridger, 2002) insists that the Potter books provide "an enormous opportunity for speaking about Christian themes and truths and ideas" (Dancy, 2002).

Legally parents have the right to monitor what their children read, and to express concern about what their children are asked to read at school. They have the right to say, "I don't want my child to read the Harry Potter books" but not the right to remove texts they object to from the classroom itself or from the school library shelves. Teachers and administrators are similarly guilty of self-censorship when they decide on their own not to purchase a potentially controversial book or to remove it from the library shelves because they think it might cause trouble. The *Newsletter on Intellectual Freedom* regularly reports such instances as the following:

> Administrators . . . will not order any new Harry Potter books for the school library, fearing that parents might object to the wizardry and witchcraft themes in the popular series. Principal Joan Bookman said . . . "We just knew that we probably had some parents who wouldn't want their children to read these books." Bookman acknowledged, however, that there had been no complaints about the books. (Censorship Dateline, *Newsletter on Intellectual Freedom*, July 2000)

Given current levels of fear and anxiety, more teachers and administrators recognize the need for established school district policies for handling challenges to books and other materials (see Brinkley, 1999, pp. 228–252). If parents express a concern about whether a book is appropriate, a teacher or administrator asks them first to read the book, *all* of it, so they can understand the context in which the offending words or passages appear. Teachers and administrators generally know to treat protesters with respect, although it is difficult when parents and community members, and sometimes even school administrators themselves, engage in highly publicized personal attacks on teachers (see Lacks, 1997, and Goldwasser, 1997).

LITERALISM, FUTURISTIC FICTION, AND RELIGIOUS FUNDAMENTALISM

A steady diet of literal and uncritical reading—the kind of reading promoted by parent protesters and by the federal Reading First initiative launched in 2002—leaves readers of any age vulnerable to those who have an agenda for which they want to enlist followers. Currently millions of adult readers are vicariously living out the ultimate fear that is described by authors who link recent events to a hastily approaching Apocalypse. Based on their literal reading of a fiction series, many parents today actually fear that they might miss the Rapture and be "left behind." Like the Potter books for kids, the *Left Behind* (1995) series by Tim LaHaye and Phillip Jenkins are a good read. They tell an exciting story with suspense and violence that describes what happens when those who are "saved" have been taken to Heaven and those who are left behind must fight the Antichrist.

The *Left Behind* books are built primarily on a literal interpretation of the Book of Revelation, but the books' subtitle ("A Novel of the Earth's Last Days") and the "About the Authors" notes at the end clearly identify the series as fiction. Ironically, religious fundamentalists and many others are reading the books as if they were based on fact, believing that the series "broke the code" for the Book of Revelation (Gibbs, 2002). The book covers say that more than 40 million copies have been sold, and *Time* reports that sales soared after September 11 (Cloud, 2002).

Surely a great many readers of the series read the books strictly as fiction, but the books' influence is remarkable. A Time/CNN poll found that 59% of respondents say they believe the events described in Revelation will come true, and nearly one-quarter think the Bible predicted the 9/11 attack (Gibbs, 2002). To the extent that the *Left Behind* books are being read by Christian fundamentalists, readers might already have identified themselves as believing in the Rapture and the Apocalypse. But it is particularly disturbing to learn that some readers, including nationally prominent political leaders, are reading the novels as "indicators of tomorrow's headlines" (Gibbs, 2002). An earlier best-selling book, *The Late Great Planet Earth*, by Hal Lindsey (1970), also predicted end times and clearly influenced high-level politicians. In 1999 Senator Orrin Hatch (R–Utah) cited Lindsey's book at a Christian Coalition meeting, warning the crowd that the end of the world might soon be at hand (Benen, 2002). Lindsey himself served under President Ronald Reagan as a consultant on Middle East affairs to the Pentagon and the Israeli government (Gibbs, 2002). Similarly, one of the *Left Behind* co-authors, Tim LaHaye, co-chaired Jack Kemp's presidential campaign until a *Baltimore Sun* reporter examined some of LaHaye's theological books and discovered that he had called Catholicism a "false religion" and said that Rome "too often gives man a false security that keeps him from seeking salvation." LaHaye resigned a few days after the newspaper reprinted the comments (Cloud, 2002).

A visit to Strandberg's (2002) "Rapture Ready" Web site (http://www. raptureready.com) reveals how literally some Christian fundamentalists read the Bible and how much influence their literal reading has on their personal decisions and views about public affairs. The site tracks 45 indicators with titles such as False Christs, Satanism, Financial Unrest, Debt and Trade, Liberalism, and Nuclear Nations. The webmaster, Todd Strandberg, uses each indicator to gauge the speed at which events are converging toward the coming of Christ.

Perhaps of more interest to those who are doubters is a PBS Web site about the Apocalypse (http://www.pbs.org/wgbh/pages/frontline/shows/ apocalypse/) that provides a collection of statements on the subject by professors of religious studies. For example, L. Michael White, Professor of Classics and Christian Origins at the University of Texas at Austin, points out that often people are surprised to learn that the Book of Revelation includes "no reference whatsoever" to the Antichrist or to the Rapture. Many interpretations of Revelation, White explains, are created by "bringing things into the Book of Revelation, into its scheme, that are not actually there and reading them as a kind of jigsaw puzzle of eschatology and last judgment." White also explains that for centuries there was controversy about whether the Book of Revelation itself should be included in the Bible. He believes that St. Augustine played a key role in being sure Revelation was included. Augustine apparently read it symbolically rather than literally, and thus may not have particularly valued it for its message, but he wanted to preserve the Bible as it was at that time and especially favored including Revelation because it included language that served as a strong warning that nothing should be added or taken away from the text. Its placement at the end of the New Testament would reduce the likelihood of "future revelations from God that will stand alongside of the New Testament itself."

On one level, it's hard to criticize the success of the *Left Behind* series. Almost everyone loves a futuristic story that involves crisis, adventure, violence, and romance. However, the amazing popularity and impact of the *Left Behind* series tell another, more chilling story. No doubt the books scare a lot of readers into becoming believers, and they leave many feeling smug about the idea of literally "being saved" among the masses who will be left behind. The books are about winning and losing, good guys and bad guys, and they provide the ultimate experience of "othering" those who do not share such narrow beliefs. Many readers express joy that they will be ready for the Rapture and self-confidently pity those who have not taken the books seriously. On the other hand, Paul Maier, professor of ancient history at Western Michigan University and an author of Christian fiction, rejects the books' depiction of God, finding in them a deity he "does not recognize," one who "can't wait to zap the Christian flight crew out of jets so they crash" (Gibbs, 2002). Surely there has never been a more crucial need for teaching student readers to distinguish clearly between nonfiction and fantasy and to become critical readers and critical thinkers.

Two days after September 11, Jerry Falwell, founder of the Moral Majority, appeared on Pat Robertson's 700 Club (Christian Broadcasting Network). Not surprisingly, their conversation focused on trying to explain how such a horrific event could occur. During the course of the conversation, Robertson made the following comments:

> We have a court that has essentially stuck its finger in God's eye and said we're going to legislate you out of the schools. We're going to take your commandments from off the courthouse steps in various states. We're not going to let little children read the commandments of God. We're not going to let the Bible be read, no prayer in our schools. We have insulted God at the highest levels of our government. And then we say, "Why does this happen?" . . . Well, why it's happening is that God Almighty is lifting his protection from us. (Falwell, November 2001)

We have come to expect some religious fundamentalists to express such opinions, and we need to be aware of the criticisms being lodged against public schools. But sometimes we also need to be ready to stand up and say, "No, you're dead wrong." Karen Armstrong, author of *The Battle for God: A History of Fundamentalism* (2000), explains that during the mid-1950s "it was generally assumed by pundits and commentators that secularism was the coming ideology and that religion would never again become a force in international affairs. But the fundamentalists have reversed this trend and gradually, in both the United States and the Muslim world, religion has become a force that every government has been forced to take seriously." (As an author, Armstrong has remarkable credentials to speak on this topic. She was a Roman Catholic nun for 7 years, taught literature at the University of London, and now teaches at the Leo Baeck College for the Study of Judaism and the Training of Rabbis and Teachers. In 1999 she was awarded the Muslim Public Affairs Council Media Award.)

RELIGIOUS FUNDAMENTALISM
AND EDUCATION POLICY

The March 1999 report of Robert Simonds, president of the National Association of Christian Educators/Citizens for Excellence in Education, claims political victory on behalf of "faithful Christians" who have supported CEE as it "put out research and then converted that information to political reality" in support of intensive phonics. What led to this claim? The federal Reading Excellence bill that was passed in 1998. Although it's not clear how big a role Simonds and his CEE members may have played in getting the bill passed, the definition of reading originally proposed to the House Committee on Education and the Workforce reflects the influence of fundamentalist thinking on phonics and reading:

> The term "reading" means the process of comprehending the meaning of written text by depending on the ability to use phonics skills, that is, knowledge of letters and sounds, to decode printed words quickly and effortlessly, both silently and aloud. (Reading Excellence Act, draft, 1997)

In this view, phonics skills lead to decoding words, and decoding is presumed to guarantee comprehension of the author's intended meaning, with no mention of the importance of even sentence-level context.

Fundamentalists have found allies among some experimental researchers who focus on isolated aspects of reading instruction, especially researchers for the National Institute of Child Health and Human Development and most of those who prepared the National Reading Panel report (NRP, 2000a). And they have found political allies, especially among conservatives (Patterson, 2002) and particularly George W. Bush, who advocated the teaching of phonics as part of his campaign for the presidency. In effect, certain experimental researchers, politicians (Metcalf, 2002), corporate publishers of materials for teaching and testing reading (Altwerger & Strauss, 2002), and fundamentalists have drawn on and even generated parents' fears that their children will not learn to read. They have succeeded in promoting phonics as the cure (Simonds, 1999; Sweet, 1989). Further, they have succeeded in legislating a phonics-first national agenda (Allington, 2002), as embodied in the Early Reading First and the Reading First initiatives that are authorized by the No Child Left Behind act of 2002.

These allies have managed to legislate a phonics-first agenda by insisting that reading instruction be based solely on "scientific" research,[2] as defined in the Reading Excellence act (1998) and the No Child Left Behind act (2002). True, both of these laws describe "scientific" research as including high quality research involving experiment or observation. In fact, however, the federal agenda for teaching reading has ignored research on the reading process, research on literacy development, research on many instructional practices, and research comparing the effects of overall approaches to teaching reading—even the experimental research (e.g., NRP, 2000a). In practice, federal agencies have promoted only that experimental research that reflects the priorities of the current Bush administration, along with certain commercial programs for reading instruction, especially *Open Court*, whose corporate owner is a long-time friend of George W. Bush (Metcalf, 2002; Strauss, 2002).

Worse yet, this federal agenda, pushed especially by fundamentalists through the early to mid-1990s (Weaver, 1994; Weaver & Brinkley, 1998), is being promoted by documents that make inaccurate, untrue statements about what this limited body of experimental research "says." The booklet that allegedly summarizes the National Reading Report (NRP, 2000b) grossly exaggerates the actually quite limited results favoring systematic phonics (NRP, 2000a). *Put Reading First* (2002), another government-disseminated booklet related to the National Reading Panel report, claims that children must develop phonemic awareness (the ability to hear and manipulate the "separate" sounds in words) before reading—but this claim is not supported by the National Reading Panel data nor by any other research. In fact, the need for phonemic awareness first is contradicted by a considerable body of other independent research, and the NRP subgroup on phonics observed that many children develop phonemic awareness while learning to read, even if they are not taught phonemic awareness (NRP, 2000a, pp. 2–33).

The Reading First initiative embodies President George W. Bush's agenda of phonemic awareness (ability to hear and manipulate the "separate" sounds in words) and phonics first, with fluency also emphasized as

---

[2]In the original staff discussion draft of the Reading Excellence Act (1997), "scientific research" was defined exclusively as experimental research. Thanks to the lobbying efforts of the International Reading Association and others, the definition of "scientific research" in the actual Reading Excellence Act (1998) was broadened to include high quality research that "employs systematic, empirical methods that draw on observation or experiment." This definition was then included in the Reading First initiative within the No Child Left Behind Act of 2002.

a precursor to reading meaningful texts. The other topics investigated by the National Reading Panel are included as the remaining "essentials" of reading instruction, but these topics—vocabulary and comprehension— have also been virtually ignored in promoting the Reading First initiative. Furthermore, comprehension is explained as getting the meaning supposedly embodied within texts, though the view that "literal" comprehension is possible has been thoroughly discredited by research into reading as a psycholinguistic process. In the Reading First legislation (2002) and in the federal guidelines for implementing it (U.S. Department of Education, 2002, p. 43), there is no suggestion of teaching children to read for deep understanding, much less to read critically. The religious fundamentalists' view of reading as saying the words and getting literal meaning from the text has won out.

Beyond the intricate professional battles and the commercial and political maneuvers that have brought about this result, as disheartening as they are, lie even more ominous prospects for the future. G. Reid Lyon, director of the Child Development and Behavior Branch within the National Institute of Child Health and Human Development (NICHD) who has been dubbed President Bush's "reading guru" by the media, gave a speech in 2001 in which he said "We're entering a period in education where Congress is asking me whether we have enough background data . . . to determine malpractice in teaching [reading]. Malpractice is defined by a departure from known fact in the treatment of human beings when, in fact, the data exists to do it in a more effective way" (Lyon, 2002). Teachers, teacher educators, and scholars who advocate a broader definition of what constitutes reading are now faced with a warning that we might be charged with "malpractice."

Thus has fundamentalists' belief in the beauty of phonics been eventually translated into federal law and policy, along with a view of reading comprehension as merely getting the literal meanings presumed to be embodied in a text (U.S. Department of Education, 2002, p. 43). And political leaders self-righteously describe how they might like to impose their agenda for teaching reading within a country that was originally built on freedom and democracy.

WHAT CAN EDUCATORS DO?

We think it is time now for all of us as teachers and citizens to stay informed about the issues and to speak boldly in defense of good teaching. In a document titled "Reading First: Cautions and Recommendations," authors Yatvin, Weaver, and Garan offer the following recommendations for developing literacy programs for schools and school districts. In that document (2002, Section 5), each of the following recommendations is briefly discussed and supporting references are cited:

1. Develop comprehensive literacy programs that include more than just the five components identified in the Reading First initiative [the five components being phonemic awareness, phonics, fluency, vocabulary, and comprehension, each taught in isolation].
2. Teach comprehension strategies from kindergarten onward.
3. Include silent, independent reading as a classroom activity.
4. Help children to expand and refine their vocabularies through both direct and indirect methods.
5. Assess even the youngest children with a wide variety of measures that emphasize comprehension and the ability to use ideas from texts in writing and discussion.
6. Make high-quality literature and informational books a central feature of literacy programs and ensure that children have continual and easy access to books of the same quality for independent reading.
7. Integrate the teaching of phonemic awareness and phonics with reading real books and with written and oral expression.
8. Use texts that capture children's interest and satisfy their curiosity, whether they are predictable, decodable, or even a little beyond the children's technical abilities.
9. Promote fluency *in conjunction with* comprehension.
10. Do not treat children's reading difficulties as evidence that they need more of the same type of instruction they have been receiving.
11. Don't allow phonics, phonemic awareness, and fluency to become gatekeepers for children's advancement through the grades.
12. Provide professional development for teachers in all aspects of literacy instruction, not just the five components of reading instruction that are required in the Reading First initiative.

In light of the issues discussed in this chapter, we present the following additional recommendations that build on those listed above and recognize the protections, challenges, and support that students and educators need in an environment that threatens good teaching practices and intellectual freedom:

13. Work with curriculum specialists, administrators, parents, and school board members to review or establish district policies for

handling challenges to books and materials, classroom activities, and teaching methods (see Brinkley, 1999, pp. 228–252).

14. Teach young readers and their parents about the differences between fact and fiction and between reality and fantasy. Teach them to become critical readers who can question what they read, actually interrogating texts rather than automatically accepting the ideas they encounter in their reading.

15. Teach young readers and their parents about protecting their right to read and to learn, about not allowing others to think for them, and about promoting intellectual and academic freedom.

Day by day we can resolve to teach boldly what we know works for students. We can teach what we have to, what our state or the federal government says we must teach, but do so while embedding narrow curricular topics in a more comprehensive context that promotes richer lifelong learning. We can be ready at any moment to explain not just what we teach but how we teach it and why we teach it that way. We can document what we do and keep students' work along with their own written responses about what they are learning; we can share these materials with administrators and parents.

On a personal level, we can make friends among our teaching colleagues and make a pact to support each other, even if that means just meeting for conversation and a drink on Friday afternoons. And we can teach each other what we know best. We can read and discuss professional journals and attend conferences. We can publish articles and present sessions about our own research and classroom experiences. We can talk to friends who are not educators, describing our love for our work, our students, and our profession. Ultimately, we can do what we can to make a positive difference and then be at peace with ourselves, with who we are and what we do personally and professionally, so that we can live out each day without apology and be a source of strength for others.

REFERENCES

Abanes, R. (2002). *Fantasy and your family: A closer look at The Lord of the Rings, Harry Potter and Magick in the modern world.* Camp Hill, PA: Christian Publications.

A Beka Book. (1996). *Home school catalog.* Pensacola, FL.

Allington, R. L. (2002). *Big brother and the national reading curriculum: How ideology trumped evidence.* Portsmouth, NH: Heinemann.

Altwerger, B., & Strauss, S. L. (2002). The business behind testing. *Language Arts, 79*(3), 256–262.

Armbruster, B., Lehr, F., & Osborn, J. (2002). *Put reading first: The research building blocks for teaching children to read.* Center for the Improvement of Early Reading Achievement

(CIERA). Distributed by the National Institute for Literacy, the National Institute of Child Health and Human Development, and the U.S. Department of Education. http://www. nichd.nih.gov/publications/pubs/PFRbooklet/pdf.

Armstrong, K. (2000). *The battle for God: A history of fundamentalism.* New York: Ballantine Books.

Averill, L. J. (1990). *Religious right, religious wrong: A critique of the fundamentalist phenomenon.* New York: Pilgrim Press.

Benen, S. (2002, December). Church, state and the 108th Congress. *Church & State, 55*(11), 4–7.

Blumenfeld, S. L. (1984). *NEA: Trojan horse in American education.* Boise, ID: Paradigm.

Blumenfeld, S. L. (1992). The "whole language" fraud. *The New American, 8*(16), 6–8.

Blumenfeld, S. L. (1996). *The whole language/OBE fraud.* Boise, ID: Paradigm.

Bonfiglio, O. (2002, November 21). Dr. Laura pulls no punches on education, family. *Kalamazoo Gazette,* p. D10.

Bridger, F. (2002). *A charmed life: The spirituality of Potterworld.* New York: Doubleday.

Brinkley, E. H. (1994). Intellectual freedom and the theological dimensions of whole language. In J. Brown (Ed.), *Preserving intellectual freedom: Fighting censorship in our schools* (pp. 111–122). Urbana, IL: National Council of Teachers of English.

Brinkley, E. H. (1995). Faith in the word: Examining Religious Right attitudes about texts. *English Journal, 84,* 91–98.

Brinkley, E. H. (1999). *Caught off guard: Teachers rethinking censorship and controversy.* Boston: Allyn & Bacon.

Caddy, B. B., Hall, T. W., & Marzano, R. J. (1996). *School wars: Resolving our conflicts over religion and values.* San Francisco: Jossey-Bass.

Censorship Dateline. (2000, July). *Newsletter on Intellectual Freedom, XLIX*(4), 103.

Chapman, J. (1986). Why *not* teach intensive phonics? Pamphlet. Pensacola, FL: A Beka Book.

Cloud, J. (2002, July 1). How an evangelist and conservative activist turned prophecy into a fiction juggernaut. *Time,* 50–53.

Cumbey, C. E. (1983). *The hidden dangers of the rainbow: The new age movement and our coming age of barbarism.* Lafayette, LA: Huntington House.

Dancy, S. (2002, November 16). Writers find glimpses of gospel in Harry Potter's world of wizards. *Kalamazoo Gazette,* p. D2.

DelFattore, J. (1992). *What Johnny shouldn't read: Textbook censorship in America.* New Haven, CT: Yale University Press.

Dobson to Californians: Quit public schools. (2002, March 30). *WorldNetDaily.* Retrieved on April 19, 2002 from http://www.worldnetdaily.com/

Falwell, Robertson: God gave U.S. "what we deserve." (2001, November). *Newsletter on Intellectual Freedom, L*(6), 240–241.

Gibbs, N. (2002, July 1). Apocalypse now. *Time,* 41–48.

Goldwasser, M. M. (1997). Censorship: It happened to me in southwest Virginia—It could happen to you. *English Journal, 86*(2), 16–20.

Goodman, K. S. (1967). Reading: A psycholinguistic guessing game. *Journal of the Reading Specialist, 6,* 126–135.

Groothuis, D. (1988). *Confronting the new age.* Downers Grove, IL: InterVarsity Press.

Holderer, R. W. (1995, September). The religious right: Who are they and why are we the enemy? *English Journal, 84,* 75–83.

Lacks, C. (1997). The teacher's nightmare: Getting fired for good teaching. *English Journal, 86*(2), 29–33.

LaHaye, T., & Jenkins, J. B. (1995). *Left behind: A novel of the earth's last days.* Wheaton, IL: Tyndale House Publishers.

Lindsey, H. (1970). *The late great planet earth.* Grand Rapids, MI: Zondervan.

Lyon, G. R. (2002, November 18). Remarks made at a conference, "Rigorous evidence: The key to progress in education?" Washington, DC: Sponsored by the Council for Excellence in Government. Retrieved on January 3, 2003 from http://www.excelgov.org/displayContent.asp?Keyword=prppcEvidence.

Marrs, T. (1987). *Dark secrets of the new age.* Westchester, IL: Crossway Books.

Marty, M. E., & Appleby, R. S. (1991). *Fundamentalisms observed.* Chicago & London.

Metcalf, S. (2002, January 28). Reading between the lines. *The Nation,* 18–22.

Miller, W. E. (1984). The new Christian Right and the news media. In D. G. Bromley & A. Shupe (Eds.), *New Christian politics* (pp. 139–149). Macon, GA: Mercer University Press.

Moffet, J. (1988). *Storm in the mountains: A case study of censorship, conflict, and consciousness.* Carbondale, IL: Southern Illinois University Press.

National Reading Panel. (2000a). *Report of the National Reading Panel: An evidence-based assessment of the scientific research literature on reading and its implications for reading instruction, reports of the subgroups.* Washington, DC: National Institute for Child Health and Human Development. [Page numbers in this text refer to the version posted online as of Nov. 2002. These page numbers agree with one of the bound but undated versions.] http://www.nichd.nih.gov/publications/nrp/report.htm.

National Reading Panel. (2000b). *Report of the National Reading Panel: An evidence-based assessment of the scientific research literature on reading and its implications for reading instruction.* [Summary booklet]. Washington, DC: National Institute for Child Health and Human Development. [We used a booklet version from 2002; the online version is not paginated.] http://www.nichd.nih.gov/publications/nrp/smallbook.htm.

Neal, C. (2002). *The gospel according to Harry Potter: A spirituality in the stories of the world's most famous seeker.* Louisville, KY: Westminster John Knox Press.

No Child Left Behind. (2002, January 8). Washington, DC: Public Law 107–110. http://www.ed/gov/legislation/ESEA02.

PBS. *Apocalypse.* Retrieved December 10, 2002. http://www.pbs.org/wgbh/pages/frontline/shows/apocalypse/

Patterson, F. R. A. (2002). The politics of phonics. In R. L. Allington (Ed.), *Big brother and the national reading curriculum: How ideology trumped evidence* (pp. 157–194). Portsmouth, NH: Heinemann.

Pearson, P. D., & Stephens, D. (1992). Learning about literacy: A 30-year journey. In C. Gordon, G. D. Labercane, & W. R. McEachern (Eds.), *Elementary reading instruction: Process and practice.* Ginn Press. Reprinted in R. B. Ruddell, M. R. Ruddell, & H. Singer (Eds.), *Theoretical models and processes of reading* (4th ed., pp. 22–42). Newark, DE: International Reading Association, 1994.

Reading Excellence Act, draft. (1997). Introduced for committee discussion by Rep. W. F. Goodling. Washington, DC: U.S. House of Representatives, Committee on Education, Labor, and the Workforce.

Reading Excellence Act. (1998). Law based on HB 2614, introduced in the House of Representatives by W. F. Goodling, and on S 1596, introduced in the Senate by Sen. P. Coverdale. Washington, DC.

Reading First. (2002, January 8). Part of the No Child Left Behind Act, Public Law 107–110. http://www.ed/gov/legislation/ESEA02/pg4.html.

Rosenblatt, L. (1978). *The reader, the text, the poem: The transactional theory of the literary work.* Carbondale, IL: Southern Illinois University Press.

Simonds, R. (1999, March). *President's report.* Costa Mesa, CA: Citizens for Excellence in Education.

Simonds, R. (2001, January). *President's report.* Costa Mesa, CA: Citizens for Excellence in Education.

Spohn, L. (1995). *An analysis of whole language.* Newsletter. Pittsburgh, PA: Public Education Network.

Strandberg, T. *Rapture ready.* Retrieved December 16, 2002. http//www.raptureready.com.

Strauss, V. (2002, September 10). Phonics pitch irks teachers; U. S. denies it's pushing commercial products. Washington, DC: *Washington Post*, p. A01.

Sweet, R. (1989). *Illiteracy: An incurable disease or education malpractice?* Washington, DC: U.S. Senate Republican Policy Committee.

U.S. Department of Education. (2002, April). *Guidance for the Reading First program.* Washington, DC: Office of Elementary and Secondary Education. Retrieved on September 1, 2002 from http://www.ed.gov/offfices/OESE/readingfirst/ReadingFirstGuidanceFINAL.pdf.

Weaver, C. (1994). *Reading process and practice: From sociopsycholinguistics to whole language.* 2nd ed. Portsmouth, NH: Heinemann.

Weaver, C., & Brinkley, E. H. (1998). Phonics, whole language, and the religious and political right. In K. Goodman (Ed.), *In defense of good teaching* (pp. 127–141). York, ME: Stenhouse.

White, M. (1994). *Stranger at the gate: To be gay and Christian in America.* New York: Simon & Schuster.

Winters, D. (1995, November/December). Is there a best way to teach beginning reading? *The Teaching Home*, 48.

Yatvin, J., Weaver, C., & Garan, E. (2002). *Reading First: Cautions and recommendations.* http://www.EdResearch.info/reading_first/index.htm.

CHAPTER EIGHT

Not in the Script: The Missing Discourses of Parents, Students, and Teachers About Success for All

Kyle D. Shanton
Teresa C. Valenzuela

To question from above holds intellectual promise; to question from below forbodes danger.

—Michelle Fine (1987)

We are supposed to be able to ask questions—that is how we open up public dialogue in a democracy, engage more critically in civic life and strive for social justice. But, in this current social moment, parents, students, and teachers know very well that the freedom to ask questions, especially about literacy teaching and learning, does not extend to everyone. It is, instead, a classified privilege, available to certain individuals, at certain times, for certain purposes. To question brings into sharp focus the blurred reality of non-negotiable agendas and undisclosed power. It is wielded by those in positions of authority, but procured from those who are not. In this chapter, we consider these problems as they relate to the mandated implementation of *Success for All* at a barrio public elementary school, in the rural southern borderlands of New Mexico. Forbidding parents, students, and teachers to ask questions, keeping them from speaking out, are acts of coercion, a degradation of their humanity. We examine what is not being heard about *Success for All*, and how such unwanted discourse is interrupted, preempted, silenced.

Since the school's opening in the fall 1998, teachers at Benito Juarez Elementary have been required to use the *Success for All* (*SFA*) program to teach students to read. According to its school district's central administration, this decision *was needed* because of the student population's previous history of substandard achievement and *continues to be necessary* because it, allegedly, has "worked" to prevent the school from being identified for corrective action by the state's Department of Education. The allure of such authoritative rhetoric has been used purposefully and repeatedly to bewilder this school's community about what has actually been accomplished in terms of improving student achievement and arrest them from asking questions that really matter. Over the past 4 years, however, a number of students, parents, and teachers have tried to ask questions and query about the substantiation of success with *SFA* at Benito Juarez School. They are not alone: parents, students, and teachers at four other schools in the same district, also mandated to use *SFA*, have tried to raise their own set of similar concerns. But, all of these questions have been denounced and their queries discredited.

RELENTLESS CONTROL AND
AN UNRELENTING CAMPAIGN

Success for All is a comprehensive school reform program, used (i.e., in most cases mandated for use) by low-performing schools to teach children who are at-risk of not reading on grade level by third grade. It is a curricular and instructional program that, as James Traub (2002), popular contributing writer for *The Times Magazine*, and ardent advocate of the program, put it, "keeps teachers and children firmly, perhaps relentlessly, focused. . . ." It is reading and teaching by the script; teachers and children are not allowed to deviate. The program's aim is to focus relentlessly, one of Slavin's favorite words, on the acquisition of arbitrarily predetermined sequences of decoding and question answering skills in order to make successful readers. Teachers do not decide what to teach based on their observations of children, or on what children know and can do; neither do they build the structure of the day, or the week. They follow the script. Similarly, students have little, if any, input into their learning. They are placed in instructional groups by alleged reading level, according to test results. And, they do not move to the next level until their test performance matches or exceeds the rank score set for that level. In other words, as Jay Matthews (2002) of *The Washington Post* first suggested, and James Traub later reiterated, SFA is teacher proof, which in their "expert" opinion, is good, even necessary.

Developed originally in 1987 as a partnership between the Baltimore City Public Schools and the Center for Research on the Education of Students Placed at Risk (CRESPAR), a federally funded research center at Johns Hopkins University, *Success for All* was piloted in five of the systems' lowest-performing elementary schools. District administrators wanted a reading program that would enable every child to read at grade level by the end of third grade, a problem identified as particularly relevant to minority and "at-risk" students. Nancy Madden, Bob Slavin and a team of researchers developed a school-wide reform model, which was implemented for 5 years and then withdrawn from all five schools. Madden and Slavin claimed success by presenting tables of statistical indices—comparing the grade level test results between students at schools using *SFA* and students at schools using regular basal-driven instruction—which reflected significant differences in favor of *SFA*.

Over the next several years, the program was expanded, with the development of *Roots and Wings*, and implemented in schools across the nation. By 1997, Slavin had launched his own campaign to influence future policy development for Title I funding. Specifically, he argued that Title I awards should be available to schools that select exemplary comprehensive school reform models—which would be identified by design competitions that focus on criteria he outlined for effectiveness. Based on a review of evaluation research methodology and results of other approaches used for Title I services, Slavin and his colleagues found *Success for All's Roots and Wings* to be the two most effective programs and, therefore, eligible for Title I funding. At about the same time, the U.S. Department of Education had called for proposals to conduct a major policy study to set a new agenda for Title I; funding was awarded to two researchers affiliated with CRESPAR, who also championed *SFA* as particularly effective. Two years later, five of the most politically powerful professional teacher and administrator organizations collaborated to commission another study focused on Title I policy through the American Institutes for Research (2000). The lead researcher selected for this project also served as a lead researcher for the 1997 U.S. Department of Education study; again, *SFA* was identified as one of the most effective reform strategies.

Although Madden and Slavin appeared to be amassing a strong evidentiary base in support of *SFA*, there were still several key questions left unanswered. How valid, or trustworthy, are these findings? What would independent evaluators find about *SFA*? Why was it significant that students instructed by *SFA* scored better than students who continued with the same traditional instruction? What was behind the "scientific" screen of Slavin's comparison methodology? And, more importantly, what did students, parents, and teachers have to say about their experiences with *SFA*? Stanley Pogrow (2000), research professor at the University of Arizona, has paid painstaking attention to the dissemination of research on *SFA* and the systematic efforts of Robert Slavin to shape the nation's Title I policy agenda. He issued this caveat emptor:

However, the biggest problem for our profession is that the impression that *SFA* and the schoolwide approach are supported by research came about as a result of a concentration of resources in the hands of a single organization that developed the program, evaluated it and its competitors, and conducted the key policy analysis that is the basis for related government and judicial action. This concentration of all of these functions in the same group of interrelated individuals associated with a single research center clearly provides the potential for conflicts of interest and for misdirecting knowledge and policy. (p. 598)

Elizabeth Jones and Gary and Denise Gottfredson of the University of Maryland were the first to take such questions seriously. In 1998, in response to Robert Slavin's and Olatokunbo Fashola's (1998) proposal to offer the U.S. Congress an answer for what works for "disadvantaged students," and what is worth the nearly $7 billion of Title I funding, they conducted an independent evaluation. Slavin and Fashola found *SFA* to be that answer. However, from their independent meta-analysis of *SFA* comparisons, Jones and her colleagues found test results for students who received *SFA* instruction averaged a zero effect size for ten of the twelve comparisons, with their estimate being approximately 4% (0.04 versus 1.13) of that reported by Slavin. Richard Venezky (1998), another independent researcher, from the University of Vermont, also considered such questions in his independent evaluation of the Baltimore research. He uncovered a failure to report the program had not met the program's primary objective—reading at grade level by third grade. In fact, students were not even reading at grade level by fifth grade; the longitudinal data illustrated that students entering sixth grade were scoring more than 2 years below grade level. It became apparent, moreover, that with additional *SFA* instruction students continued to fall further behind national norms. He also uncovered serious biases in the selection of alleged matched comparison groups (e.g., the majority of students identified for special education were withdrawn from the *SFA* group, whereas those in the comparison group remained). Extending his critique of bias in the evaluation methodology, and thereby echoing questions about the validity of claims of success for *SFA,* Herbert Walberg and Rebecca Greenberg (1999) outlined four major infractions made invisible by the omissions of Slavin et al.: 1) selection of participants—in terms of both teachers and students; 2) coherence between program design and evaluation measure; 3) relevant data, analysis and interpretation; and, 4) impartial disclosure in reporting results (i.e., CRESPAR internal reports record negative results that have not been disclosed in publication; see also Venezky).

Despite the emerging counter evidence from independent evaluations of *SFA*, Slavin continued on his unrelenting campaign. Consider the following events:

- 1996—the U.S. Department of Education awards funding for its key policy analysis research on the future of Title I to CRESPAR where *SFA* was developed;
- 1997—Slavin argued that due to the overall ineffectiveness of Title I, significant sums of money should be invested in design competitions to identify exemplary programs, which would be judged according to criteria he suggested, and encourage schools to adopt these programs;
- 1998—a member of Slavin's research team at Johns Hopkins University participatcd as an invited member of the Committee on the Prevention of Reading Difficulties in Young Children, which reported *SFA* to be remarkably successful;
- 1999—another of Slavin's research associates helped author a research evaluation report commissioned through the American Research Insititute by the five largest teacher and administrator organizations, finding *SFA* to be one of three programs with strong research support and effectiveness;
- 2001—Slavin was named as a panelist on the National Literacy Panel on Language Minority Children and youth, commissioned by the U.S. Department of Education/Institute of Education Sciences to conduct a comprehensive, evidence-based review of the research literature relevant to the development of literacy among language minority children and youth;
- 2002—the U.S. Department of Education awarded the National Opinion Research Center at the University of Chicago a grant of $6.1 million to evaluate 30 *SFA* sites and 30 comparison sites, to determine the effectiveness of the program; and,
- 2002—Slavin served as an advisory board member of the Coalition for Evidence-Based Policy, which prepared a report to the U.S. Department of Education and suggested that it institute a sweeping effort to a) build the knowledge base and b) provide strong incentives for the widespread use of identified programs.

The campaign for *Success for All* is being mounted at a time when students, parents, and teachers are being deliberately discouraged from trying to see or address the problems they face in their schools. Their focused attention is, in other words, being diverted. Instead, they are being urged to narrow the range of their vision and read only the approved script of teaching and learning, a script edited by those politically positioned to do so. It presents a very particular view—one that is framed around only what is supposed to be seen—of teachers, children, teaching, and learning. The campaign for *Success for All* rejects any alternative explanations of teaching and learning and refuses any questions about the legitimacy of its claims. The realities of program capacity, political agenda, and educational equity have become distorted into illusions by the magic of so-called scientific researchers, political representatives, concerned business leaders, the media, and public philanthropists who have coalesced to take control of U.S. education from policy to practice. With this in mind, we speak out with those who have dared to speak out. Ours is indeed counter-discourse to the disingenuous rhetoric of those who disregard, even silence, what they do not want to hear. Through our narrative inquiry we are trying to open up spaces for parent, student and teacher to voice their dissent missing in the discourse on *SFA*. In the spirit of what David Purpel (1998) called foundational inquiry, "[We] refuse to sever [our] concerns with the issues of schooling and education from [our] own moral and political commitments, from [our] outrage about all that weighs so heavily on the youngest and most vulnerable" (p. xvi). And, like Stanley Pogrow, we ask: Whose interests are really being served? And, why are alternative ones interests being ignored?

SUCCESS FOR ALL COMES TO LAS MESAS

Las Mesas is situated in a region of the United States known as the borderlands, a geographic expanse of nearly 2,000 miles along the political borders of the United States and Mexico. The city sits in a river valley nestled among several adjacent mesas from which the eye can see into the distance for what seems like almost forever. It is a unique contrast of both rural and urban, with a population of more than 75,000. Las Mesas has been home to families of Mexican descent for generations; today it is being billed across the United States as a "best place" for retirees. English and Spanish are spoken in most public places, although English predominates.

By the spring of 1998 the literacy programs at five schools in Las Mesas had adopted *Success for All*. Because students at each school had accumulated a record of "poor performance" on standardized tests, principals were directed to bring in reading programs that would improve the test scores immediately. Acting on behalf of the schools' principals, the district's Director of Federal Programs contacted Title I directors across the nation, researched the Title I literature on effective literacy programs and observed the implementation of *SFA* at an elementary school in a neighboring district. She came to the conclusion that *SFA* was a program that would improve reading scores in the least amount of time. Although 80% of the teaching staff are expected to agree in order to adopt the program, this protocol was not followed exactly at each of the schools in Las Mesas

(Valenzuela, 1999). In fact, the faculty at Benito Juarez Elementary had no choice in the matter. The adoption was an administrative decision made prior to the hiring of the teaching faculty; there was no opportunity for teachers to give voice to their questions or consider other options. Neither was any input sought from parents.

Benito Juarez sits on top of what local residents refer to as the east mesa. It is a primary (K–2) school, serving a student population of approximately 500 students, about 77% are Hispanic, 20% White, 2% African American, and 1% American Indian. And, it is situated adjacent to the campus of its sibling intermediate school (3–5), Soledad—the community's original K–6 elementary school. Due to overcrowding at Soledad, district officials decided to restructure it as an intermediate school and build a new K–2 school. As a result of that decision, primary grade students were reassigned three times, attending foster schools, two of which are located more than 10 miles from their neighborhood—one requiring travel across a major state highway and the other across an interstate freeway—and the third approximately five miles away, over an 8-year span before Benito Juarez was built. During this period of transitions, the decision was made to give priority to build one of the foster schools—which has served a student population of less than 300 from upper-middle and upper-class neighborhoods—before Benito Juarez.

According to the *SFA* Foundation, retention is virtually eliminated through the implementation of *SFA*. But, at Benito Juarez over 1/3 of the second graders (65 of 180) were identified as at-risk for retention in the spring of 2002 and placed on the state's Academic Improvement Contract, after 3 years of *SFA* instruction, because they could not read at grade level. Thus, the goal of *Success for All* has not become a reality at Benito Juarez. Moreover, what we find most interesting is that at another school in the district, with a nearly identical student population (i.e., in terms of a majority percentage of students of color and who qualify for free and reduced lunch), but at which teachers have had greater regard for their professionalism and more freedom to design and implement reading instruction, students achievement results are consistently higher:

- test scores on the annual standardized, norm-referenced test for the last three years are consistently between 5 and 8 *nce*s greater for the comparison school than for Benito Juarez; and,
- holistic scores on the district's writing assessment for the comparison school were the highest in the district for each year reported and below district average each year for Benito Juarez.

This, however, has not deterred the administration from re-adopting *SFA*. The questions that still remain are: Why? What is this really about?

MAKING TROUBLE—A PARENT SPEAKS OUT

Juliet was raised in Las Mesas and graduated from one of the public high schools in town. She describes herself as Hispanic, fully bilingual and very proud of her community. She has been a stay-at-home mom, raising her only child, Timothy, and helping her husband with their family-owned restaurant.

For as long as she could remember, she did many of the same things with her son that her mother did with her: singing to him, telling him stories, and reading to him. She recalls that Timothy, somewhat to her surprise, actually liked books from very early on. He would often pick several for her to read to him; and, by the time he was a first grader, he was reading his favorite books by himself at home.

Long before *SFA* came to Benito Juarez, then, Juliet had taken very seriously the importance of actively supporting her son's literacy development. For instance, she mentioned, "Since he started school, I would always visit classrooms, but not just to do the 'chores,' you know making copies and all that that parents usually get to do, but to get to know the teachers and kids." She cares about who is teaching her child, and her friends and neighbors' children, as well as what they are doing to help children learn.

Juliet told us that, shortly after Timothy started second grade, she began to worry about what was happening at school. She could sense he was growing frustrated. She remembers he told her that there was a new reading program called *SFA*. She asked him, "What's *SFA*?" Timothy replied that he did not know a lot about it but, "it was boring." So, Juliet went to school and talked with the teacher to find out more about this program. Within the next few days, she decided to sit in during the ninety minute reading block because she "wanted to know what it was about." This was not unusual for her; in her eyes, "[She] needed to do that to become more aware of what was really going on."

Following that observation, she began asking Timothy's teacher and the principal questions about *SFA*. Juliet was told that because the school had been on academic probation, due to low test scores, *SFA* was adopted as the reading instruction program. "It was supposed to raise test scores so the school would get off probation."

By the beginning of third grade, however, Juliet had noticed that Timothy seemed even more frustrated and he was having problems with reading, problems he had not experienced before *SFA*. She recalled how she had watched saw her son "shutting down and not wanting to read anymore." He seemed despondent and "depressed about reading." She could detect an unfamiliar anxiousness in his voice when she tried to talk to him or encourage him to read. He no longer asked her to read with him, and he no longer brought out books to read by himself. Juliet, therefore, decided to meet with his *SFA* reading teacher, then the *SFA* facilitator, and finally the principal. Regrettably, none of them offered any meaningful relief or support for her son. She had wanted to discuss her observations of what had been happening to him since *SFA* instruction first began. She also wanted to discuss what they had observed about her son; she wanted to know how well they had come to know him. To her disappointment, they listened only briefly to her. And, almost immediately, the discussion turned to focus on their appraisal that Timothy suffered from test anxiety. "He needed more practice in order to overcome this anxiety," they suggested. She had wanted to discuss the obvious change in her son's attitude and behavior toward reading; she had wanted to talk about her son. The teacher, facilitator, and principal, however, were focusing strictly on the program. At this point, the facilitator recommended Timothy be tested more frequently, almost every week, in order to gain some practice with taking tests and to better identify his what else he needed to read at grade level. Juliet became numb with frustration over this decision. As she recalled, "Well, after you're getting tested practically every week over the same thing, over and over and over, why bother? You're not learning, and they're not moving you. You're still stuck in one place." She realized she would have to figure out how to help her son. She found herself facing what did not make any sense. "Their bottom line was that *SFA* [was] a proven program. It [would] work. Timothy just needed to keep trying in order to overcome his problem." Something she doubted very seriously.

Juliet then started talking to other parents about her concerns and to find out theirs. She learned that "other parents, [and] kids, [were] going through the same things that I went through with [Timothy]." Although she knew that most parents in the community were to go to the school and talk with teachers, she emphasized that she had not realized the extent of their fear. "They're scared to go in and say anything. And myself and my friend, we have told them, 'No, these are our kids! We need to be advocates for them. You can't just let your kid go by; you can't do it. Something needs to be done.' " Through this process, she found she had to talk more openly with teachers, too. Juliet described that "the majority of teachers at Benito Juarez do not support the program, but they don't or can't say anything." From her perspective, she sees that teachers are frightened to speak out about this, but she does not know exactly why. She suggested that, "Maybe they are afraid of losing their jobs?" Juliet has had conversations in which a teacher will share her frustrations about *SFA*, but she made Juliet promise that if she were to say anything to the administration she would share these as anonymous concerns. She is puzzled as to why teachers will not speak out. And, she wishes they would because, as she put it, "They need to be advocates for what really is best for children. That is part, an important part, of what it means to be a teacher."

Instead, Juliet believes that teachers are acquiescing to an adversarial system, one that hurts children because it focuses on what they did not do on a test and treats them as though they are all alike. "It just labels them and then puts them together by the labels." Other parents tell her they have tried to show how their children can read, because they, too, are aware of and worry about the labeling. But, the response is: "Well, [your child] may read at home, but I'm sorry [she's] not doing good in *SFA*. So, [she's] going to be in a lower group until she improves." Juliet reiterated that this did not make any sense to her. "How can they not listen to us and believe us when we see what these kids can do?" She thinks the program's emphasis on testing, and prescription, instills in children, especially those struggling to move from one level to the next, a sense that they are incompetent. Juliet is worried that it has discouraged students to the point of "having complexes about themselves and reading, and then they don't want to try anymore. They just give up on school because it gave up on them."

For the remainder of his third grade year, and through most of his fourth grade year, Juliet stopped asking him what or how he was doing in school, and talked to him about things that seemed to matter most to him—those things outside of school, like his friendships and family. She also enrolled him in private tutoring, which required less than half the amount of testing and focused more clearly on teaching her son rather than a particular program. Gradually, Timothy began talking openly with her about "feeling sad because he didn't like to read in *SFA* and wasn't a good reader any more." She said that as "[H]e started to read again at home he also started to realize he was not the problem." And, as she spoke, her voice resonated with a painful sense of joy in knowing Timothy could again see himself the way she had always seen him.

But, Juliet has not given up her struggle with these issues of power that allow children to be treated this way, for the sake of a program that is supposedly based on "scientific" research. She speaks out about what she has learned from her son's experience; and, she challenges the way programs are used to censor, coerce and control parents, children, and teachers. "[I] see a lot of kids who are struggling worse now," although the district claims that test scores are higher and probation was rescinded. She is still deeply concerned that because most of the parents in her community are afraid to challenge the school, nothing will change and more children will be debilitated by *SFA*. "When I think about the fact that teachers aren't able to, or maybe they really don't want to, take a stand against *SFA*, and the district administration is trying to force them into silence also, I just feel overwhelmed. But, so many children are falling through the cracks, and we should be protecting them from feeling as if they are failures. We should be allowed to talk openly about these things. And, we have to something different." In the midst of this struggle, Juliet has come to be known by several of the teachers and *SFA* staff as a trouble maker. She knows this because when she walks into the school, she "can feel people staring at me, and I hear them say 'Here comes trouble'! I know what they think of me."

For Juliet, if there are no changes made in the next several months, the only alternative left is to organize several other parents go with her before the local school board and voice these concerns directly to them. She reminded us: "I'm in the school constantly, at least once a week and sometimes twice, and I see kids struggling. They don't want to do *SFA*. They don't even want to read. They talk to me because I know them and they know me. You see, I go over to their houses and they come to mine. We know each other. And, they say they can't wait to leave, to just get out."

MISSING THE POINT—A STUDENT SPEAKS OUT

Juliet's son, Timothy, is definitely aware of his mother's critique of *SFA*; he has heard her talk openly about her concerns. He has watched Juliet talk with his peers and their parents about on-going struggles with the program's restricted teaching and their feelings of frustration, embarrassment, and boredom. In and out and across these dialogic moments, he gradually opened up to his mother about his own struggles. Timothy has become more articulate about what has troubled him. And, he has his own story to tell.

Timothy remembers that he wanted to learn to read, and used to like to read. In fact, as a first grader he was particularly proud of the books he would bring home to read to his mom and those he would take from home to school to show his teacher. He is Mexican American, an only child born to working class parents. Timothy is now a fifth grader who, like most of his peers, cannot wait to go to middle school. His reasons are typical of most young adolescents, although one is rather unusual. He wants to go to middle school so that he can be a reader again.

Timothy started attending Benito Juarez School as a second grader, 3 years ago, the year the school opened. "I was in second grade when they first started *Success for All*. I took a test, and they put me in second-grade reading. But, then, when I was in third grade they put me in second grade reading again. It didn't make any sense, because I could already read those stories. And, I didn't want to read them again. I just got even more bored. Now I've been in *SFA* for second, third, fourth and fifth grades. It's the same thing every year. But, next year, at the middle school, they don't do *SFA*. So, then, I can just really read like I already know how to do."

Until then, Timothy has to "do the *SFA* program," which, is "just about taking a test so that they can put you into different classes and do what the wall chart and teacher's book say you're supposed to do." As he, unequivocally, suggested, it is about testing and grouping, not about reading—or teaching and learning for that matter. His descriptions of what happens in practice plainly portray a routine series of step-wise procedures that teachers and students carry out within strict time constraints because the script says so:

STAR Story—"The teacher reads a story aloud and you just listen to it, but we can't talk about it because there isn't enough time."

Reading—"You read silently by yourself and then out loud with a buddy, but you can barely do it, because the teacher tells you when you're done."

Think-Pair-Share—"You have to get your partner and then you wait for the teacher to say think, that's the question, and you're supposed to think quietly; then the teacher says, 'Pair,' and you share what you thought; you're only supposed to say one thing because you only have like 2 minutes, so you can't really talk about the story."

Story Retell—"You get this practice book and your notebook, and you just answer the questions, like 'Where did the dog go?' and, you answer, 'The dog went to the neighbor's house,' but sometimes you can't finish it either."

Meaningful Sentences—"You have to use the red words, from the word wall, and you pick two; you do the steps of making definitions that are six parts long (e.g., who, what, where, when, how, and why) and putting all of that together to come up with one sentence for each word, but you don't have enough time, really."

Two Minute Edit—"The teacher looks in the *SFA* book and writes down a sentence on the white board, and it's misspelled and needs a little correction; then someone goes up, corrects it and sits down, and then you have to copy it correct before the 2 minutes are up."

Adventures in Writing—"You do all the steps in the writing process (e.g., brainstorming, rough draft, revision, editing, final draft) one at a time, one on each day, and you have to get them all done in a week; then you do it all over again the next week for a different story."

Although he ascribed "learning how to write the definitions of a word" and "maybe how to correct sentences the teacher writes on the board," he also came to the conclusion that "it really doesn't help that much . . . because it is boring and [he has] no idea what it's for." But, even more problematic for him was the disingenuous ways that some teachers treated him, and his peers, during the daily *SFA* period. He recalled that teachers wanted students to "just finish all the activities on time." And, at the end of every 8 weeks, when it was time to test again, they "put a lot of pressure on us" because "they always say: 'You better pass that test; I would hate to have you back again.' "

He was unapologetic about the fact that he neither took any interest in *SFA* nor thought he had learned anything useful through the program. He substantiated his argument further by explaining how he preferred the longer periods of time he is able to spend in his homeroom class, working on projects and reading, as well as free time to visit the school library. These he named as his most rewarding academic experiences.

Timothy pointed out that despite his boredom, frustration, and mere grade level placement in the *SFA* program, he knows he is a good reader. In his eyes, his mother helped him figure this out, encouraging him to read what he wanted to read and respecting what he had to say. "In *SFA* they only let me read 5.1 or 5.2 books, but I can really read 6.1 books and higher." For example, since the beginning of school this year, he has read and re-read *Harry Potter and the Sorcerer's Stone*, *Little House on the Prairie*, and *The Lion, the Witch and the Wardrobe* at home. Timothy explained that he "can read these better because the books are better. They are more like real stories that you can think about, and you know why you're reading them."

With his eye on next year, and being a reader again in middle school, Timothy recommended that "[a] teacher should, first of all, let kids pick the stories they want to read, and let them read. Let kids choose when they want to read something again, not make them always read the story again. They need to let kids read books at different levels, at lots of levels, and give more time to read and write. There should also be fun activities with reading a book, like letting kids talk and draw—with chalk, sketching pencils and colored pencils—about what they think. And, they should read fun stories to kids, too."

MARKED ON THE "BLACKLIST"— A TEACHER SPEAKS OUT

Kelly always wanted to be a teacher. He believes his desire grew out of the strong impressions of several unforgettably awful teachers he had as a kid, as well as his stubborn passion to read. From his perspective, he sees as the purpose of teaching to do something different for kids, to actually teach with them in mind.

When Kelly began teaching 8 years ago, he remembers that he tried to do what Yetta Goodman (1982) called *kidwatching*, that is, learn about children by carefully watching them learn. From the very beginning he noticed that if you ask first graders, "How many of you know how to read?" most of them look away immediately, and very few say they can. Yet if you let them read, and talk about their reading, then as a teacher you can support their emergent literacy. He sees over and over again how all of them look to a teacher continually to affirm their hope that they are somehow becoming readers. Kelly has come to realize that a teacher is indeed powerful enough to "make or break" how a student understands what reading is, and, therefore, whether or not she considers herself a reader, by the things he does or does not say. This raises serious concerns in his mind about how he approaches teaching. He now spends long periods of time wondering "What did I say?" or "Why didn't I say something else?" At Benito Juarez School where Kelly now teaches, his experiences with *Success for All* have only worsened these concerns. He has seen how his students' sense of themselves as readers and reading are dulled by the program's intractable structures, routine activities and indifferent strategies toward different children. He put it this way: "You can go in there . . . and read the script, like you're 'supposed' to, but if you don't know where the kids are coming from, and you can't relate to them, none of that matters."

This is Kelly's fourth year teaching at Benito Juarez. When he started 3 years ago, he helped open the school. Kelly recounted how he followed *SFA* instructions religiously the first 2 years, although he was becoming bored and completely disinterested with teaching. His students were disengaged from reading but, ostensibly, on task throughout the minute-by-minute routine. And, many were failing. That is, during those first 2 years more students than he and his colleagues could count were not scoring at grade level and had to repeat the previous 8-week module all over. Kelly started to ask questions: first, to himself, and then, gradually, but quietly, to trusted colleagues because he couldn't understand "where the success was in *Success for All*." Other, more experienced, colleagues were, however, speaking out against what was happening. The more he turned this problem over in his mind, the more clearly he could see what was hidden behind the structures of the program. He began to see how standardized, norm-referenced testing and the predetermined and fixed scope and sequence actually placed barriers in children's way, especially those who struggled in school, before they ever got started. "If a student is just beginning second grade, but her test score didn't match, even though she reads books leveled by the *Accelerated Reading Program* at second, and third, grade level, then she's 'behind' before she even begins. More crucial than that, if her scores on the 8-week post-test didn't place her into the next semester's module, then she repeats everything she just did, exactly as she had done it before. Word by word, sentence by sentence, story by story, day after day and week after week. How is this supposed to help a child who didn't 'get it' the first time?"

Kelly knew he had to be very careful of what he said about the program because "the walls listen, and very shortly after you talk you get called in by 'downtown.' They want to meet with you because they've heard that you're 'not in support of the reading program,' or that you've made some 'unprofessional comments' about *SFA*." Kelly insisted that no questions about the effectiveness of the program were ever allowed at staff meetings, school presentations or *SFA* conferences. As he put it: "If you challenged the program in any way, you were either ignored or chastised, and then, you were put on the blacklist."

In his third year teaching at Benito Juarez, he had had enough. Four of the ten students Kelly was teaching now had to repeat the same module for the third time and two for the fourth. Kelly was feeling overwhelmed with stress as he watched these second graders become further depressed about themselves and their abilities to read and write. They showed no interest in coming to his classroom for *SFA* or reading anything during their *SFA* instructional time; in fact, they regularly resisted his efforts to encourage them to participate by arguing that they "didn't know how to do that," or acting silly as a last resort.

Kelly talked privately with a few of his colleagues, who shared his concerns, but these conversations came to an abrupt end. The school's assistant principal had somehow found out about their private forum. All of them received disciplinary action for "unprofessional behavior." There were three with whom he spoke regularly about frustrations and his skepticism. One was tireless in her quest to pinpoint problems and voice concerns in public about *SFA*. Having taught for more than 15 years in the district, she had been recognized as a master teacher of reading, frequently asked to provide professional development workshops by district administrators, teachers, and colleagues from around the state. Regardless, she was placed on an improvement plan, and disallowed to transfer to any other school in the district. She finally resigned her teaching position in the district. The two others received written warnings about their actions. They both decided to stop talking about *SFA* and follow through with the objectives of the program. Eventually both transferred to other schools that were not mandated to use *SFA*. For reasons he could not explain, Kelly thought this meant he was somehow exempt—that he would not face these consequences, or have to pay such a price, for what he had to say.

Kelly's concern for his students, and now his colleagues, led him to look more carefully at the history of *SFA*'s record at the school. Annual test scores were not rising; the scores were unmistakably flat-lined. His query led to more questions: "Why do we stick with *SFA* if test scores aren't improving? Why is *SFA* being used with all students in our school, even for special needs students whose exceptionality is reading? What will really make a difference for our kids?" Then as he scrutinized the testing and placement records of students in his classroom, who had been repeating *SFA* instructional modules, he found that even those who were being tutored were not faring any differently on the tests. So, Kelly, unaware that he was about to make the most serious mistake of his career, decided it was time to say something.

He confided in the school's new assistant principal because he had a sense that she was interested in what teachers had to say. He was right in thinking that she would listen to teachers, but he was wrong about her reasons for doing so. On a Friday afternoon in late October of 2001, he told her about his frustration with students' lack of improvement and the program's lack of flexibility. He explained further that he had recently noticed that four of his *SFA* students who were tested by the school diagnostician, and recommended for Child Study Team, had qualified for Special Education with reading as their exceptionality. Kelly, therefore, asked her: "What kind of services were these kids going to receive?" She said that they would continue in the *SFA* program. His response was: "You know, there is a problem with that. What justice are we doing these kids? We need to offer them an alternative." Kelly knew that he needed to be politically savvy, so he also mentioned that he was not trying to derail *SFA* at Benito Juarez. Instead, he explained that he wanted to make a case for good instruction—that is, it always allowed for alternatives in order to address what had been overlooked, or not working well, to meet a child's needs.

As he looks back on this today, he now realizes that she only appeared to be listening. The last thing he remembers about the conversation was that she said she was sorry he was so worried, and "there is really nothing else we can do." Because he was worried about his students, and he believed he was doing the right thing, he felt a deep sense of relief at having finally expressed what he really felt.

Two days later his principal called him, unexpectedly, into his office. He told Kelly he wanted to talk to him alone before the assistant principal joined them. He started with "Kelly, you know what, you're giving me gray hair." Kelly recalls that he wanted to laugh at first, but he quickly detected that his principal wasn't joking. So, he immediately began thinking, "What did I do?" And, it did not take him long to remember each of his colleagues who had asked questions, or spoken out publicly, about *SFA* and the consequences they had to endure. "Don't ruin your career, because that's exactly what you're doing right now." Kelly just looked at him, thinking, "This can't be happening." He didn't actually say anything at that point.

His principal continued, "You've got to play the game. You need a pay-check just like I do. Don't ruin your career." He then told Kelly that, for disciplinary appearances, and more importantly his own safety, he was as-signing him something else to do during the daily *SFA* period. He sug-gested that because Kelly's classroom was located outside the main build-ing, in a portable, he could do his own thing. They were not going to come around checking on him anymore that year. Kelly wanted to argue back, "No, I want you to come in. We should be looking at what we're do-ing here with all our kids."

His principal then informed him that the administrator in charge of Ele-mentary Education at the district's central office was concerned about this situation. Apparently, the assistant principal had suggested to this admin-istrator, and the principal, that Kelly was not a "good" teacher because of his alleged infidelity to the *SFA* model, and his attitude was insubordinate toward the school's commitment to it. When she entered the office, she barely spoke to Kelly. But when she finally did, she very clearly outlined one more consequence: she would not write in support of his application to the local university's administrative degree program. Her support was necessary in order to be accepted for the required internship. His princi-pal did not have to say anything; Kelly knew this meant that he could not support him either.

As he walked away from the office, he grew more and more bewildered about what was happening to him. He kept repeating to himself: "Why can't I ask questions? Why can't I express my concerns? How can I just go in my classroom and do this?" For the first time in his career he thought se-riously about throwing in his towel. Kelly had always thought he would be proud to be a teacher: he had found it both enormously challenging and rewarding. And, he had believed that he would be respected as a thought-ful and knowledgeable teacher, especially because he had recently been named as a finalist for State Teacher-of-the-Year. But now he was no long-er sure. None of this made any sense.

For the remainder of that year he decided to go as unnoticed as possi-ble, doing the program exactly as it was outlined. However, he has since continued to struggle, mostly in silence, with his questions about the right of children to be able to learn to read by really reading, the right of teach-ers to ask questions and change their practice in keeping with students' needs, and the right of both to pursue education as a practice of these freedoms.

Before *SFA* was put in place at Benito Juarez, teachers were supposed to have a say in the matter. That was never the case. After 3 years they were supposed to have direct input as to whether or not to continue. But that would not be the case either. Kelly had originally believed that *SFA* was based on best practices, and it could provide students, and teachers, what they needed in order to learn and achieve. He no longer believes this. Kelly is not exactly sure what purpose a packaged program like *SFA* serves, other than to control curriculum, teaching and achievement; but he knows what purposes it does not serve. He is aware that the *SFA* program is not really about collaboration between teachers, students, parents, and district administrators to improve a school. And, it is certainly not about real teaching or reading. And, he knows where the problem really lies. As he put it: "The program is nothing more than a script, a schedule and some materials. The problem is that teaching and reading are about people—the teachers, kids, and parents. They're completely missing from the *SFA* equation."

MATTERS OF (OP)POSITION

Through these narratives, it is possible to see how the campaign for *Success for All* has positioned certain special interests in opposition to its own, treating them as adversarial and systematically omitting them from the current conversation on "best evidence of" and "what works" in teaching and learning for literacy. We have seen how a parent, child, and teacher may be questioned "from above" (i.e., by those placed in positions of authority in the *SFA* hierarchical scheme) about their actions and interests, but the reciprocal—to question "from below"—is not allowed. It is, in fact, dangerous.

For us, these narratives are about the ways in which discourses are positioned in oppositional stances, against one another, in a discursive hierarchy. And, there is no mistaking which is the opposition. Linguist James Gee (2001) explained, "Discourse-defined positions from which to speak and behave are not, however, just defined internal to the discourse, but also as standpoints taken up by the discourse in its relation to other, ultimately opposing, discourses" (p. 2). In the case we examined, then, the campaign for *SFA* is able to claim success because it defines parent, child, and teacher as failures. As such, their discourses, their narratives about who they are and how they are literate, are problematic, even unnecessary.

An unyielding claim of authority over teachers, and their teaching, and children, and their learning, resonates across all channels of the authorized discourse about *Success for All*. Such pejorative, even hateful, rhetoric toward teachers and children has been used to defend unexamined assumptions about the responsibility, and right, of everyone—except teachers and children—to make sure that this kind of "common sense" approach is followed. It has legitimized sanctimonious public sentiments on "what works," as if these were expert opinions based on sound evidence.

And, as David Purpel (1998) clarified, this discourse of stigmatization has persuaded the public to overlook the ways in which we have violated our moral, spiritual, and political traditions of liberty, equality and justice, as well as our commitment to public education for all people. Inherent in this discourse are political transactions, based on a deeply-seeded value of competition and a fundamental belief in the idea of winners and losers, that aim not for consensus but control. There is, perhaps, no regard for parents, students, and teachers, because we have lost sight of our common human ties with them. Instead we shame and exclude them.

But, why do teachers and children need to follow a script? Which teachers and children are unfocused? Who says so? Based on what evidence? It is by no means a coincidence that Madden, Slavin and their colleagues acquired so much acclaim for their work. Slavin's 1997 proposal to award Title I funding based on design competitions is now required by the U.S. Department of Education's Institute of Education Sciences. The results of their initial review of effective programs have been replicated by renowned organizations (e.g., the National Academy of Sciences and the American Institutes of Research), which also found *SFA* to be one of the most successful. Moreover, they have attracted the attention of the two most prestigious and widely-circulated newspapers in the nation, both of which have offered a carte blanche endorsement. What we find at the same time fascinating and disturbing is that the errors in research strategy, misrepresentation of findings and antithesis evaluations by suitable independent researchers are not sufficiently discussed. In fact, in most instances they are not even mentioned. Clearly, Madden, Slavin and others have created a powerful political alliance that draws on the reach of the federal government, professional organizations, scientific community, and mainstream public media. In so doing, they have organized a prominent and powerful critical mass, strategically positioned to omit any counter evidence or silence any counter discourse.

We, too, are implicated in this problem of positioning. As researchers, we have spoken for Juliet, Timothy, and Kelly; we have represented them with the signature of our own voices (Clandinin & Connelly, 2000). Although not entirely ours, nor mostly ours, the story scripts are ultimately ones we penned. We have found a forum in which to speak openly. Juliet, Timothy and Kelly remain outside that forum, unable to truly speak for themselves. We are the "authenticating presence" (Alcoff, 1995).

The *SFA* script reads like a contemporary *manifest destiny*, claiming authority and, therefore, dispensation to take over the public education of children, in particular that of children of color, English Language Learners, and children in poverty. The authors have written over the voices of parent, student and teacher. The *SFA* script was written without the drama of the classroom in mind—there is no space for local knowledge and language, human curiosity and inquiry, or the unpredictable dynamics of human interaction and literacy. It is a script with a single-minded voice and a one-size-fits-all message. The focus is on following a protocol of teaching, learning and literacy, without a vision of whom, by whom and for whom. There is no mention in the script, no place in its production, for those involved in these human endeavors. In this way, it has failed to address what teaching, learning and literacy actually are: human endeavors.

CONCLUSION

The *Success for All* campaign marches on toward the goals of improving instruction and student achievement. What is at issue, however, is neither a teaching nor learning problem. Rather it is a problem of power. Through the narrative lenses of Juliet, Timothy, Kelly and the *SFA* campaign we can clearly see how power is structured. The problem is obvious in the positioning of one party against another: the school against the parent, the curriculum against the student, and the program against the teacher. According to this arrangement, there is no room for Juliet, Timothy, or Kelly to articulate what they think, feel, and understand about their experiences with the program. There is no reason to listen to them speak their concerns or questions. By way of interrupting their queries, silencing their questions and censuring their participation, they have been excluded. Teaching, learning and literacy are defined, then, in terms of the script alone, not in terms of real human beings and their endeavors. In facing this problem, we turn our attention to bell hooks (1994), who called for opening up the spaces of teaching and learning. We argue that there must be space for the parent to share how she participates with her child in literacy events, for the learner to bring forward his knowledge, language and practice of literacy, or for the teacher to draw on what he knows about literacy and his students in order for school to be about teaching, learning, and literacy.

Reflecting on each, we are humbled by what each had to do in order to give voice to what they had to say. We see Juliet as an example of what it means to "do" social justice—she deeply cares about and is determined to take action on behalf of her son's and her neighbors' children's education. She has engaged in the struggle at hand to voice her concerns and questions even in the midst of being dismissed as ignorant, and harassed as a troublemaker. We see Timothy as an outstanding example of how articulate children can be about their literacy education. As Eugene Gordon (1999) pointed out, children's sense of awareness are heightened by their close relationship to, and the freedom to participate with, a family member who is actively working with many people in the community to better understand significant issues. And, we see Kelly as remarkable because he struggled with his concern for his students' and his own freedom in the classroom. He tried to confront the duplicity inherent in the current system that, on the one hand, suggests children and families be able to contribute to the design of an education but, on the other, only to the extent that what the school has identified as important is what ultimately matters. Each one has found the courage to face daunting odds and serious risk.

We want to conclude this essay by focusing again on the narratives of parent, student and teacher. We want to remember, as Leslie Marmon Silko (1996) explains, "the boundless capacity of language . . . [to] bring us together, despite great distances" (p. 59). With their narratives, we realize that it is possible to bring together attitudes, ideas, feelings, language, perspectives, and practices in order to rehumanize teaching, learning and literacy.

Your silence will not protect you. (Audrey Lorde)

REFERENCES

Alcoff, L. (1995). The problem of speaking for others. In J. Roof & Wiegman (Eds.), *Who can speak? Authority and critical identity* (pp. 97–119). Chicago: University of Illinois Press.

Baron, J., Boruch, R., Crane, J., Ellwood, D., Gueron, J., Haskins, R., Hoyt, R., Hull, B., Kessler, D., Ravitch, D., Robinson, L., Sawhill, I., Seligman, M., Slavin, R., Solow, R., & Zill, N. (2000). *Executive summary: Bringing evidence-driven progress to education.* A report of the Coalition for Evidence-Based Policy.

Clandinin, J., & Connelly, M. (2000). *Narrative inquiry.* San Francisco: Jossey-Bass.

Fashola, O., & Slavin, R. (1998). Schoolwide reform models: What works? *Phi Delta Kappan, 82*(1), 38–40.

Fine, M. (1987). Silencing in public schools. *Language Arts, 64*(2), 157–172.

Gee, J. (2001). What is literacy? In P. Shannon (Ed.), *Becoming political, too* (pp. 1–9). Portsmouth, NH: Heinemann.

Goodman, Y. M. (1982). Kidwatching: Evaluating written language development. *Australian Journal of Reading, 5*(3), 120–128.

Gordon, E. (1999). *Education and justice: A view from the back of the bus.* New York: Teachers College Press.

Herman, R. (2000). What we know about comprehensive school reform models. Report for the U.S. Department of Education, Office of the Under Secretary of Education, Planning and Evaluations Service, American Institutes for Research, Washington, DC.

hooks, b. (1994). *Teaching to transgress.* New York: Routledge.

Jones, E., Gottfredson, G., & Gottfredson, D. (1998). Success for some: An evaluation of the Success for All program. *Evaluation Review, 21,* 643–670.

Marmon Silko, L. (1996). *Yellow woman and a beauty of the spirit.* New York: Touchstone.

Matthews, J. (2002, July 21). Success for some: Critics of a controversial method for teaching poor children claim its benefits are overrated. The question is, what's the alternative? *The Washington Post,* p. W. 30.

Owocki, G., & Goodman, Y. (2002). *Kidwatching: Documenting children's literacy development.* Portsmouth, NH: Heinemann.

Pogrow, S. (2000). The unsubstantiated success of *Success for All*. *Phi Delta Kappan, 82*(1), 38–40.

Purpel, D. (1998). Foreword. In S. Books (Ed.), *Invisible children in the society and its schools* (pp. ix–xiii). Mahwah, NJ: Lawrence Erlbaum Associates.

Slavin, R. (1997). Design competitions: A proposal for a new federal role in educational research and development. *Educational Researcher, 26*(1), 22–28.

Success for All Foundation. (2000). *A proven schoolwide program for the elementary grades: Success for All* [Brochure]. Baltimore, MD.

Traub, J. (2002, November 10). No Child Left Behind: Success for some. *The New York Times,* Education Life Supplement.

U.S. Department of Education. (2002, March). *Mini-Digest of educational statistics* (NCES 2002-026). Washington, DC.

Valenzuela, T. C. (1999). *Reading program adoption: "Success for All" arrives in Las Cruces, New Mexico*. Unpublished manuscript.

Venezky, R. (1998). An alternative perspective on Success for All. In K. Wong (Ed.), *Advances in educational policy, Volume 4* (pp. 145–165). Greenwich, CT: JAI Press.

Walberg, H., & Greenberg, R. (1999). Educators should require evidence. *Phi Delta Kappan*, 132–135.

PART THREE

THE MEDIA

The chapters in Part III function to broaden the focus of the book from dealing with issues within the community of "literacy" and illustrate the wide-ranging effects of creating fear and disempowering teachers. These two chapters do not focus strictly on literacy, but rather take a wider lens on the media's role in promoting the conservative and corporate agenda.

CHAPTER NINE

Unelected Policymakers:
Conservative Think Tanks
and Education

Eric Haas

If you followed the education debates in Congress during 2001, there was a good chance that you saw a citation to the Heritage Foundation's Krista Kafer. If you attended the April 26, 2001, press conference of Rep. John Boehner, Chairman of the House Education and the Workforce Committee, you heard him sing the praises of the House of Representatives' No Child Left Behind (NCLB) bill. Boehner was ecstatic because a Heritage Foundation report gave their bill high marks on education reform, and he urged his fellow Representatives to read it (Schnittger & Lara, 2001). In that report, Kafer cited the recently released National Assessment of Education Progress (NAEP) scores to conclude that it is wasteful to spend federal money on public education and that it should be replaced with a system of vouchers, charter schools, and national testing.

What Boehner did not say in his press conference was that Kafer, who authored the Heritage Foundation report, entitled "B+ for H.R. 1's Education Reforms," is not an expert on education. Kafer, although billed as such by the Heritage Foundation, has only a B.A. in history and no experience working in education.[1] If he had, his listeners might not take Kafer's incomplete report and simplistic assessment very seriously.[2]

---

[1]Krista Kafer's Heritage Foundation biography can be found on the Heritage Foundation Web site at http://www.heritage.org/About/Staff/KristaKafer.cfm (downloaded January 18, 2003).

[2]Kafer's Heritage Foundation report did not discuss such issues as total spending on students who are not in special education has not been rising and in some cases has been decreasing (Bracey, 2002a; Molnar, 1999); the United States spends less than most other industrialized countries on education (Berliner & Biddle, 1995; Bracey, 2002a; Kozol, 1991);

Now you might dismiss this lack of full disclosure as expected in a poli-
tician and turn to reputable newspapers for more complete coverage of
education. You would be disappointed there, too. In the following
months, both the *New York Times* and the *Washington Post* cited Kafer as
an expert commentator on NCLB.[3] The *New York Times* described her as a
"policy analyst for the Heritage Foundation, a conservative research organization" whereas the *Washington Post*, in two different articles, described her only as "an analyst for the Heritage Foundation" and "of the
Heritage Foundation" (Alvarez, 2001; Fletcher, 2001; Fletcher & Milbank,
2001). These reports did not mention Kafer's lack of expertise in education, and they did not inform the readers that her level of expertise is typical of Heritage Foundation personnel. Readers certainly would not know
that Heritage Foundation "experts" have been described as some of the
least qualified of all Washington, D.C. think tanks, and that their lack of expertise is so pronounced that a *Time* magazine reporter once suggested
that they should be dubbed "advocacy" tank, not think tank (Wilentz,
1986). As is discussed later, that description aptly describes the Heritage
Foundation's current crop of education experts.

You will also find the Heritage Foundation on the U.S. Department of
Education Web site.[4] The second Bush administration placed the Heritage
Foundation on its NCLB Web site as a source for information on education.
The NCLB Web site provides no description of the Heritage Foundation.

Thus, all of these sources, Rep. Boehner, the *New York Times*, the
Washington Post, and the U.S. Department of Education Web site, have
left out vital information for judging the quality of what the Heritage
Foundation produces and they then disseminate. They do not say, for
example, that the Heritage Foundation describes itself as a "second-
hand dealer" of conservative ideas (Smith, 1991, p. 201) and that the Heritage Foundation attributes its success in influencing the media, politicians
and the public to "mission, money, management, and marketing," not in-

---

federal spending is only about 7% of overall education spending—most comes from states
and local districts (Symonds, 2001); NAEP scores do show improvements in student achieve-
ments (Berliner & Biddle, 1995; Bracey, 2002a; Molnar, 1999); students spend only 9% of
time in school—so other factors strongly influence learning and test performance (Bracey,
2002c); and studies of the performance of students who attend charter schools, who use
vouchers to attend private schools, or who attend schools run by the private Edison Schools,
Inc. most often show that there is insufficient data to judge the reason for student performance (positive or negative) or that these students perform about the same as public school
students (Bracey, 2002b; Horn & Miron, 2000; Miron & Applegate, 2000).

[3]No Child Left Behind is a renaming of the Elementary and Secondary Education Act
(ESEA).

[4]The Heritage Foundation is listed as an information source on the "Resources" page of
the U.S. Department of Education's No Child Left Behind Web page. It is available on the
Internet at http://www.nclb.gov/next/where/index.html (downloaded on January 18, 2003).

formation derived from rigorous research (Kuttner, 2002). Nor would you know from any of these sources that what the Heritage Foundation packages as research has been described as "sophomoric" (Soley, 1992, p. 62).

Sadly, these examples from the Heritage Foundation are not aberrations; they are the norm of conservative think tanks. The Heritage Foundation is the guiding force in a coordinated movement of conservative think tanks, many of which model their operations on the marketing techniques of the Heritage Foundation. The marketing technique is this: package provocative claims and incomplete information as easy-to-use research reports and through readily-available, media savvy experts so that this information can be used by the media, politicians and policymakers to lend an air of credibility to conservative policies and programs that are not supported by more rigorous scientific research and more qualified experts (Howe, 2002; Kaplan, 2000; Shaker & Heilman, 2002). In education, conservative think tanks are marketing experts and research to promote and support the growing fear that public education is in crisis—a crisis caused by governmental bureaucracy and teachers unions—a crisis that can only be solved by private school choice such as charter schools, tuition tax credits, and vouchers. The following are some representative examples of what conservative think tanks are disseminating as experts and research and how each falls way short of that mark when closely (or not so closely) scrutinized.[5]

UNQUALIFIED EXPERTS

The Heritage Foundation produced more than 25 writings on education during 2001 and 2002.[6] These writings characterize public schools as horrific, school choice as the only solution, and politicians who do not support vouchers and school choice as "hypocrites" (Garrett, 2001a–d). The majority were written by seven staff members—Krista Kafer, Megan Farnsworth, Jennifer Garrett, Stuart Butler, Robert Moffit, Mike Franc, and Tom Hinton—listed as education "experts" on their Web site. According to

---

[5]In essence, all scientific research, whether it be in education or any other field, should endeavor to be "utterly honest" in its methods and reporting (Feynman, 1985, p. 311). As such, educational research, if it is to be deemed scientific, should entertain and discuss counter evidence, provide a transparent account of its research process sufficient for readers to assess the rigor of the research methods and analytical reasoning utilized, and be submitted for critical peer review prior to release to the media and general public (American Educational Research Association, 1992; National Academy of Science, 1992; Shavelson & Towne, 2002). None of the think tank publications discussed in the chapter met this standard.

[6]Heritage Foundation publications on education can be found on their Web site at http://www.heritage.org/Research/Education/index.cfm (downloaded on January 18, 2003).

their staff biographies,[7] five of the seven have neither studied nor worked in education. Tom Hinton has B.A. degrees in political science and Christian education, but no experience working as a teacher or administrator.[8] Their most qualified expert on education is Megan Farnsworth. According to the Heritage Foundation, she earned a master's degree of education from UCLA and is "an alumna of Harvard's Graduate School of Education with a degree in reading instruction and school reform."[9] She has worked as a teacher, curriculum specialist, and school evaluator, although it is not clear for how long. At most, only one of the seven education "experts" has either extensive study or extensive experience working in education.

Of these "experts," the news media cited Krista Kafer most often during 2001 (Haas, Molnar, & Serrano, 2002). In giving statements in the press, she was most often presented as an expert, labeled as an "education analyst," "policy analyst," or "of the Heritage Foundation" (Haas, Molnar, & Serrano, 2002). No one reading these news reports or the press releases and writings produced by Krista Kafer and disseminated by the Heritage Foundation would know her utter lack of qualifications—a B.A. in history and no experience working as a teacher or school administrator.[10]

This lack of expertise appears to be typical for Heritage Foundation staff. Writing in 1992, Professor Lawrence Soley described the Heritage Foundation personnel as follows:

> Among beltway [Washington, DC] think tanks, Heritage associates have the weakest scholarly credentials, but are nonetheless the capital city's most active policy advocates. Of its 34 permanent "fellows, scholars, and staff" members, only 7 have Ph.D.'s. None are renowned scholars in their fields. The biggest names in this think tank are not thinkers, but former Republican officials. (p. 60)

Such a description remains true today. Nevertheless, the Heritage Foundation personnel continue to be recognized as education experts. As just noted, they are regularly cited in the news media as education experts and the second Bush administration placed the Heritage Foundation on the U.S. Department of Education's NCLB Web site as a source of expert information.

---

[7]The biographies of the Heritage Foundation "experts" on education can be found on the "Research: education" section of their Web site at http://www.heritage.org/Research/Education/index.cfm (downloaded on January 18, 2003).

[8]Tom Hinton's Heritage Foundation biography is located at http://www.heritage.org/About/Staff/ThomasHinton.cfm (downloaded on January 18, 2003).

[9]Megan Farnsworth's Heritage Foundation biography is located at http://www.heritage.org/About/Staff/MeganFarnsworth.cfm (downloaded on January 18, 2003).

[10]See note 1.

MISINFORMATION AS RESEARCH

In an examination of recent policy campaigns of conservative think tanks, Trudy Lieberman describes the efforts of the Cato Institute to abolish Head Start. In a chapter entitled, "Masking Ideology as Research: Bringing Down Head Start," Lieberman details how the Cato Institute promoted its anti–Head Start campaign with rhetoric masked as research that was widely and uncritically disseminated by the press (Lieberman, 2000). The campaign turned on the Cato Institute's 1992 Policy Analysis No. 187 entitled, "Caveat Emptor: The Head Start Scam," written by John Hood, research director at the John Locke Foundation, a conservative state-level think tank in North Carolina (Hood, 1992). Although its analysis had numerous quotes and citations, making it look like rigorous research, it fell way short of that standard. Instead, No. 187 used a "rhetorical style of unbridled scorn" (p. 102), in which Hood labeled Head Start supporters as "hucksters," early childhood intervention a "fad," and all positive Head Start evaluations as "fleet averaging gimmick(s)" that told "Head Start whoppers" that, he concluded, resulted in a "Head Start myth" (Hood, 1992, online). Hood backed his accusations mostly with news reports and frequent out-of-context quotes and mischaracterizations of research studies that turned the words of Head Start supporters into criticisms. According to Lieberman, the Cato Institute then used these "criticisms" to support its conclusions that Head Start should be eliminated or replaced with a preschool voucher program. She concludes that this report "dress[ed] up ideology as objective evaluation" (p. 101) and that "[a] careful reader should have discerned that the think tank's . . . report [was] intellectually dishonest" (p. 102).

Even so, the Cato Institute promoted this paper as credible and it received extensive, supportive coverage in the press. The news media, through numerous hard news and syndicated opinion columns in newspapers across the country, presented No. 187 as "research" and its author as a "researcher," "expert," and "academic" although he had minimal to no credentials in child development or education (pp. 108–109). Further, the Cato Institute itself was also given quite favorable coverage for it was presented as either having "expertise" in child development (p. 110) or with such lackluster descriptors as "Cato Institute" or "Washington-based research organization" from which readers could not discern Cato's ideological orientation (p. 110). Taking all this together, Lieberman concludes:

> Cato's attack also exemplifies the media's gullibility, intellectual laziness, and eagerness to run with a story without researching what was behind it. The media gave a massive amount of attention to Cato's one-sided analysis, failed to do its own digging to verify its claims, and allowed Cato to portray Head Start in a way that was both incomplete and misleading. (p. 102)

The Cato Institute continues to produce education documents and the news media continue to look to them for expert commentary on education.[11] Many of these documents persist in arguing for the termination of Head Start.[12] Several of these were written by Darcy Olsen, who was the Director of Education and Child Policy at the Cato Institute (Olsen, 1997, 2000; Olsen & Olsen, 1999). She is now the president and CEO of the Goldwater Institute, a conservative state-level think tank in Arizona. Her weak research skills are discussed in the section "campaigning for school choice with dubious evidence."

POOR SCHOLARSHIP RELEASED
AS RIGOROUS RESEARCH

In February 2001, the Manhattan Institute issued a report entitled "An Evaluation of the Florida A-Plus Accountability and School Choice Program" (Greene, 2001). Its author, Jay Greene, a Manhattan Institute Senior Fellow, calculated that schools that received a failing grade from the state, thus making their students eligible for tuition vouchers to attend another school if they failed again, achieved much larger test score gains the following year than did other schools. From this, he concluded:

> This report shows that the performance of students on academic tests improves when public schools are faced with the prospect that their students will receive vouchers. These results are particularly relevant because of the similarities between the Florida A-Plus choice and accountability system and the education initiatives proposed by President George W. Bush. (Greene, 2001, executive summary)

The Manhattan Institute report received extensive and positive coverage in the press (Molnar, 2001). Newspaper headlines included "The Wonderful Voucher Threat" in the *New York Post*, "Florida Schools Shape Up Amid Voucher Threat, Findings Could Boost Bush's National Plan" in *USA Today*, and "Threat of Vouchers Motivates Schools to Improve, Study

---

[11]Cato Institute writings on education are located on their Web site at http://www. cato.org/research/education/index.html (downloaded on January 18, 2003).

The Cato Institute lists many of its media citations on various pages of its Web site, including its "Press Room" located at http://www.cato.org/pressroom/experts-on-tv.html, its "Multimedia" page located at http://www.cato.org/media/index.html and on the pages of its various policy experts (see, for example, David Salisbury's biography page located at http:// www.cato.org/people/salisbury.html) (downloaded on January 18, 2003).

[12]Cato Institute writings on Head Start are located on their "Child Care" Web page located at http://www.cato.org/research/education/childcare.html (downloaded on January 18, 2003).

Says" in the *New York Times* ("The Wonderful Voucher," 2001; Henry, 2001; Schemo, 2001). Rep. Boehner said that Jay Greene's Manhattan Institute report "will have 'significant impact' on the congressional debate" (Henry, 2001). Researchers, who had access to the study only after it was released to politicians and the press, found it riddled with errors.

Re-examining the study's research methodology, Professors Gregory Camilli and Katrina Bulkley of Rutgers University had "serious questions regarding the validity of Greene's empirical results and conclusions" and found "that it is simply not clear whether or not the threat of vouchers is having a positive impact on student test scores" (Camilli & Bulkley, 2001). "It is overly simplistic," Camilli and Bulkley concluded, for Greene "to assume that the voucher threat was the only active agent, or that other causes were contingent on the voucher threat" (2001). More likely, the test score gains were due to a number of possible factors, including changes in teaching materials and staff, that Greene either did not take into account or assumed were the result of the voucher threat alone (Camilli & Bulkley, 2001).

Professor Haggai Kupermintz of the University of Colorado also examined Greene's study. He found that Greene "over-stated" the effect that the vouchers threat had on failing schools in Florida because of important statistical issues "that Greene either paid no attention to in his report or dismissed as unimportant" (Kupermintz, 2001). Re-analyzing Greene's statistics, Kupermintz found that the threat of vouchers had little effect on failing schools—except in writing. Here, according to Kupermintz, the "voucher effect" likely had an unintended and negative consequence. He believed that failing schools made considerable improvements in their writing test scores because the teachers and administrators in those schools taught to the test. Kupermintz's analysis of the test score data suggested that the teachers were probably using teaching methods that they expected would guarantee a passing grade of D in as many students as possible, but could risk doing little more. With Florida having no other measure of successful teaching beyond pass or fail and given the dire consequences if the school failed again, it appears that the voucher threat scared educators in these failing schools to develop writing abilities in their students that were a mile wide and an inch deep.

Kupermintz found the consequence of the "voucher effect" to be consistent with a prior newspaper article that investigated why Florida students appeared to be writing better. Quoting the article he wrote, "Out of fear and necessity, Florida educators have figured out how the state's writing test works and are gearing instruction toward it—with constant writing and, in many cases, a shamelessly formulaic approach" (Kupermintz, 2001). Thus, vouchers might be bullying educators into getting more kids to pass the state writing test, but it isn't scaring the students into writing well, just passing the test. In rather understated language, Kupermintz concluded that "the reader of the Manhattan Institute's laudatory report is offered a false sense of dramatic success" (Kupermintz, 2001).

Jay Greene's report does not appear to be an isolated incident at the Manhattan Institute, but in line with their preresearch conclusion that "there will be a need for school vouchers" in school reform (Spring, 2002, p. 32). Such a research agenda led Joel Spring (2002) to write this about the Manhattan Institute:

> The institute's research on vouchers is not a search for truth but a search for justifications for its political program. An objective program would seek to find out if vouchers are an effective means of improving school conditions . . . [Instead], the goal of the institute's support of research is not to prove whether vouchers are effective but to create arguments supporting voucher plans. Objective research is replaced by political polemics. (pp. 31–32)

Sadly, the press continue to present Jay Greene and the Manhattan Institute as education experts. For example, a *New York Times* article of December 28, 2002, that questions the benefits of high stakes testing, quoted Jay Greene, "a senior fellow at the Manhattan Institute," and presented him as an education expert who supports high-stakes testing (Winter, 2002). The article also mentions that Greene is currently working on his own study about the effects of high-stakes testing. The *New York Times* did not mention that his recent study on the effect of high-stakes testing combined with the threat of vouchers was found to be methodologically unsound and his conclusions overly simplistic. Additionally, the second Bush administration placed the Manhattan Institute on the U.S. Department of Education's No Child Left Behind Web site as a source of expert information.[13] The NCLB Web site does not present these criticisms of Greene and the Manhattan Institute.

CAMPAIGNING FOR SCHOOL CHOICE
WITH DUBIOUS EVIDENCE

The National Education Association (NEA), a teachers union and a staunch defender of public schools, reports that a number of state-level think tanks belonging to the State Policy Network, a loose federation of conservative think tanks and interest groups, have been simultaneously and very ac-

---

[13]Like the Heritage Foundation, the Manhattan Institute is listed as an information source on the "Resources" page of the U.S. Department of Education's No Child Left Behind Web page. It is available on the Internet at http://www.nclb.gov/next/where/index.html (downloaded on January 18, 2003).

tively promoting school choice efforts to legislators (NEA, 2000; State Policy Network, 2002). For example, the NEA credits the Goldwater Institute with being a significant force in the passage of Arizona's tuition tax credit law in 1997 (NEA, 2000). The Arizona law currently allows individuals to receive a dollar-for-dollar tax credit up to $500 for contributions to School Tuition Organizations that award tuition scholarships to students for use at private schools. Another provision of the tuition tax credit law provides a $250 tax credit for individual donations to public schools to fund extracurricular activities. In March 2002, the Goldwater Institute's president and CEO, Darcy Olsen, issued a report entitled, "Education Scholarships: Expanding Opportunities for Students, Saving Taxpayers Money" (Olsen, 2002). In the report, Olsen advocates extending the tax credit to corporations to enable even more poor students to escape the public schools while saving the taxpayers $53 million over 5 years. Unfortunately, examinations of Arizona's tuition tax credit program and Olsen's report determined that Olsen's assertions were unfounded, wishful thinking.

One of Olsen's key contentions is that the tuition tax credit program should be expanded because it is currently helping so many needy children leave failing public schools to attend better private schools. Olsen writes that "more than 80 percent of the [tuition tax credit] scholarships were awarded on the basis of financial need" (Olsen, 2002) and she footnotes a Cato Institute survey in support of this figure. In reviewing the report, Professor Kevin Welner of the University of Colorado, tried to find the origin of this figure. He could not. Instead, he found that the Cato Institute survey cited a Goldwater Institute employee as the source for this figure, but without a hint of where the 80% figure came from.[14] To Welner, "this sort of circular reference amounts to little more than an academic version of money laundering: citing 'the guy down the hall' but depicting the authority as independent" (Welner, 2002). Finding numerous other shortcomings in Olsen's report, Welner concluded that "little in the present proposal offers empirical support for the proposition that this is a sensible way to channel [the business] community's financial contributions" (Welner, 2002).

Further, an analysis of the first 3 years of Arizona's tuition tax credit program, directly contradicts Olsen's claim that it assists mostly poor students. In his report entitled, "The Equity Impact of Arizona's Education Tax Credit Program: A Review of the First Three Years (1998–2000)," Glen

---

[14]Footnote 8 of Olsen's Goldwater Institute report cites Cato Policy Analysis No. 414 (September 17, 2001), "The Arizona Scholarship Tax Credit: Giving Parents Choices, Saving Taxpayers Money," by Carrie Lipps and Jennifer Jacoby (available on the Internet at http://www.cato.org/pubs/pas/pa-414es.html (downloaded January 18, 2003)). Footnote 17 of the Lipps & Jacoby's Cato Institute report, in turn, cites a representative of the Center for Market-Based Education, which is part of the Goldwater Institute, for the 80% figure.

Wilson of Arizona State University analyzed data from the Arizona Department of Revenue, the Arizona Department of Education, and the U.S. Department of Education's National Center for Education Statistics (Wilson, 2002). He calculated that "approximately 76 percent of the private school tuition tax credit grants are going to current private school students" and that "public schools in the wealthiest quarter received more than five times as much money from the [extracurricular tax credit] program as public schools in the poorest quarter" (Wilson, 2002). Wilson concludes that it is primarily wealthy students, those already in private schools and those in wealthy public schools, who benefit from these tax credits. Low-income children receive relatively little (Wilson, 2002). This might explain why Olsen had to invent her 80% figure.

More distressing than the dubious research, is the possibility that helping middle class and wealthy parents, not poor families, may have been the real goal of the Goldwater Institute's support for this program. It appears that the initial emphasis on assisting low-income students is a ruse to get the tuition tax credit legislation foot into the legislative door. In his review of the Goldwater Institute's report, Welner made the following observations about their motives:

> Notwithstanding the rhetorical use of poor families in passing and defending the law, however, the "scholarships" awarded through the tuition tax credit program have provided few actual benefits to these low-income parents.[15] Only days before the release of *Education Scholarships*, its author, Darcy Olsen, was quoted in *The Arizona Republic* acknowledging the strategic use of poor kids. Olsen admitted that the present system "probably" helps the middle-class and wealthy more than the poor; she also said that attempts to sell the program as helping poor kids would have been "only an angle."[16]
>
> To its credit, the new Goldwater proposal differs from the original tax credit law in that it expressly limits student beneficiaries to those who attended public school in the previous year and who qualify for the federal free and reduced-price lunch program. Even so, some skepticism may be warranted. In the paper, Olsen writes: "This scholarship program is a starting point for reform, designed to assist the neediest students in public schools first."[17] The statement strongly suggests that the new proposal tar-

---

[15]Bland, Karina (2000, April 9). "School tax credits wide open to abuse: Millions are diverted from needy students." *The Arizona Republic*, A1.

See also: Wilson, Glen (2002). *The Equity Impact of Arizona's Education Tax Credit Program: A Review of the First Three Years (1998–2000)*. Tempe, AZ: Education Policy Studies Laboratory, Arizona State University.

[16]Kossan, Pat. (2002). "School tax credits fail poor." *The Arizona Republic*, March 23, 2002. Available on the Internet at http://www.arizonarepublic.com/special12/articles/0323 taxscam.html (downloaded on January 18, 2003).

[17]Olsen (2002, pp. 1, 11). See also similar statements on pages 4 and 7.

gets poor children only to gain a policy foothold, and that its supporters' ultimate aim is to ratchet up the system in the future. (Welner, 2002)

It appears that little is accurate and straightforward in the Goldwater Institute report. Nevertheless, Arizona continues its tuition and public school extracurricular tax credit program.

Similarly in Michigan, the Mackinac Center for Public Policy, a local think tank, has been credited with helping spur the state's expanding charter school program. Like the Goldwater Institute, it belongs to the State Policy Network and it produces research to promote school choice. The Mackinac Center is a strong supporter of continuing to increase the number of charter schools in Michigan as well as an active promoter of school vouchers and a universal tuition tax credit plan,[18] similar to the one in Arizona. And, like the Goldwater Institute, its research has received stinging criticism. Professor Peter Cookson and Dr. Katie Embree from Columbia University and Professor Alex Molnar from Arizona State University analyzed all 14 pieces of original and interpretive research on education produced by the Mackinac Center from 1990 through 2001. Using guidelines from the American Psychological Association, they found that only a few studies met the standards of publishable university research. Specifically referring to their school choice research, Cookson, Molnar and Embree had this to say:

> The analyses in this report suggest that much of the work of the Mackinac Center retards rather than advances public understanding of the issues that it has addressed. In the area of school choice, for instance, the work of the Mackinac Center systematically ignores evidence that charter schools may reinforce the social stratification of schools; no where in Mackinac sponsored research is there any evidence that school choice may lead to re-segregation; no where in Mackinac sponsored research is there any indication that the record of school choice plans in promoting student achievement is mixed and ambiguous; and no where in Mackinac sponsored research is there any indication that there is evidence that suggests privatizing reforms have had little effect on student achievement. The way in which Mackinac Center sponsored research characteristically frames questions is biased and the methodology employed of little social science merit. (Cookson, Molnar, & Embree, 2001)

Despite these criticisms, the Mackinac Center was recently cited by the *Washington Post* as an expert source on education (Pierre, 2002). The *Washington Post* article did not mention these criticisms of the Mackinac

---

[18]Information about the education policies, writings and spokespersons promoted by the Mackinac Center can be found on their Web site at http://www.mackinac.org/# (downloaded on January 19, 2003).

Center's education research, although they did print a letter to the editor that pointed them out (Haas, 2002).

What does all this mean to education policy and practice? The work of conservative think tanks should be approached with caution. As the previously mentioned examples demonstrate, conservative think tanks substitute the principles of marketing for those of education research and thus produce experts with little experience and knowledge about education and research that is inaccurate, inflammatory, simplistic, and unsound. When it comes to conservative think tanks, one should not judge a research report by its cover.

Professor Kenneth Howe likens conservative think tanks to salespeople who use research to sell cars (Howe, 2002). Car salespeople market research—their own and others—to make their claims about their car's performance appear more credible. They search for any information that looks like a study to support their latest model and present it to the shopper. Their list of research usually ignores conflicting information, because their overriding goal is to sell you this car. They are not interested in educating shoppers about which car, of all possible cars, is right for them.

Likewise, conservative think tanks present education "research"—their own and others—in order to convince the press, policymakers, and the public that their ideas of a crisis in the public schools and the need for charter schools, vouchers, and tuition tax credits are credible and trustworthy. Yet numerous analyses of their research including the representative examples just discussed, show that it falls well short of the "utter honesty" and rigor of real scientific research (Feynman, 1985, p. 311). No one should take a car salesperson's research as scientific; it is assumed to be biased to serve their purposes. The research of conservative think tanks should be held in the same regard.

Citations in news media reports on education are no guarantee that the spokesperson is expert or that the research is credible. All of the conservative think tanks and their spokespersons and writings just discussed received extensive and uncritical coverage in the press. Apparently the news media are not investigating these think tanks to the extent that they should. Even the second Bush administration's editing of the U.S. Department of Education Web site to include the Heritage Foundation and Manhattan Institute now makes the reliability of government information suspect.

All this boils down to the idea that education policy and practice is almost certainly undermined—made ineffective or possibly harmful—to the extent that it relies uncritically on conservative think tank research. This is not to say that there are not problems in the U.S. education system—there are. But, to the extent that educators, policymakers and the public focus on charter schools, vouchers, and tuition tax credits as the solution because they are well, though deceptively, marketed, rather than seeking adequate funding, trained teachers, and reasonable class sizes for all schools—policies and practices supported by extensive, scholarly research (Berliner & Biddle, 1995; Molnar, 2002)—then we do our students and our nation a disservice.

What could be reliable information from well-endowed conservative think tanks is not and that is disappointing, possibly dangerous. Its prevalence in the news media, the words of politicians and U.S. government Web sites means that educators must be critical in examining what they are presented as research in education. It means, too, that educators must continue to educate themselves about the best sources of research. Educators from university professors to classroom teachers must become more involved in the development of a communal dialogue that demands that knowledge derived from rigorous education research be included, and educators must utilize sound educational research in a manner such that all who are involved and concerned about education can become better informed.

Educators must actively challenge the onslaught of misinformation produced by conservative think tanks. This is a daunting task as knowledgeable educators are already behind in the minds of many and are clearly outgunned. Given the educational trends of NCLB and the push for school choice, it appears that opting out of the debate cannot be an option. So, then, educators must ask themselves, if movement conservatism can move education policy with a lack of expertise, how do we harness our wealth of knowledge to put it back on track?

REFERENCES

Alvarez, L. (2001, May 24). House votes for new testing to hold schools accountable. *New York Times*, National Desk, A1.

American Educational Research Association. (1992). Ethical standards of the American Educational Research Association. *Educational Researcher, 21*(7), 23–26.

Berliner, D., & Biddle, B. (1995). *The manufactured crisis: Myths, fraud, and the attack on America's public schools*. Reading, MA: Addison-Wesley.

Bland, K. (2000, April 9). School tax credits wide open to abuse: Millions are diverted from needy students. *The Arizona Republic*, A1.

Bracey, G. (2002a). *The war against America's public schools: Privatizing schools, commercializing education*. Boston: Allyn & Bacon.

Bracey, G. (2002b). Charter schools, vouchers and EMOs. In A. Molnar (Ed.), *School reform proposals: The research evidence*. Greenwich, CT: Information Age Publishing. Also available on the Internet from the Education Policy Studies Laboratory at Arizona State University. Retrieved on January 18, 2003 from http://www.asu.edu/educ/epsl/EPRU/epru_ 2002_Research_Writing.htm.

Bracey, G. (2002c, January 16). What they did on vacation: It's not schools that are failing poor kids. *Washington Post*, Editorial, A19.

Camilli, G., & Bulkley, K. (2001). Critique of "An evaluation of the Florida A-Plus Accountability and School Choice Program." *Education Policy Analysis Archives, 9*(7), March 4, 2001. Retrieved on January 18, 2003 from http://epaa.asu.edu/epaa/v9n7/.

Cookson, P., Molnar, A., & Embree, K. (2001). Let the buyer beware: An analysis of the social science value and methodological quality of educational studies published by the Mackinac Center for Public Policy (1990–2001). Tempe, AZ: Education Policy Studies Laboratory, Arizona State University. Retrieved on November 3, 2002 from http://www.asu.edu/educ/epsl/EPRU/documents/EPRU%202001-102/epru-0109-102.htm.

Feynman, R. (1985). *Surely you're joking, Mr. Feynman*. New York: W. W. Norton.

Fletcher, M. (2001, July 24). With school testing, unresolved questions; Hill, White House differ over standards. *Washington Post*, A3.

Fletcher, M., & Milbank, D. (2001, August 2). Bush urges realistic education standards. *Washington Post*, A2.

Garrett, J. (2001a, April 26). Hypocrisy on vouchers. *Scripps Howard News Service*.

Garrett, J. (2001b, April 27). Hypocrisy on school choice. *The Deseret News*, Opinion, A17.

Garrett, J. (2001c, April 29). Hypocrisy rife on school vouchers. *Chattanooga Times/Chattanooga Free Press*, Perspective, F1.

Garrett, J. (2001d, May 8). Hypocrisy on school vouchers. *Washington Times*, Final Edition, Part A, Commentary, A16.

Greene, J. P. (2001). *An evaluation of the Florida A-Plus Accountability and School Choice Program*. New York: The Manhattan Institute. Retrieved on January 18, 2003 from http://www.manhattan-institute.org/html/cr_aplus.htm.

Haas, E. (2002, August 2). "Nonpartisan" think tank. *Washington Post*, Letter to the Editor.

Haas, E., Molnar, A., & Serrano, R. (2002). *Media impact of think tank education publications 2001*. Tempe, AZ: Education Policy Studies Laboratory, Arizona State University. Retrieved on January 18, 2003 from http://www.asu.edu/educ/epsl/EPRU/documents/EPRU%202002-115/EPSL-0205-115-EPRU.htm.

Henry, T. (2001, February 16). Florida schools shape up amid voucher threat, findings could boost Bush's national plan. *USA Today*, News, 1A.

Hood, J. (1992). *Caveat emptor: The Head Start scam*. Cato Policy Analysis No. 187. Washington, DC: The Cato Institute. Retrieved on January 18, 2003 from http://www.cato.org/pubs/pas/pa-187.html.

Horn, J., & Miron, G. (2000). *An evaluation of the Michigan charter school initiative: Performance, accountability, and impact*. Kalamazoo: The Evaluation Center, Western Michigan University. Retrieved on January 18, 2003 from http://www.wmich.edu/evalctr/charter/michigan/.

Howe, K. (2002, April 10). Free market free-for-all. *Education Week*. Retrieved on November 3, 2002 from http://www.edweek.org/ew/ewstory.cfm?slug=30howe.h21& keywords= howe.

Kaplan, G. (2000). Friends, foes and noncombatants: Notes on public education's pressure groups. *Phi Delta Kappan, 82*(3), K1–K12.

Kossan, P. (2002, March 23). School tax credits fail poor. *The Arizona Republic*. Retrieved on January 18, 2003 http://www.arizonarepublic.com/special12/articles/0323taxscam.html.

Kozol, J. (1991). *Savage Inequalities: Children in America's schools*. New York: Crown.

Kupermintz, H. (2001). The effects of vouchers on school improvement: Another look at the Florida data. *Education Policy Analysis Archives, (9)*8, March 19, 2001. Retrieved on January 18, 2003 from http://epaa.asu.edu/epaa/v9n8/.

Kuttner, R. (2002, July 15). Philanthropy and movements. *American Prospect*. Retrieved on November 3, 2002 from http://www.prospect.org/print/V13/13/kuttner-r.html.

Lieberman, T. (2000). *Slanting the story: The forces that shape the news*. New York: New York Press.

Miron, G., & Applegate, B. (2000). *An evaluation of student achievement in Edison Schools opened in 1995 and 1996*. Kalamazoo: The Evaluation Center, Western Michigan University. Retrieved on January 18, 2003 from: http://www.wmich.edu/evalctr/edison/wmu_edison_ rpt.pdf.

Molnar, A. (2001, April 11). *The media and educational research: What we know versus what the public hears*. Paper presented at the 2001 AERA annual meeting, Seattle, WA. Retrieved on January 18, 2003 from http://www.asu.edu/educ/epsl/EPRU/documents/cerai-01-14.htm.

Molnar, A. (2002). *School reform proposals: The research evidence*. Greenwich, CT: Information Age Publishing. Also available on the Internet from the Education Policy Studies Laboratory at Arizona State University. Retrieved on January 18, 2003 from http://www.asu.edu/educ/epsl/EPRU/epru_2002_Research_Writing.htm.

National Academy of Science. (1992). *Responsible science: Ensuring the integrity of the research process (Volume I)*. Washington, DC: National Academy Press.

National Education Association. (2000). *The story behind America's voucher movement: Right-wing advocates and emerging players promote "choice" at public education's expense*. Washington, DC: National Education Association.

Olsen, D. (1997). *The advancing nanny state: Why the government should stay out of childcare*. Cato Policy Analysis No. 285. Washington, DC: The Cato Institute. Retrieved on January 18, 2003 from http://www.cato.org/pubs/pas/pa-285es.html.

Olsen, D. (2000, September 1). It's time to stop Head Start: A Cato commentary. *Human Events*. Retrieved on January 18, 2003 from http://www.cato.org/research/education/articles/stopheadstart.html.

Olsen, D. (2002, March 26). *Education scholarships: Expanding opportunities for students, saving taxpayers money*. Phoenix, AZ: Goldwater Institute.

Olsen, D., & Olsen, E. (1999). *Don't cry for me, Head Start*. Washington, DC: The Cato Institute. Retrieved on January 18, 2003 from http://www.cato.org/dailys/04-15-99.html.

Pierre, R. (2002, July 28). Detroit still skeptical about school vouchers and who really profits: Despite failing classrooms, voters rejected move. *Washington Post*, A3.

Schemo, D. J. (2001, February 16). Threat of vouchers motivates schools to improve, study says. *New York Times*, National Desk, A12.

Schnittger, D., & Lara, D. (2001, April 26). Foundation gives H.R. 1 high marks; Chairman Boehner urges colleagues to read Heritage Foundation report on education plan. *U.S. News Wire*. National Desk, Education Reporter.

Shaker, P., & Heilman, E. (2002). Advocacy versus authority—Silencing the education professoriate. *AACTE Policy Perspectives, 3*(1), 1–6.

Shavelson, R., & Towne, L. (Eds.). (2002). *Scientific research in education*. Washington, DC: National Academy Press.

Smith, J. (1991). *The idea brokers: Think tanks and the rise of the new policy elite*. New York: The Free Press.

Soley, L. (1992). *The news shapers: The sources who explain the news*. New York: Praeger.

Spring, J. (2002). *Political agendas for education: From the religious right to the green party*, 2nd ed. Mahwah, NJ: Lawrence Erlbaum Associates.

State Policy Network. (2002). "Background" web page. Retrieved on November 10, 2002 from http://www.spn.org/about_spn/background.asp.

Symonds, W. (2001, October 29). School reform gets an incomplete: Education initiatives feel the pinch of the war on terror [Electronic version]. *Business Week*. Retrieved August 7, 2003, from http://www.businessweek.com/magazine/content/01_44/b3755075.htm

Welner, K. (2002). Review of "Education scholarships: Expanding opportunities for students, saving taxpayers money" Darcy Olsen (Goldwater Institute, March 26, 2002). Tempe: Education Policy Studies Laboratory, Arizona State University. Retrieved on January 18, 2003 from http://www.asu.edu/educ/epsl/EPRU/peer_reviews/EPRU%202002-111/EPSL-0204-111-EPRU.doc.

Wilentz, A. (1986, September 1). On the intellectual ramparts. *Time*, pp. 22–23.

Wilson, G. (2002). *The equity impact of Arizona's education tax credit program: A review of the first three years (1998–2000)*. Tempe: Education Policy Studies Laboratory, Arizona State University. Retrieved on January 18, 2003 from http://www.asu.edu/educ/epsl/EPRU/documents/EPRU%202002-110/epru-0203-110.html.

Winter, G. (2002, December 28). Make-or-break exams grow, but big study doubts value. *New York Times,* National Desk, A1.

The wonderful voucher threat. (2001, March 1). *New York Post*, Editorial, p. 30.

CHAPTER TEN

Bilinguaphobia in the New Millennium

Christian Faltis
Cathy Coulter

The passage of Proposition 227 in California (1998), Proposition 203 in Arizona (2000), and Question 2 in Massachusetts (2002) represents the culmination of efforts by a nationalistic, neoconservative movement in the United States to restrict and repress the use of non-English languages for teaching and learning in school, thereby hampering their promulgation in society. This movement stems from an orchestrated web of historical and contemporary policies designed to advance the causes of cultural assimilation and the restriction of immigration by non-English-speaking working-class peoples, with the ultimate goal of dismantling civil rights policies that, beginning in the 1960s, opened the door to affirming ethnic and language diversity in school (Dixon, Green, Yeager, Baker, & Franquiz, 2000).

One of the most powerful forces to motivate and result from these conservative causes, especially with respect to divesting bilingual education, was, and continues to be, *bilinguaphobia*, the excessive fear of bilingualism, biliteracy, bilingual communities, and any educational approach for promoting the acquisition and use of nondominant languages prior to or simultaneously with the learning of the dominant one. In the case of California, Arizona, and Massachusetts this particular fear has been directed primarily toward the acquisition and use of Spanish and Chinese (Mandarin and Cantonese), the languages of the two fastest growing bilingual, working class minority communities nationwide.

BILINGUAPHOBIA AS A DISCOURSE OF FEAR

Our view of bilinguaphobia posits a relationship between socio-political forces and the creation of certain texts, real and imagined, which contribute to a Discourse, in this case, a Discourse of fear. By *Discourse* (Gee, 1989, 1999), we mean standing for certain manners of being that are recognizable by the way members of the Discourse act, talk, think, and believe. Members of a Discourse show their affinity for particular beliefs, attitudes, and meanings through the language they use to convey their stances. According to Gee (1999), Discourses always integrate language with ways of thinking, valuing, and believing to enable members of a particular Discourse to enact an identity with respect to certain positions and meanings. Members of this particular Discourse of fear, bilinguaphobia, can be identified by their stance toward cultural assimilation, coupled with their support for anti-affirmative action, immigration restriction, and English-only legislation. "This is America," they insist, "speak English and leave your old ways behind." It is important to understand that this statement is not isolated; rather, it belongs to a Discourse comprised of people who stand for and assert through speech and in writing a recognizable set of beliefs, attitudes, and meanings about bilingualism, biliteracy, and bilingual education.

Bilinguaphobia as a Discourse of fear has a long and lugubrious history in the United States (Flores & Murrillo, 2001; MacGregor-Mendoza, 2000). Beginning with World War I, suspicions about the patriotism of German-speaking communities surfaced, prompting fearful political leaders to embrace the new political mantra of one nation, one language. President Teddy Roosevelt, elaborating on the mantra, revealed his bilinguaphobia in this 1917 speech to the nation:

> We must have one flag. We must also have but one language. That must be the language of the Declaration of Independence, of Washington's farewell address, of Lincoln's Gettysburg speech and second inaugural. We can not tolerate *any attempt to oppose or supplant the language* and culture that has come down to us from the builders of this Republic. (emphasis added, cited in Flores & Murrillo, 2001, p. 194)

At that time, Roosevelt was referring specifically to German-English bilinguals, but he also cast a wide net of suspicion over all bilingual communities nationwide. An effect of this early Discourse of fear about bilingualism was to ban the use of German for teaching and learning in bilingual schools and to eliminate it as a foreign language in high schools. It was not until the late 1920s that German was re-introduced as a modern foreign language (Molesky, 1988).

Post-World War I saw the introduction of intelligence tests, ushering in a different, but nonetheless pernicious blow to bilingualism. In comparisons on intelligence tests between bilingual and monolingual English speakers, the bilinguals performed significantly lower, leading researchers to conclude that bilingualism negatively affected intelligence. Never mind that the tests were culturally biased toward white, middle-class monolingual English-speakers or that none of the working class bilinguals taking the tests were English-dominant, the alarm was sounded: "bilingualism is bad, . . . a foreign home language is a handicap" (Sánchez, 1997, p. 127).

The onset of World War II once again brought about the extirpation of the German language from all public schools. Students who wished to study a modern foreign language were allowed only to learn how to read, but not speak or understand its spoken form, lest they be suspected of un-American activities (Chastain, 1976).

SHIFTING TO A DISCOURSE
OF AFFIRMING DIVERSITY

Bilinguaphobia and the sociopolitical forces that promoted it waned considerably during the Civil Rights era (1965–1980), when ethnic and language diversity were asseverated legally, socially, and educationally. In 1968, bilingual education, dating back to Roman and Greek times, was introduced through Title VII of the Elementary and Secondary Education Act as a way to enable non-English-speaking children (mainly Spanish-speaking children of working class families) access to, participation in, and benefit from schooling in their native language while they acquired English as a second language. Bilingual education required bilingual teachers, literacy materials in languages other than English, and bilingual pedagogy; in short, innovative ways of talking, writing, thinking, and teaching about as well as believing in the widespread benefits of educating children bilingually. The point being stressed here is that bilingual education needed a recognizable Discourse that affirmed to the public and teachers alike, the value of teaching, learning, and communicating in two languages.

During this Discourse period, researchers and policymakers alike touted highly developed bilingualism as desirable, based on findings that associated it with cognitive and economic assets (Baker, 2002; Faltis & Hudelson, 1998). Moreover, modern foreign language study enjoyed a resurgence in popularity, reaching its greatest enrollment ever.

Seeing a connection between poverty and ignorance, President Lyndon Johnson, circa 1968, declared a war on poverty, proclaiming education as the key to victory. Johnson began pouring vast quantities of federal money into education in general, and into bilingual education in particular, under the auspices of Title VII of the ESEA. Bilingual education spread with celerity throughout the Southwest and Northeast, bolstered legally by the 1974 Supreme Court decision in Lau v. Nicholas, which found that

> (t)here is no equality of treatment merely by providing students with the same facilities, textbooks, teachers, and curriculum; for students who do not understand English are effectively foreclosed from any meaningful education. (Lau v. Nichols, 414.U.S. 563, 1974)

Bilingual education became the preferred (but not most widely implemented) approach for addressing the educational needs of non-English-speaking children until it began to be challenged in the 1980s.

BILINGUAPHOBIA RESURFACES

With the election of President Ronald Reagan in 1980 came renewed support for the leitmotif of one nation, one language that had begun some 60 years earlier. With support from the Reagan administration, the National Commission on Excellence in Education issued its national reform report, *A Nation at Risk* (1983), the same year Baker and de Kanter published *Bilingual Education: A Reappraisal of Federal Policy*. Both publications set the tone for a re-entry into the Discourse of fear, sending the dominant group message that the United States was indeed a "nation at risk" of losing its educational prominence if it persisted in catering to the needs of non-White, non-English-speaking minority families and their children. In the span of a decade (1980–1990) conservative policy makers and government funded researchers, using disinformation myths and fraud, were able to manufacture a perception that America's schools were in a crisis and in need of reform (Berliner & Biddle, 1995). The reform the new policymakers had in mind to address this manufactured crisis (Berliner & Biddle, 1995) was the introduction of vouchers and charter schools to support right wing religious and back-to-basics education (phonics and basal readers), along with the re-introduction of high stakes testing in response to powerful textbook and testing company lobbies.

Baker and de Kanter's reappraisal of bilingual education also pointed to a crisis in the learning of English that they believed could be fixed by replacing bilingual education with Structured English Immersion (SEI), an English-only approach modeled after the French immersion programs in Canada that were successful for middle-class English-speaking children learning academic content through French. Their report was replete with inaccuracies, misleading conclusions, and disinformation about the effectiveness of bilingual education (Krashen, 1991; McQuillan & Tse, 1996). But, it supported the agenda for re-establishing neoconservative control over the nation's education system, and in doing so, to regain the power base for this group's English-speaking, right wing constituents.

Under this new reform movement, bilingualism and bilingual education once again became targets of fear and suspicion, as the eminent, conservative historian Arthur Schlesinger Jr. makes clear in the following passage:

> Bilingualism shuts doors. It nourishes self-ghettoization, and ghettoization nourishes racial antagonism . . . institutionalized bilingualism remains another source of fragmentation of America, another threat to the dream of "one people." (1991, pp. 108–109)

Schlesinger's bilinguaphobia makes sense only in the context of a Discourse of fear that is distressed by the conviction that America is too diverse (Cummins, 2000), and that English is being learned as a *second* language rather than the *only* language.

It was in this context that proponents of a growing movement to declare English the official language of states and the federal government began to flex their political muscle. The very idea that the federal and state governments were spending public money to accommodate non-English-speakers by printing tax returns and driver's tests in languages other than English, despite a minimal cost, struck many English-only advocates as un-American (Crawford, 1997).

The English-only movement gained momentum with the rise of anti-immigration sentiments in the 1990s, especially in the state of California, which in 1994 sought to eliminate health and educational services for undocumented immigrants through Proposition 187. Congressional Republicans, seeing an opportunity to exploit the anti-immigrant mood, introduced H.R. 123, known as the "English Language Empowerment Act of 1996." In the bill, they portrayed bilingualism as a hazard to national unity. English, they claimed, needed "legal protection" to preserve America's "common bond" (Congressional Record, 1996; cited in Crawford, 1997, p. 6). Newt Gingrich, commenting on the need for such a policy, declared that English was "at the heart of our civilization." Language diversity, he asserted, could lead to its eventual "decay" (Crawford, 1997, p. 6).

PLUS ÇA CHANGE, PLUS C'EST LA MÊME CHOSE
(THE MORE THINGS CHANGE,
THE MORE THEY STAY THE SAME)

Following Proposition 187 and H.R. 123 an engagé multimillionaire software developer named Ron Unz conceived, financed, and orchestrated a statewide ballot initiative in 1998 to dismantle California's bilingual education programs, his personal bête noir, and replace them with 1-year

English immersion programs heralded as effective nearly 2 decades before by conservative policymakers, Baker and de Kanter. Designated Proposition 227, Unz named the initiative *English for the Children* to bring attention to what he considered to be the primary solution to the most serious problem faced by urban schools: that children were learning in languages other than English, and not learning English.

The premise on which Unz based *English for the Children* stems from classic symptoms of bilinguaphobia; namely, the unfounded fear that: Bilingualism is responsible for school failure; it hinders the acquisition of English; and it promotes un-American allegiances. It should come as no surprise that Unz has no children of his own, has never set foot in bilingual classrooms, has no teaching experience in public schools, and has no academic background in language acquisition or literacy (Shultz, 1998). (Parenthetically, Unz is proficient in several nonhuman computer languages in addition to English.) *English for the Children* proposes a solution that reflects not only his fear of bilingualism, biliteracy, and bilingual education, but also his complete lack of knowledge about teaching and learning in school settings, especially those involving students becoming bilingual.

Nonetheless, *English for the Children* resonates with hoi polloi and English-speaking voters. Who would not want immigrant children to learn English? What many voters do not seem to divine is that this question obscures a false choice between teaching children English and giving them bilingual education (Crawford, 1997). The choice is spurious because it implies that bilingual education does not enable children to learn English, a deception easily dispelled in the research literature (Krashen, 1996).

FALSE CLAIMS AND DISINFORMATION

Unz based his *English for the Children* campaign in California (and subsequently in Arizona, Massachusetts, and Colorado) on false claims and disinformation in the media, which have provided him widespread and generally, uncritical coverage. Two examples of rather egregious false claims that Unz made and proclaimed repeatedly are that:

> 95 percent of English learners in California fail every year to learn English.

and

> Anyone who wants bilingual education for his or her children can still have it by just asking for a waiver. (Schultz, 1998, p. 22)

These inaccurate statements have been cited in numerous newspaper articles about the Unz initiatives.

What Unz and the articles injudiciously failed to point out is that *two thirds of the English learners* Unz is referring to were in English-only classrooms, *not* bilingual ones. Moreover, Unz wrote the initiatives so that parents would have a difficult time admitting their child to bilingual classes. Parents cannot simply choose bilingual classrooms; in fact, parents have to place their child in an English-only class for the first month of every school year, and then request permission for school administrators to change to a bilingual classroom.

Disinformation is deliberately false information provided to intelligence agencies and media for the purpose of confusing consumers of that information. Disinformation was especially prevalent during the Cold War, and more recently, politicians have used disinformation in the media to confuse voters. From California to Massachusetts, Unz's initiatives have relied on disinformation to foment bilinguaphobia, confounding voters into believing myths and fabrications about the goals and benefits of bilingualism and bilingual education.

Unz's disinformation campaign was started by the media coverage of the 1996 boycott by Spanish-speaking parents of the Ninth Street School in Los Angeles, California, where parents pulled their children out of school in a highly publicized effort to gain more English instruction for their children. According to an article in the *Los Angeles Times*,

> Using a civil rights tactic to further a cause dear to conservatives, dozens of Latino parents have pledged to keep their children out of a downtown Los Angeles elementary school today to protest bilingual education. . . . The parents poised to boycott, led by Skid Row community activist Alice Callaghan, maintain that their repeated requests for English-only classes at Ninth Street School have been ignored, despite district guidelines that allow parents to choose the language of instruction. (Pyle, 1996)

As presented in the article, the case seems clear: Parents want their children to be taught English, and the school is refusing to comply with parents' requests. Parents, led by a "Skid Row" community activist, must resort to grassroots tactics to be heard by an unmovable bureaucracy, a bureaucracy that is imposing bilingual education on unwilling participants, a bureaucracy that will not even address parents' concerns. However, beneath the surface the case is not exactly limpid. According to James Crawford (1997),

> What actually happened at Ninth Street was more complicated. The protest was orchestrated by Alice Callaghan, an Episcopal priest and community activist who ran a daycare center on which the boycotting parents depended;

whether all of them participated freely in the protest remains a matter of dispute. Before pulling their children out of school, none of the parents had ever requested transfers to all-English instruction—an option that would have spared the students two weeks of disrupted schooling. (1997, p. 3)

Every one of the boycotting parents relied on the daycare provided by Alice Callaghan. Additionally, Eleanor Vargas Page, the principal of the Ninth Street School at the time, said that every one of the parents who participated in the boycott signed consent forms for bilingual instruction when they enrolled their children in school (Crawford, 1998). Further, they always had access to the school's alternative, intensive-English program; they had only to request it. Vargas Page repeatedly offered to address the group of boycotting parents, but Callaghan refused, saying that she did not believe the school would change the program without pressure from higher ups (Pyle, 1996). Patently, the school was making an effort to listen to parents' requests. Complying with their requests would simply have meant transferring students to the already existing English-only classes. But, apparently, Callaghan did not want resolution. She wanted media attention, and that's what she got.

In spite of "the other side of the story," and despite the complexities surrounding the case, the media perpetuated the Ninth Street Myth, enabling Unz to disinform voters about bilingual education and bilingualism ever since. Articles ran disinforming headlines such as, "Bilingual Schooling is Failing, Parents Say," or "80 Students Stay Out of School in Latino Boycott" or "Parents Seek More English-Only Classes" (Crawford, 1998). A disinformation campaign was launched in which bilingual education was put on the defensive, pegged as the "bad" guy, the monster that denied children access to the language of power in the United States, English, whereas Unz's *English for the Children* was shrouded in language of prochildren, pro-immigrant sentiment, but underneath the language was just the opposite. And how was the public to know? When the media continually depicts a slanted view, such as those based on the Ninth Street Myth, how is the public to discern the truth from the disinformation? How can it argue for bilingual education when, according to the newspapers, not even the parents of affected children want it? How is the public to know that bilingual education is not to blame for increasing dropout rates, low test scores, failing students?

Another pertinent example of disinformation manifested by the Unz initiatives is found in one of the newer forums for Unz's English-only endeavors: Colorado. A September 22, 2002 article in *The Denver Post*, written by Rita Montero, chairwoman of *English for the Children* in Colorado, leads with the headline, "The language of Learning Amendment 31 on the November ballot wants Coloradans to make English-language immersion mandatory, but foes say it's not a good idea. PRO: Teach our children English." The article is seeped in antibilingual education rhetoric, replete with inflammatory language, and unapologetically biased, pleading to voters to stop the iniquity that she contends bilingual education represents.

Although Montero is up front with her role as chair of the *English for the Children* campaign in Colorado, she also relies heavily on her role and identity as a Latina parent, relating what happened to her as a testimonial to the woes of bilingual education. Montero claims that her son was forced nolens volens to attend a Spanish-language class. Her complaints were allegedly met with refusal to release him, so she eventually switched schools. And although her claim is dubious, her accusatory riposte was not:

"The real culprits are the Spanish-only bureaucrats who inflicted this suffering on innocent children." At the beginning of the article, Moreno implores the voters of Colorado to "help rescue our immigrant children from the disaster that is 'bilingual education' " writing the following piece of disinformation:

> For more than 20 years, so-called "bilingual education" programs have destroyed the educations and even the lives of tens of thousands of young children. The classes may be called "bilingual," but in most classes Latino children are segregated in Spanish-speaking educational ghettos, where students spend years learning barely any English at all, despite the wishes of their parents.
>
> Other students are place in English-only classes (English as a Second Language), where they do not understand 90 percent of the instruction and then are pulled out of the class for 30 to 45 minutes and are given help in their own language. As a result, immigrant children often leave Colorado schools never knowing how to read or write or sometimes even speak English properly. As illiterates in two languages, they can't get good jobs or go on to college, and are forced to work as janitors or laborers or become trapped in a life of welfare or crime.

Montero goes on to assert that her goal is to "stop these discriminatory educational attacks against Hispanic and other immigrant children," and that under the English for the Children Amendment, all children will be taught English in English-only classes by "specially trained teachers."

Although Montero's article is glaringly one-sided, it relies on rhetoric and disinformation that may not be quite so conspicuous. Montero's claims ride on lines of discourse that were played out in both California and Arizona: That bilingual education is represented by self-interested bureaucrats who do not care about children, indeed, who will willfully harm children in order to maintain the status quo; that advocates of bilingual education do not want immigrant children to learn English, nor to lead successful lives in this English-dominant nation; that most Latino parents want English-only programs, but bilingual educators refuse to comply with their wishes.

In fact, within the spectrum of philosophies that accompany bilingual education, it is safe to say that no one in the field argues that immigrant children should not learn English. Indeed, learning English is a main goal of bilingual education (Faltis & Hudelson, 1998). But bilingual educators also express the desire to promote bilingual abilities in children, both English and their native language, as well as to facilitate the learning of content areas while the children develop their bilingualism in school.

Discourse that accuses bilingual educators of "attacking" immigrant children and "inflicting" Spanish-only classes on them is not only incendiary, it is disinformative as well. But *English for the Children* advocates could not pass their initiatives by telling voters the truth about bilingual education.

It must be said, however, that one does not have to look beyond Montero's article to find the inconsistencies. Recall the second option Montero describes in bilingual education, the alternative to what she calls the Spanish-speaking educational ghettos:

> Other students are placed in English-only classes (English as a Second Language), where they do not understand 90 percent of the instruction and then are pulled out of the class for 30 to 45 minutes and are given help in their own language. As a result, immigrant children often leave Colorado schools never knowing how to read or write or sometimes even speak English properly.

What alternative does Montero suggest? English-only classes, where it is likely students will not magically be able to understand any more than the 10% Montero says they did in the classes she described above, even if they are taught by "specially trained teachers." Indeed, there is no such special training that can perform this kind of magic, even in the best of university teacher education programs.

In the meantime, what information do voters have to rely on? When the media provide a definitive slant in its reporting, as evidenced by the coverage that created and sustained the Ninth Street Myth the answer has to be, "Not much." And when the media play into the current state of bilinguaphobia in our nation, the public does not have far to stretch to believe false claims and disinformation that are found in articles such as Montero's.

Articles such as Montero's are ultimately detrimental to bilingual children and bilingual schooling. The fact is that 63% of Latinos voted against Prop. 227 in California. The fact is that children who come to the United

States speaking a language other than English will need more support than the sink-or-swim alternative Montero and *English for the Children* hope to have mandated (successfully in California, Arizona, and Massachusetts). The fact is *English for the Children* is a thinly disguised attempt to discriminate against children of immigrant children by robbing them of the very opportunities bilingual education was endeavoring to give them. The fact is that articles such as Montero's disseminate false claims and disinformation about bilingual education, the preferences of immigrant parents, and what's best for their children. The fact is that *English for the Children* is spreading new fear among teachers and their students, fear that if they use language other than English to make sense of school work, teachers could face legal sanctions or even lose their jobs (Gutiérrez, Baquedano-López, & Asato, 2000). The fact is that teachers, as a result of *English for the Children* initiatives, are now forced to use pedagogy that contradicts their specialized preparation for teaching immigrant children who come to school speaking a language other than English.

WHAT'S NEXT? FABIAN RESISTANCE

Bilinguaphobia will continue to exert formidable influence on U.S. education policy. Driven by fear of bilingualism, biliteracy, and bilingual education, there appears to be no dearth of Ron Unz acolytes who are willing to push for the prohibition of languages other than English for teaching and learning academic content and literacy. We know however, that fear and suspicion of foreigners and foreign languages can be overcome with gradual and persistent resistance that interrupts and subverts efforts to dismantle bilingual education and spread fear about bilingualism and biliteracy. We refer to this type of opposition as Fabian resistance, named after the Roman general Quintus Fabius Maximus, who defeated Hannibal by a prolonged and gradual use of subversion without direct confrontation. Fabian resistance to bilinguaphobia requires local acts of subversion to interrrupt and alter the impact of policies that affect the quality of teaching and learning in schools with children who are becoming bilingual. Moreover, Fabian resistance to bilinguaphobia requires a sustained dialogue about the benefits of bilingualism for meaningful learning, peaceful coexistence, and enhanced commerce. Many bilingual and language specialist teachers throughout the United States are resisting the policies brought about from bilinguaphobia (for examples, see Beykont, 2000; Constantino & Faltis, 1998; Shannon, 1995). Their resistance ranges from concealing and using non-English-language children's literature prohibited by the school to organizing small parent groups to discuss ways of promoting and enhancing *literacy in languages other than English*.

It is important to note that present day fears about bilingualism, bi-literacy, and bilingual education differ little from those expressed and felt at the beginning of the 20th century, when the apothegm was "English for the nation." Then, as now, the goal was to Americanize non-English speaking immigrants by having them learn English at the expense of their own native language. Immigrant children (as well as Native-American peoples) were punished severely for using their non-English languages at school. While the days of derision and punishment are for the most part over, for teachers, the specter of fear about sanctions and job loss remains real and ominous. There are, however, ways to resist policies based on bilingua-phobia, and to ensure that children who are becoming bilingual meaningfully participate in and benefit from schooling. It can be done with discussion, commitment, and caring.

REFERENCES

Baker, C. (2002). Bilingual education. In R. Kaplan (Ed.), *The Oxford handbook of applied linguistics* (pp. 229–242). New York: Oxford University Press.

Baker, K., & de Kanter, A. (1983). *Bilingual education: A reappraisal of federal policy.* Lexington, MA: Lexington Books.

Berliner, D., & Biddle, B. (1995). *The manufactured crisis: Myths, fraud, and the attack on America's public schools.* Reading, MA: Addison-Wesley.

Beykont, Z. (Ed.). (2000). *Lifting every voice: Pedagogy and politics of bilingualism.* Cambridge, MA: Harvard Education Publishing Group.

Chastain, K. (1976). *Developing second-language skills: Theory to practice.* Chicago: Rand McNally College Publications.

Congressional Record. (1996). Debate on H.R. 123, Vol. 142, No. 116, Pt. II, H9738–72.

Constantino, R., & Faltis, C. (1998). Teaching against the grain in bilingual education: Resistance in the classroom underlife. In Y. Zao & H. Trueba (Eds.), *Ethnic identity and power* (pp. 113–131). Albany: State University of New York Press.

Crawford, J. (1997). The campaign against Proposition 227: A post Modem. *Bilingual Research Journal, 21*(1), 1–29.

Crawford, J. (1998, May 25). The Ninth Street myth: Who speaks for Latino parents? *Hispanic Link Weekly Report.* Retrieved on November 21, 2002 from http://ourworld.compuserve.com/homepages/jwcrawford/HL3.htm.

Cummins, J. (2000). *Language, power, and pedagogy: Bilingual children in the crossfire.* Clevedon, England: Multilingual Matters.

Dixon, C., Green, J., Yeager, B., Baker, D., & Franquiz, M. (2000). "I used to know that": What happens when reform gets through the classroom door. *Bilingual Research Journal, 24*(1 & 2), 1–14.

Faltis, C., & Hudelson, S. (1998). *Bilingual education in elementary and secondary school communities: Toward understanding and caring.* Needham Heights, MA: Allyn & Bacon.

Flores, S., & Murillo, E. (2001). Power, language, and ideology: Historical and contemporary notes on the dismantling of bilingual education. *The Urban Review, 33*(3), 183–206.

Gee, J. (1989). Literacy, discourse, and linguistics: Introduction. *Journal of Education, 171*(1), 5–17.

Gee, J. (1999). *An introduction to discourse analysis: Theory and method.* New York: Routledge.

Gutiérrez, K., Baquedano-López, P., & Asato, J. (2000). "English for the Children": The new literacy of the old world order, language policy and educational reform. *Bilingual Research Journal, 24*(1 & 2), 1–21.

Krashen, S. (1991). *Bilingual education: A focus on current research.* Washington, DC: National Clearinghouse for Bilingual Education.

Krashen, S. (1996). *Under attack: The case against bilingual education.* Culver City, CA: Language Education Associates.

Lau v. Nichols. (1974). 414 u.s. 563.

MacGregor-Medoza, P. (2000). Aquí no se habla español: Stories of linguistic repression in Southwest schools. *Bilingual Research Journal, 24*(4), 333–345.

Molesky, J. (1988). Understanding the American linguistic mosaic: A historical overview of language maintenance and language shift. In S. L. McKay & S. C. Wong (Eds.), *Language diversity: Problem or resource* (pp. 29–68). New York: Newbury House.

McQuillan, J., & Tse, L. (1996). Does research matter? An analysis of media opinion on bilingual education, 1984–1994. *Bilingual Research Journal, 20*, 1–27.

Montero, R. (2002, September 22). The language of learning Amendment 31 on the November ballot wants Coloradans to make English-language immersion mandatory, but foes say it's not a good idea. PRO: Teach our children English. *The Denver Post,* p. E1.

National Commission on Excellence in Education. (1983). *A nation at risk: The imperative for national reform.* Washington, DC: Author.

Pyle, A. (1996, February 13). Latino parents to boycott school bilingual plan. *Los Angeles Times.*

Sánchez, G. I. (1997). History, culture, and education. In A. Daarder, R. D. Torres, & H. Gutiérrez (Eds.), *Latinos and education: A critical reader* (pp. 117–134). New York: Routledge.

Schlesinger, A. (1991). *The disuniting of America.* New York: W. W. Norton.

Shannon, S. (1995). The hegemony of English: A case study of one bilingual classroom as a site of resistance. *Linguistics and Education, 7*, 175–200.

Shultz, J. (1998, November/December). Bilingual education: Politics first, children second. *Thrust for Educational Leadership,* 22–24.

PART FOUR

TOWARD LIBERATORY EDUCATION

This section brings the book to a close with another story of resistance and a concluding chapter that describes the existing local, state, and national organizations engaged in resisting, fighting, and changing the educational policies driven by the corporate and political right.

CHAPTER ELEVEN

Cracks in the Wall?
Initiating Actions Against
Federal Policy

Richard J. Meyer
Tom Keyes
Penny Pence
Sylvia Celedon-Pattichis
Ruth Trinidad Galván
Leslie Poynor

Almost 10 years ago, Seymour Sarason presented at AERA at a celebration of his years of work studying, supporting, and venturing into educational change. He began his presentation with a discussion of views of change and then told a story about a friend of his who was renting a room in the old city of Jerusalem. Each day, as Sarason's friend labored on a manuscript, the friend would pause and look out the window that faced the wall at which many Jews came to pray. He saw an old man praying every morning, afternoon, and evening; the old man faced the wall and prayed and prayed for hours. After weeks of observing, Sarason's friend left his manuscript and approached the man as he completed his prayers one evening.

"Excuse me," he said to the old man. "I've seen you praying here everyday."

"I do pray every day," the old man responded.

"What do you pray for?" the writer asked.

The old man explained that he had a routine, praying for peace in the morning, health in the afternoon, and understanding in the evening—the same things each day.

"What's that like?" the writer asked, "to pray for these things every day?"

"Like?" asked the old man. "What's it like? It's like talking to a wall."

Educators seem to face a litany of walls constructed by special interest groups, legislatures, and even religious groups. This article is about a few moments when we faced the wall formed by government's agenda for education. Our actions may not lead to sustained change within the government," but they were a change for us and the beginning of something. We changed from fairly compliant nonactive, but reflective, researchers and teachers to activists who dared to act in an arena in which compliance is the norm.

Each of us was frustrated with the climate in which *No Child Left Behind* (NCLB) emerged as legislation and became law. We saw the appearance of one government sponsored text (Adams, 1990), then another (Snow, Burns, & Griffin, 1998) and, most recently, the *Report of the National Reading Panel* (n.d.). The panel report is the backbone of the NCLB sections on reading, in spite of a minority view (Yatvin, in the NRP report). That minority view is attached as an appendix in the full report of the NRP, but it is not part of—nor even mentioned—in the 33-page summary of the report that is much more widely circulated than the full report. Further, reading researchers' responses noting the shortcomings of the NRP report (Allington, 1997, 2002; Coles, 2000; Garan, 2001b) have not been acknowledged as legitimate by the Federal government. Even the common press carried articles that presented evidence suggesting that the best interests of children learning to read were not at the heart of the report (Metcalf, 2002). None of these concerns appears to have been considered when NCLB was written.

In April, not long after the passage of NCLB, Rod Paige, Susan Newman, and other individuals from the federal level (including one of our federal senators and one representative) helped to kick off the 25 city tour intended to promote an end to illiteracy because no child would be left behind. The event took place at the National Hispanic Cultural Center in Albuquerque, a new and exciting center that serves our diverse population through artistic, cultural, and community events. The Center has a large outdoor amphitheater that has tall, steep concrete bleachers, much like the local university football stadium. A variety of speakers and diverse performers, even the one New Mexican who won the skeleton event at the winter Olympics, spoke about the importance of learning to read. The backdrop for these speakers was hundreds of children from the local elementary, middle, and high schools. They walked or were transported from their schools to sit in the bleachers and cheer. Some were handed signs that were two feet by three feet reading: "Results for Student Achievement," "Using Solid Research for Instruction," "Information and Options for Parents," and "Flexibility and Local Control." Everyone was given American flags that they waved during the many pauses for applause.

The New Mexican sky was its typical spring deep blue and the sun was hot and bright. Speaker after speaker acclaimed the new legislation and after each there were songs and music and dance. One of the Head Start programs brought young pueblo dancers. A high school pep squad cheered "R E A D read!" New Mexico is the first state made up of a majority of minorities and the schools near the Center are very diverse. Each speaker was backgrounded by the steep bleachers packed with diverse children, their teachers, and some families. Finally, a patriotic song came over the loudspeaker and Rod Paige, our secretary of education, appeared—at the top of the bleachers. All rose and cheered and waved their flags as he made his way down the bleachers, stopping to shake children's hands, hug them, and wave to their teachers. After his speech, during which he highlighted the signs the children held, he walked towards our senator and representative. Music came up and a loud noise scared all present. No one noticed the cannons next to the platform. Huge plumes of white smoke rose, the music played, and within the smoke was red, white, and blue confetti. As each person left, man, woman, or child (all covered with confetti), they were given what appeared to be an oversized videotape container. Inside were two booklets, two CD-ROMs, a pen, a pencil, a bookmark, and an American flag on a stick (like the ones being waved about). On the cover of the container are photos of President Bush, Secretary Paige, and children. Everyone got one of the "kits." No one was left behind.

As Rick left, he thought, *where are the protesters? Where is the dissent, the other side? I know there's one because it is the one to which many of my colleagues and I subscribe*.

Months later, just weeks after the start of a new school year, leaflets began appearing all over the state of New Mexico. Reid Lyon (the Chief of the Child Development and Behavior Branch of the National Institute of Child Health and Human Development at the National Institutes of Health), the man who assembled and oversaw the National Reading Panel, was coming to New Mexico to tell teachers what must be done to fix the reading problem. This government intervention was occurring with sufficient advance warning for us to act. And we did.

RICK MOVES FIRST

Rick is one reading faculty at the local university. He's been keeping track of the legislation, its influence on the state, and studied the way one of the preferred programs for teaching reading unfolded in a classroom (Meyer, 2001). He talked with the other authors of this article, most having expressed interest after a faculty meeting at which Rick announced a need to act. We decided to have a protest on the day of Lyon's talk and to follow it, on the next day, with a teach-in at which we could further inform interested individuals about the controversies surrounding the report of the National Reading Panel. Pragmatic realities such as time, the difficulty of assembling large numbers of protesters, and finding a venue and speakers for a teach-in led us to tabling the teach-in strategy. Rick called the president of the local teacher's union, an activist who has visited his classes. She was honest and explained that teachers would not leave their classrooms to protest. She could not use any district mail delivery systems or electronic servers to advertise a political event. Rick contacted colleagues from other universities around the state. They originally thought they could get sympathetic colleagues, parents, and teachers to attend, but their efforts fell through.

Rick also called the convention center in the city where the event was to take place. He was told he needed a permit to protest. The police would not grant him one, saying they did not have the authority. The mayor's office did not return his calls. The convention center did not return his first call, so he called again. The event organizer there said she would look into it. Rick explained that the convention center was a public forum funded by tax dollars. She called back and informed Rick that the city attorney said it was not a public forum and any protesters could not go inside, but we could use the sidewalk in front of the center. The problem with that was that the sidewalk would not be used by most attending the event. They would enter directly from the attached garage.

Rick called the ACLU, the Southwest Organizing Project (SWOP is local, political, and active, particularly in human rights issues), and an anti-death penalty activist he knows. The latter was the most helpful. She connected him with a first amendment lawyer who offered advice. The lawyer said that we could go in, but to desist as soon as we were asked to. If we did not, we would probably be arrested. He explained that *public forum* is not a generic term and that it is judged case by case. He thought we could win a case if we were arrested because there was not a forum in which to reach people who attended the presentation unless we did enter the building. Rick decided that whomever helped would carry the lawyer's phone number until all the action subsided.

THE MEETING

Two days before Reid Lyon's presentation, Rick arranged a meeting to flesh out the course of our actions. Seven of us sat in chairs and on the floor deciding what to do in light of the short timeline for planning and knowing that the turnout would be limited to us in spite of our efforts to mobilize teachers. We talked about what we would do, knowing that we were about to engage in nonviolent civil disobedience. We were not allowed to be in the building distributing contrary literature, but we were going in anyway. We were tired of talking to the wall.

Because there were so few of us, we decided not to picket because a small number of picketers would give the impression of being a radical fringe element and because no one would see us outside. Instead, we would engage in three actions. First, some of us would distribute flyers inside the large meeting room where the teachers would be seated. Rick drafted a flyer (see Fig. 11.1 Fact Sheet) prior to the meeting to see if all would be comfortable distributing it if we were to picket. He would also get fluorescent green copies made, using money donated by a colleague who wanted to help but was not sure she could attend; she ultimately did attend as an observer. The flyer uses language and content from the Minority View of the National Reading Panel Report.

The second action would involve the setting up of a table at which participants could get a copy of the Minority View, articles about the report,

---

Fact Sheet #1

What Caring & Informed Teachers Need to Know and Ask

KNOW that
- ☙ The research you are hearing about today views reading very narrowly
- ☙ Such views are not particularly useful to teachers, administrators, and policymakers
- ☙ Such views are NOT addressing the issues that make our schools a "battleground for . . . opposing philosophies and prey for purveyors of quick fixes"
- ☙ The National Reading Panel did NOT rely upon classroom-based research or the realities of classroom life
- ☙ The Panel's work is resulting in mandated instruction that is difficult—even impossible—to implement
- ☙ The report of the Panel is unbalanced and largely irrelevant

*Questions you should ask **today:***
1. Why aren't broader views of reading being listened to and presented today?
2. How much of the research presented today has been studied carefully in classrooms?
3. What will policymakers do to insure that research-based programs are balanced?
4. Why weren't more teachers asked about the policies that were developed from this report?

Tell the panel about children in your class that are being left behind by legislation and policies rooted in the *Report of the National Reading Panel.*

FIG. 11.1.   The Fact Sheet distributed by our group. This was formatted to fit one sheet of paper. *Source:* Report of the National Reading Panel: Teaching Children to Read. Minority View.

and engage in discussion. Tom was most excited about this action. The third action arose because it turned out that Lyon would be in town for 2 days. On the first day, the event was open to anyone that wanted to attend. The second day was by invitation only. Rick was invited along with a small number of others. Rick would attend the closed meeting on Friday, as an invitee, and engage in distribution of the flyer and response to the session.

The final part of the meeting involved reiterating some of the precautions we agreed to take. The lawyer suggested that no one act alone and that someone be present with a video camera and also take notes, especially if the police got involved. The lawyer said that the tendency since September 11, 2001 has been for the police to be aggressive in response to dissent. Each of us would have a colleague shadowing us or right beside us as a partner in order to hear and record responses we received. No one wanted to carry a video camera, so we decided on a still camera (which was never used) and the use of not-too-distant observers to take notes and serve as witnesses. Observers would write down badge numbers and officers' names if police became involved. They could also take photos, especially knowing that officers that confiscated cameras from anyone were involved in illegal seizure, according to the lawyer. Having qualitative researchers as note takers seemed quite fitting as they were used to taking field notes.

TOM'S JUSTIFICATION AND PLANS FOR ACTION

Tom's decision to act was rooted in his belief that the discrepancies between the whole report of the NRP (600 pages) and the 33-page summary were systematically perpetrated by Widmeyer Baker, the company that wrote the summary of the NRP report (Metcalf, 2002). He was angry knowing that most people would not read the entire report; rather, they would rely on the summary and the video (both composed by the same company). The biggest client of that company was McGraw Hill (Metcalf, 2002). Although the authors of critiques of the panel report were fast becoming his heroes, he did not know how to engage in ways that he considered mindful. Tom had never been an activist involved in any form of nonviolent civil disobedience.

Tom was anxious about acting alone and was relieved that the ACLU and the first amendment lawyer Rick had contacted agreed that acting alone was not effective or safe. Tom stressed that any action that was not planned could hurt our cause, making us look thoughtless, senselessly radical or even mean-spirited. He was glad to know that Ruth would observe him so that if someone claimed that he was resistant, there would be another point of view present.

Tom wanted teachers to have access to more of the dissenting and explanatory articles (Garan, 2001a; Metcalf, 2002), copies of the Minority View (Yatvin, 2002), and the flyer. Tom's view of the minority view is akin to a minority view of the supreme court in which there may be one winning view but there is also much to learn from the dissenting opinions. He wanted teachers to know that dissent exists. Tom's plan was to go into the convention center, set up a table, and distribute the $130.00 worth of materials he photocopied at his own expense. He later called this, "The best $130.00 I've ever spent." He thought that because New Mexico is pretty relaxed, he would not be noticed. If anyone challenged his presence, he would state that he was representing the same report being discussed, so why would they ask him to leave. Further, he did not know whom to call to get permission to be at the event but, more importantly, he could not imagine that they would not want him present because his information was from and about the same report that was the focus of the day's event.

Rick provided everyone at the meeting with a slip of paper that had the name and phone number of the first amendment lawyer. We would all carry that with us through the entire event because none of us trusted that dissent would be welcome, much to Tom's chagrin.

THE WAY IT CAME DOWN FOR TOM

On Thursday, the Lyon presentation at the convention center was scheduled to begin at 9:00 a.m. Tom knew this from the State Department of Education flyer he had received in his mailbox. He wanted to be at the convention center by 8:15, but he and Ruth, the colleague he was supposed to meet, misunderstood each other's directions and wasted precious time in the parking lots of two different McDonald's separated by about a mile. They finally found each other and arrived at the convention center at 8:50, expecting to find all the attendees inside the convention's Ballroom A, which holds about 400 people. Tom was relieved to find hundreds of teachers milling about with coffee and donuts. Tom brought a camping table (longer than a standard bridge table) and opened it. He placed it near the nametag table and put a blue tablecloth on the table as Ruth positioned herself close enough to hear his interactions with others but far enough away so as not to seem connected to him. He reached for the NRP report to place it on the table when two women approached him. He had been there for 30 seconds. He kept setting up the table as they talked. He pulled out the NRP report, the video, the summary, copies of the Minority View, and the articles he had photocopied. Tom shook their hands and said, "I'm Tom Keyes, a parent and a teacher." He said he was there to represent the minority report. They asked if he had permission to be there.

He said no and that he did not know he needed it because he was present in order to represent the report that was being discussed today. Before any more could be said, a teacher interrupted and asked Tom if the handouts were there to be taken. He said yes. The original two women were flustered and Tom thought they really wanted him to go away but did not ask him to. Teachers were overhearing the conversation and began to form a line to get the materials he had available. The two women left.

Two minutes later, someone would be back. But before that, Tom decided to make one point, over and over, for each group of teachers that huddled around the table, took materials, and left, making way for the next huddle of teachers. His point was this: the summary and the video did not accurately represent the findings of the panel. Today's presentation would be based on the summary and the video, but not the full report. He offered the teachers one example of this: *the full report* says that there is no evidence that intense phonics instruction improves reading for second through sixth-grade struggling readers. The *summary* says that such instruction *is* successful with *all* second through sixth graders, including those that are struggling.

Tom had handwritten posters on 8½ × 11-inch white paper but never had time to tape them to the wall. He had one with the Web site (http://www.nichd.nih.gov/publications/NRP/report.htm), phone number, and address for teachers to request a copy of the full report. He also had a poster with facts from the full report that were inaccurately represented in the summary. These were placed to the side and not hung up as he planned. The only sign he had time to post was on the front of the table; it read: *National Reading Panel Report: Minority View*.

Each new huddle of teachers, about one huddle per 30 seconds, heard Tom's thoughts and took handouts, including the brightly colored flyer that was being distributed inside Ballroom A. Tom noticed one of the two original women hovering near the table. She was listening to what he presented to the teachers. She withdrew when the State Department of Education's Director of Special Education (one of the key organizers of the event) approached the table. Tom knew him. He approached Tom asking, "What are you doing here?"

Tom explained, as teachers listened and took handouts, that he was representing the NRP report. The director told him, "You're not supposed to be here."

Tom said, "I am here . . . representing the same document you'll be discussing all day today."

The director said, "This doesn't have anything to do with what we're discussing today."

Tom said that he was representing the dissenting view. Tom spoke loud enough for teachers to hear him and so that Ruth could hear as well. The director asked Tom to step aside from the table and speak with him alone. The director was upset. His face was red. He moved about 15 feet away from the table and motioned to Tom. Tom would not leave the table, and calmly told the director, "If you have anything to say to me you can come back here. . . . I'm talking to people over here." The director returned to the table and said, "I'm sorry to have to say this in front of other people, but this is inappropriate."

Tom said, "I'm sorry you feel this way." He kept on talking to teachers and distributing handouts, and then turned to the director and said, "The original findings are greatly distorted in the summary and video."

At this point, the director lowered his voice and said, "If you had called me . . . I could have got you a spot here . . . maybe even a face to face meeting with Reid Lyon."

Tom told the director that Reid Lyon was "the wrong audience" because he would not change. Tom's goal, he told the director, was to get information that made a difference to his own understanding of the report to as many people as possible. He wanted others in the state to know what had upset him. The director walked away. To truly appreciate this encounter, we wish that readers could hear how soft spoken and see how gentle Tom is. He has a mild nature and a warm wide smile, all of which he maintained through all of his interactions with those whom he was making so uncomfortable by his presence. The Tom that teachers saw was genuine, clear, kind, and respectful.

For almost 15 minutes Tom spoke to huddles that surrounded the table as a long line of people waited to listen to him. A representative of the convention center approached him and wanted to know what he was doing at this event. She wanted to know if he was part of the event and if he had called for permission to be present. If not, he would have to leave. Tom told her that he did not call (we had all agreed about the importance of being honest) but that he was here to represent the exact same report being discussed all day. His pattern of sticking to a simple explanation, delivered calmly and in a very friendly manner, was getting him the time he needed to get his message out. She listened to Tom and said, "I think you need to get permission from the person running the event," and then she offered to find her so that they could get that permission. The woman was clearly sent by the director of special education, but the contradictions that Tom offered confused her. Friendliness paid off.

She asked Tom to come with her to find the event organizer. Tom left the table and went with her as the orderly line of teachers that had formed continued to take the remaining handouts. When they could not locate the organizer, the convention center representative suggested to Tom that he return to his table! When Tom returned to the table, all the handouts were gone. They were in the hands of teachers. Some people were coming out of Ballroom A to ask him questions about the flyer and to see if there were more handouts. They wanted to know how to get the full report and he showed his small poster so they could copy the information they needed.

Then, the convention center person returned with a man carrying a walkie-talkie. Tom thought it was center security. That man asked Tom what he was doing at the convention center and after listening to Tom's response told him that he had to leave the building. Tom said he would and that he appreciated how they treated him. He said he did not understand why the event organizers would not want him present (as teachers listened and watched) but that he would leave as requested.

Tom folded up the table as Leslie and Sylvia walked right past him, having completed their actions inside Ballroom A. Then Penny (the observer for Sylvia and Leslie) came out and greeted Tom and Ruth. The convention center woman asked, "Do you have people in the Ballroom passing out green flyers?" Tom said he did not have people anywhere. The woman said, "You have to leave the building." Then she said that she was calling security, although Tom thought he had already been addressed by security. They all left, Tom, Ruth, and Penny together, eventually catching up to Leslie and Sylvia. They never saw security.

INSIDE BALLROOM A: SYLVIA, LESLIE, AND A SEA OF GREEN

Leslie and Sylvia arrived as the event was getting under way, just after 9:00. They did not know why Tom and Ruth were late and were inside Ballroom A when Tom and Ruth arrived in the large open hallway outside of the Ballroom. Leslie and Sylvia entered with the bright green flyers inside Leslie's backpack and sat in the middle of a row near the rear of the Ballroom. As more and more people found seats, they finally decided to make their move. They brought out their flyers, and turned to the teachers next to them. Passing the flyers in opposite directions, Leslie and Sylvia said, "Someone asked me to take one and pass the rest," to the teachers that sat next to them.

They could see a sea of green flyers spreading across the rows and aisles and eventually making their way to the front rows. Leslie and Sylvia decided to leave as the first speaker approached the microphone. Their departure was part of the plan: get in, distribute, and leave without being recognized or noticed. They had not planned to stay for the entire talk because of other responsibilities (and they knew what the content would be). They walked past Tom at high speed but with a feeling of having done something. They got the information out.

Back on campus, Leslie and Sylvia found Rick teaching and interrupted his class for a few minutes to let him know what had happened. Rick could not believe how thrilled and energized they were. Leslie kept saying, "It was amazing; this was pure genius." From Tom, Leslie, and Sylvia's responses, we all got the sense that teachers wanted to know. They wanted to know there was a group that dissented; they wanted to know that there was a voice willing to talk, even in the form of a sea-green whisper.

Leslie suggested changing the color and format of the flyer for the next day's activity. She was concerned that one flash of green could result in instant expulsion because the convention center staff and security might be looking for such actions. Rick went home and reformatted the flyer and made copies on white. He anticipated about 50 people being at Friday's events.

FRIDAY'S ACTIONS

Rick and a colleague that did not attend the planning meeting (but has been an activist for many causes) arrived at the convention center together at 8:25. They found the smaller room that would be the venue of Friday's meeting, scheduled to begin at 9:00. A third colleague joined them; she was not at the planning meeting, but expressed interested in participating when Rick met her in the hall later in the day of the planning meeting. The room had eight round tables with about ten chairs at each. They placed flyers around the tables. The third colleague was unable to stay for the meeting and returned to campus as Reid Lyon arrived.

When about a dozen people were present, a member of the State Department of Education introduced herself and invited others to do so. New Mexico has an open meeting law that demands that public meetings be accessible to all interested attendees. However, we are not sure that the Friday meeting would be considered a public meeting because it appeared that one could attend only by invitation (although Rick's colleague had no invitation). In order not to violate anyone's confidentiality, we will be vague about exactly who attended and what they said, except for Rick's words and actions. Lyon was there; so was Robert Pasternack, a speaker from Thursday described as the Assistant Secretary for the U.S. Department of Education, Office of Special Education and Rehabilitative Services. There were two in-state district administrators, one active in a national organization for administrators. Other members of the state's department of education, the special education director that confronted Tom on Thursday, special education faculty from two different state universities, a dean from a college of education within the state, the state superintendent, an officer from one of the state's teacher organizations (unions) who is also a teacher, a state legislator, Rick, and Rick's colleague. Although the colleague was not on the signature-ready attendance list (which no one signed), he was not asked to leave. The special education director was running another meeting and attended the one with Lyon only sporadically.

Following introductions, Lyon spoke for almost 30 minutes. The contents of his talk was predictable (NRP summary) and will not be iterated here. He did say that the Higher Education Act was up for renewal and that there "will be changes." He did not explain what those changes might be. He said that NICHD was conducting studies now of second language learners because there is "nothing of quality" in the present ESL/bilingual literature, nor have there been studies "in the last 20 years . . . [that have] intellectual scientific strength." Pasternack interjected that the President requested that Pasternack and Lyon "meet with bodies all over the country" to talk about "standards of evidence by scientific bodies." In other words, the research with or on English-language learners and bilingual children and teachers is now dismissed in favor of the *science* that will be coming out of the NICHD.

Lyon said that teachers need to be involved in sustained staff development that includes ongoing conversations about how to meet the needs of their students. Someone would refute this later in the morning during an explanation of what is really happening with staff development in the shadow of the NRP report summary; she explained that there is no room for conversation, dissent, or thinking outside the NRP report summary.

After almost 30 minutes, Rick interrupted, "I do not mean to be rude, but I was invited to a conversation and that's not what is happening here. If others are not invited to speak, I will need to leave."

Lyon responded that there would be a conversation and that he only had a little more to say. He spoke for a few more minutes and then the state's superintendent interrupted him. Again, to preserve confidentiality, I will not report many of the specifics of the superintendent's frustrations and uneasiness about what to do to serve his state best. He did say that the NRP report addressed only 38% of his state's children and that left the majority of teachers and districts not knowing what to rely on for guidance in shaping a reading program. He expressed other concerns about teachers, culture, language, and diversity and the shortcomings of the report.

Another person in attendance made said that "we don't have answers" for the specifics of our state and another added that funding was tied to answers that did not apply to the state. Lyon said that the new research being conducted would address these issues in 2 years. Some said they did not have that much time because of pending state sanctions based on test scores. One person said that staff development most recently is only about specific programs and that there is not room for the conversations Lyon said are essential. One person said that when her district could rely on conversations, the scores rose. Another said that they could not find exemplary in-state programs to follow.

Rick noted the mounting frustration in the room as each person spoke, particularly when their concerns were dismissed by Lyon as already solved or being solved with the present line of NICHD-funded research. Then Pasternack said, pointing to the flyer, that he was enraged by the contents of the flyer. Rick, not acknowledging that he brought it (but sure most in the room knew he had) pointed out that it states that the NRP report is the source of the information. Lyon said the information was not from the report. Rick said he was pretty sure he could find the pages it came from. Then Pasternack said that if he still lived in New Mexico (where he worked in special education at the state department of education) that he would use the type of language he wanted to use to respond to the flyer. But, because he was working for "our president" he could not do that. Someone present said, "He's not my president." There was some laughter.

Rick said that Pasternack's response to the flyer was indicative of the deeper problem occurring right now. Rick explained that harassment and being harsh in response to a flyer indicated the lack of tolerance for dissent at the present time in our country. Further, teachers are convinced that their own decision-making is a form of dissent and, as such, is not welcomed. Rather, it is almost forbidden. Then Rick said that No Child Left Behind is not the president's idea, but that of Marion Wright-Edelman, founder of the Children's Defense Fund. She intended it to signify wrap around services for children that would include physical, psychological, and other needs being met. Rick also said that alternative licensure programs are hurting the state's children by putting underqualified teachers in classrooms. Such teachers rely on purchased reading programs and are not equipped to identify and address individual differences.

Rick's strategies were to take notes while others spoke, ensure that all voices could be heard, and develop a list (on the spot) of issues that were of concern to those around the table. He was not talking to Lyon or Pasternack; he was talking to the others around the table, the ones that might listen. The responses to Rick's remarks were two-fold. One was that Lyon and Pasternack dismissed them. The second was that some around the table agreed and told of specifics of their situations in which children would not be served well by the present climate and legislation.

Lyon responded by talking about differences between qualitative and quantitative research (something only he brought up and kept referring to). He talked of quantitative studies as *causal*; he said, "If A causes B, we should be doing A." Rick explained the difference between causal and correlational statistics and reminded Lyon that none of the studies in the

NRP report were causal. Lyon dismissed this and said that we know what causes children to read. Rick's hope was that some of those attending heard; Lyon did not.

Thirty minutes before the session ended, Rick excused himself to go meet a teacher-researcher that was working on a final draft of her study. He thought that such an exit was more effective than the quiet drifting out that often occurs at such meetings.

WHAT WE LEARNED

We are not sure we influenced federal reading policy—a wall is still a wall. But we learned some things. We learned that small well-planned acts of nonviolent civil disobedience can dramatically alter how people see an issue. The sea of fluorescent green flyers gradually filling a large conference room is a powerful image that will stay with those who saw it. That sea effectively competed with the huge video screens, scripted language, and amplified voices of the government's presentation. As the flyers passed from hand to hand, it changed the setting for the presentations from that of domination and acquiescence, to one of dialogue—a whispered dialogue, but one that could grow louder as the meeting went into its second day and as meetings are held around the country. People in the crowd who disagreed with what was being said could know that they were not alone, and people who were seeking a simple answer to "the reading problem" might begin to see complexity. And the powers-that-be received a strong message that some educators will not collapse into compliance under the weight of autocratic policies.

We also learned about the value of succinct language to make a few cogent points. We are a group of researchers and teachers who can talk for hours about reading and readers. Some of us have published articles and books on the topic. We are capable of creating streams of language that can drown those for whom reading is a necessity, tool, or even a joy. This situation called for a different approach. We needed to counter the sound bites, bullets, and glamour of No Child Left Behind with our own sound bites and bullets. We could not afford the glamour. The process of reducing our concerns to a one-page low budget flyer clarified our thinking and taught us that our first step was to open space between the two views and create a desire to know more. In that space, we could provide information. Our limited funds turned out to be an asset in the long run because we learned that we seek not to glorify with glitz but to educate with earnestness.

That earnestness was borne out in our physical presence as well. Tom became our hero as we watched him deal with the state and convention center staff peacefully, embracing them with the logical reasons for his right to be there. His courage and composure in the face of conflict taught us to take the floor gracefully and strongly, to keep it for just long enough, and to relinquish it gracefully when we have spoken our truth. And Rick was an activist who raised the volume of our collective voice from a whisper to a clear call for conversation rather than indoctrination. He used his presence to begin the conversation and them framed that work with a strategically planned exit.

But most of all, we felt alive and involved, rather than helpless and despairing in the face of No Child Left Behind. We found that our actions were less risky and more effective than we anticipated and that there are organizations and lawyers out there to help. We learned to value the energy we created with each other in the convention center, enabling us to let go of our expectations of changing the Federal government. We realized that the government will only change when enough of us begin to say we have had *enough*—enough of blaming children and teachers; enough of the view of teachers and children as diseased; and enough of holding up programs and reports as though they are a vaccine. There are other "*enoughs*" to consider: when *enough* of us point out the dissonance between educational policies grounded in democratic dialogue and legislated autocracy; when *enough* of us who work with children daily name aloud the difference between meeting the needs of the nation's children and standardizing practice; and when *enough* of us believe that our voices are important and we keep talking to each other, to anyone who will listen and to the wall; *then* we may see the wall crack, daylight stream in, and sense restored to an education system that has lost sight of so much of what we know about reading pedagogy and, most importantly, lost sight of children.

NEXT STEPS

We debriefed our experiences in smaller groups as we met for coffee, lunch, or interrupted each other's classes to talk about what occurred. We found that arriving late may be a good strategy because we did that on Thursday, acted quickly, and left. Friday's dynamic was different and arriving early worked best there. Timing is a key consideration.

As of this writing, some of us are planning the teach-in. We need to think about the goals and audiences of such an event and the president of the local teacher's union, hearing about our actions, approached us with the offer of siting the teach-in at union headquarters. We're also planning to write letters to the editor and op ed pieces because we want the public to be informed of the issues. And we are planning to have an intrastate meeting of teacher educators and other interested individuals in higher education. This meeting will serve to inform and open dialogue among our colleagues across the state. We need to collectively shape our goals as we work to move from enhanced consciousness to further actions.

FINAL REFLECTION (FOR NOW)

After our local action and the local actions of others around the country *some* national organizations became increasingly vocal, partly because their national conventions were sites of informational sessions, debates, unrest, and disagreement. The International Reading Association continued to take the official line that Reading First is an "opportunity to provide excellent reading instruction to children in high-poverty areas" (IRA, 2003, p. 1). The National Council of Teachers of English disagreed in a formal NCTE resolution stating that Reading First is "potentially harmful to children for several reasons" (NCTE, 2002, p. 1). But primarily resistance has remained that of the "guerilla option" in which teachers and university educators have quietly worked within the system to subvert the damaging effects of NCLB.

At the time of our own resistance efforts, we were silenced or dismissed in virtually every political forum in which we sought to engage in discussion about our concerns. We had attended state board of education meetings, legislative committee meetings at the state level, and meetings within our college. We felt desperate and as though we were lone voices in a huge abyss. Perhaps that sounds dramatic now, but at the time no one seemed to be listening. All actions grow out of contexts and our context was one of desperation and frustration.

But now, with the official position statement of NCTE, and with several of the Democratic Presidential candidates calling for the repeal of the NCLB act, the momentum seems to moving in a new direction. In each context, groups must work to understand what is going on and what actions they want to take to get their voices heard (see chapter 9 of Meyer, 2001, for ideas). They also need to consider possible repercussions and assess how willing they are to live with them. We can not provide a formula for action, but we know that the one action that perpetuates things we do not like is doing nothing. Doing nothing makes us complicit in keeping the wall in place. To that end all of us have continued the resistance individually and collectively. Tom has continued his work with local school systems and teachers' union. Rick and Leslie collaborated on a guest editorial criticizing the reading policies of the local and state super-intendents that was prominently featured in the local newspaper. All of us have continued to raise these issues in our graduate and undergraduate courses. It is through our local, state, and national actions that we will have our voices heard and do the work that will support teachers as pro-fessional decision-makers. Our hope is that locally generated action, now in conjunction with some national organizations and their state affiliates, will result in a wall so cracked that it will fall in upon itself.

REFERENCES

Adams, M. J. (1990). *Beginning to read: Thinking and learning about print.* Cambridge, MA: MIT Press.

Allington, R. (1997, August/September). Overselling phonics: Five unscientific assertions about reading instruction. *Reading Today,* 15–16.

Allington, R. (Ed.). (2002). *Big brother and the national reading curriculum: How ideology trumped evidence.* Portsmouth, NH: Heinemann.

Coles, G. (2000). *Misreading reading: The bad science that hurts children.* Portsmouth, NH: Heinemann.

Garan, E. (2001a, March). Beyond the smoke and mirrors: A critique of the National Reading Panel Report on Phonics. *Phi Delta Kappan, 82*(5), 500–506.

Garan, E. (2001b, September). What does the report of the national reading panel really tell us? *Language Arts, 79*(1), 61–71.

International Reading Association. (2003). IRA survey examines process for Reading First applications. *Reading Today, 20*(4), 1 & 3.

Metcalf, S. (2002, January 28). Reading between the lines. *Nation,* 18–22.

Meyer, R. (2001). *Phonics exposed: Understanding and resisting systematic direct intense phonics instruction.* Mahwah, NJ: Lawrence Erlbaum Associates.

National Council of Teachers of English. (2002). NCTE resolution of the Reading First Initiative. http://www.ncte.org/resolutions/readingfirst2002.shtml downloaded August 7, 2003.

National Reading Panel. (n.d.). *Teaching children to read: An evidence-based assessment of the scientific research literature on reading and its implications for reading instruction. Report of the subgroups.* Washington, DC: National Institutes of Health.

Snow, C., Burns, S., & Griffin, P. (Eds.). (1998). *Preventing reading difficulties in young children.* Washington, DC: National Academy Press.

Yatvin, J. (2002). Babes in the woods: The wanderings of the National Reading Panel. *Phi Delta Kappan, 83*(5), 364–369.

CHAPTER TWELVE

Where Do We Go From Here?

Leslie Poynor
Paula Wolfe

Many of the chapters in this book have served to describe the reality of our current political economy and its implication for public education in this country. And, the reality is harsh. Using a variety of scare tactics, the corporate and political right are exerting economic and political pressure to institute more for-profit scripted programs to be evaluated by for-profit standardized tests, which are culturally, linguistically, and economically biased against diverse populations of children. When those populations score poorly on such tests, the corporate and political right use those scores to claim that the teachers are not making "adequate progress" even with the for-profit scripted program. The right can then take over the school; sell it to a private corporation; blame colleges of education for failing to train teachers, and dismantle colleges of education so that there is no voice of protest in this process. This is a pretty bleak scenario. But, it is not the only scenario. For example, in chapter 1, *Relatively Speaking: McCarthyism and Teacher-Resisters,* Carole Edelsky begins by painting a distressing picture of the new McCarthyism and its impact on classroom teachers, but she also leaves us with a glimmer of hope as she describes how twenty educators across the country are engaging in acts of resistance in the areas of testing and curriculum. Likewise, in the preceding chapter, Rick Meyer along with several of his colleagues at the University of New Mexico describe the subversive acts of nonviolent civil disobedience in which they engaged in order to counter act the sophisticated, well orchestrated, and well funded misinformation events of the corporate and political right. The acts of these classroom teachers and teacher educators are encouraging and hopeful to all of us and it is that sense of hope that we want to build on, expand, foster, and nourish as we bring this book to a close.

In an effort to end on a hopeful note we offer a literature review of organizations actively involved in exposing and/or opposing the corporate and conservative agenda. We have loosely organized this review into three sections: philosophical, pedagogical, and overtly political.

The philosophical section can also be considered the alternative media section as it describes alternative media sources as well as organizations that offer more depth, more breadth, and more contextual reporting and information on educational issues and on the intersection of educational, political, and corporate agendas. This section is appropriate for educators seeking detailed information on what is happening "out there." The next section we have named the pedagogical section because it describes organizations that offer specific pedagogical suggestions and resources for teachers and teacher educators who are seeking to make social justice an active part of their classroom curriculum. The last section is the overtly political section. We say "overtly political," because we agree with Shor and Pari (1999) that *education is politics*, but this section refers to parent groups, coalitions, and organizations who have begun to actively challenge the conservative agenda through petitions, litigation, media campaigns, and protests. This section is for educators ready to become politically active for social justice.

All of the organizations listed in this chapter are accessible through the World Wide Web and most of the organizations have their own resource list that will lead to additional information, groups, and organizations. This review is only intended to be an introduction, a starting point. Because this is a listing of online organizations, this entire chapter is also accessible online at (http://www.erlbaum.com/poynor) to facilitate searching the resources included in this chapter.

PHILOSOPHICAL

Rethinking Schools (www.rethinkingschools.org)

Rethinking Schools is one of the most important sources of information for classroom teachers and teacher educators today. It is a quarterly education journal offered in both print and online versions that is "committed to equity and to the vision that public education is central to the creation of a humane, caring, multiracial democracy" (Rethinking Schools, 2003a). It was founded in 1986 in Milwaukee when a group of classroom teachers wanted to address problems with basal readers, standardized testing, and textbook-driven curriculum (sound familiar?). Today the journal is still a "small nonprofit organization directed by editors and editorial associates who volunteer their time" (Rethinking Schools, 2003a), and it still addresses the needs and concerns of classroom teachers teaching for social justice. Some of the issues that this journal has tackled are bilingual education, the education of gay, lesbian, and transgender students, the No Child Left Behind act, school vouchers, the Civil Rights movement, minority, education, sex education (or the lack thereof), teen pregnancy, teachers unions, creationism in public schools, and many, many other important and timely topics.

In addition to the quarterly education journal and the Web site, *Rethinking Schools* has published 12 books that address many of the above issues as well as others. For example, one of their publications is *Rethinking Globalization: Teaching for Justice in an Unjust World* (Bigelow & Peterson, 2001). This 400 page "comprehensive new book from Rethinking Schools helps teachers raise critical issues with students in grades 4–12 about the increasing globalization of the world's economies and infrastructures, and the many different impacts this trend has on our planet and those who live here" (Rethinking Schools, 2003b). Although it is reasonably priced ($18.95) educators do not have to purchase the book in order to benefit from the information and resources inside. Much of that information is also available free of charge online. And, finally, *Rethinking Schools* provides a resource list much like the one in this chapter only more comprehensive with "clickable" links to each site mentioned.

Substance (www.substancenews.com)

Another equally important, if less well known, publication is *Substance*. *Substance* is a monthly newspaper written by and for classroom teachers. Started in 1975, *Substance* has had as its mission to "report facts and provide interpretations of the news about public schools unhindered by the biases against public education that currently infest both the 'liberal' left and the 'conservative' right. We are also pro-union, pro-child, and pro-democracy" (Substance, 2003a). *Substance* reporters engage in investigative journalism and report on issues such as misuse of educational funds by boards of education, activities of teachers unions to support teachers, efforts to resist the conservative and corporate agenda and other little reported events in public education.

Substance is perhaps best known for the 1999 lawsuit filed against the newspaper and then editor George Schmidt for publishing the "complete text of six of the 22 Chicago Academic Standards (CASE) examinations" (Substance, 2003b). *Substance* printed the text of the examinations *after* the tests had been given as part of its ongoing critique of the misuse of standardized tests in Chicago. The Chicago Board of Education filed the lawsuit on January 26, 1999 asking for $1 million in damages and Schmidt lost his high school teaching position on February 1, 1999. Local newspapers, *The Chicago Tribune* and *The Chicago Sun Times* have run articles against both Schmidt and *Substance*, who have now filed a counter lawsuit for violation of First Amendment rights (Substance, 2003c).

EdResearch.info (www.edresearch.info)

For any educator interested in the use of educational research to determine or change current education policy as well as classroom practice the Web site *EdResearch.info* is an important source of information. Prominent scholars in the field of literacy education have organized the findings on current educational research on reading, writing, and testing. According to the Web site home page:

> *EdResearch.info* seeks to make the findings of independent, peer-reviewed, replicated research on reading and writing education, as well as information on publicly reported tests of reading and writing achievement, accessible to busy parents, educators, and policymakers in order that they may make informed decisions about education and educational policies. (EdResearch. info, 2003)

From the home page an educator can click on *Reading Research* and find a list of topics such as beginning reading instruction, comprehension, phonemic and phonological awareness, phonics, reading at grade level, scripted reading programs and many more topics related to reading. Each topic includes a definition of terms (i.e., what exactly is a phoneme?) in lay language accessible for parents or novice teachers and more importantly a presentation of research concerning the topic. The scholars associated with this Web site have organized the research in the following manner:

1. seminal research, what were the findings of the original study;
2. replication research, what were the findings of subsequent studies on the same issue; and
3. research review, what were the findings of a multiple studies on the same issues.

This Web site provides parents, teachers, and administrators with the replicated research findings necessary to support or change the instructional programs used at their school.

Fairness & Accuracy In Reporting (www.fair.org)

These three organizations just mentioned have dealt exclusively with alternative sources of information on educational issues, but the organization *Fairness & Accuracy In Reporting* (FAIR) is the national media watch group, that critiques media bias and censorship. We include FAIR in this review because public perception about education and educational issues is largely formed by the manner in which those issues are presented by the national media. Founded in 1986, FAIR has been active in "scrutinizing media practices that marginalize public interest, minority and dissenting viewpoints" (FAIR, 2003). FAIR not only offers educators an alternative new source, it offers us the opportunity to let FAIR know about the real education news that is often not reported. In addition to the online resources, FAIR publishes the magazine *Extra!*, and produces the weekly radio program *CounterSpin*.

CorpWatch (www.corpwatch.org)

As with FAIR, we include the organization *CorpWatch* in this review because much of what is happening to public education today is driven by the corporate agenda. *CorpWatch* works "to foster democratic control over corporations by building grassroots globalization—a diverse movement for human rights, labor rights and environmental justice" (CorpWatch, 2003). *CorpWatch* is most well known for their efforts to expose the working conditions in Vietnamese sweatshops producing Nike shoes and products. Their Web site includes information on how to conduct research on corporations for activist campaigns including how to develop a research plan and specific links on corporations and politics. This Web site is useful for anyone seeking to expose corporate control over public education.

Home Pages

We conclude this section with a list of three home Web pages of prominent education scholars. Using their own Web page, these scholars work to keep the public informed about important events, issues, policies, and legislation that affects public education and schooling. No doubt, there are more, but we select these three because they resonate with themes addressed in this book.

Susan Ohanian (www.susanohanian.org)

Susan Ohanian speaks out about a wide variety of issues ranging from the No Child Left Behind Act to standardized testing to what she describes as educational atrocities. It is an excellent source of information on what is happening "out there" with real parents, teachers, and students. Ohanian also has a comprehensive list of resources for educators who would like to become politically active (some of which are reviewed in this chapter).

Alfie Kohn (www.AlfieKohn.org)

Alfie Kohn addresses several issues on his Web site including parenting and classroom management, but, perhaps, the most important issue that he tackles is the standards and testing movement. In addition to providing a list of books and articles related to this topic, Kohn provides educators with four important links related to resisting the movement:

1. **why** we should oppose it;
2. **how** we can oppose it;
3. **whom** to contact; and
4. **where** to find more information.

Jill Kerper Mora (http://coe.sdsu.edu/people/jmora)

Jill Kerper Mora maintains a comprehensive Web site designed for students in teacher education courses at San Diego State University, for classroom teachers and administrators, for university colleagues, and for parents and other members of the community. Mora's Web site provides information about Cross-cultural Language and Academic Development (CLAD) for preservice and practicing teachers, tests for teacher candidates in California, and policy and legal issues. Mora provides an exceptionally thorough and detailed analysis of Proposition 227, the antibilingual, anti-immigrant proposition discussed in chapter 10.

PEDAGOGICAL

In this section we turn to those resources that provide teachers and teacher educators with specific pedagogical strategies that may be used to resist the current conservative and corporate agenda. This is not to say that the previously mentioned resources do not or could not provide pedagogical strategies, certainly they could and do, but their mission is also one of informing teachers, teacher educators, and the public at large about educational issues. The organizations that we list next also have as their mission informing the public, but they include specific pedagogical practices as part of their mission.

Teaching Tolerance (www.tolerance.org/teach/)

Teaching Tolerance is one of the many sister sites of *TOLERANCE.ORG*, a Web project of the Southern Poverty Law Center in Montgomery, Alabama. As with the organizations previously listed, *TOLERANCE.ORG* provides the public with information about the problem of hate and intolerance. *Teaching Tolerance* was founded in 1991 in an effort to help classroom teachers and other educators promote acceptance of racial diversity. Through the Web site and the print magazine entitled *Teaching Tolerance,* this organization "serves as a clearinghouse of information about anti-bias programs and activities being implemented in schools across the country" (Teaching Tolerance, 2003a).

On the Web site educators can find classroom activities for promoting peace, social justice, and tolerance as well as free resources such as videos, handbooks, texts, and posters. For example, one of the free curriculum kits offered is entitled "America's Civil Rights Movement," and includes the video, "A Time for Justice," the text, "Free at Last," and a teachers' guide for middle and upper grades. In addition to activities and resources, *Teaching Tolerance* offers grants of up to $2000 to classroom teachers attempting to create an antibias education initiative. In particular they fund grants that are "small-scale, resourceful and student-focused, promoting acceptance of diversity, peacemaking, community service or any other aspect of tolerance education" (Teaching Tolerance, 2003b). This Web site is for any educator looking for practical ways to bring equity and social justice into the curriculum.

Educators for Social Responsibility (www.esrnational.org)

Although not as comprehensive as *Teaching Tolerance, Educators for Social Responsibility* offers sample lesson plans, lists of children's literature, professional development programs (for a fee) and professional literature (for a fee) regarding conflict resolution, peace education, and intergroup relations. Their mission is to "make teaching social responsibility a core practice in education so that young people develop the convictions and skills needed to shape a safe, sustainable, democratic, and just world" (Educators for Social Responsibility, 2003). The free resources available to educators include links to downloadable information and materials to be used in the classroom as well as suggested classroom activities. One such link is to a description of Peter Elbow's "Believing Game" in which readers are provided information about the theoretical premise behind the game as well steps for playing the it with students. There are similar links to sites that deal with understanding propaganda, what teachers can do to address anti-Arab discrimination, how to handle bullying and many other issues peace and democracy.

The Gay, Lesbian, and Straight Education Network
(www.glsen.org)

The Gay, Lesbian, and Straight Education Network (GLSEN) "is the leading national organization fighting to end anti-gay bias in K–12 schools" (GLSEN, 2003). Because of its targeted mission to end antigay bias, this Web site is necessarily smaller than the preceding two; however, it does offer educators important downloadable (PDF) information for teachers interested in promoting safer classrooms and schools for gay, lesbian, bisexual, and transgender students. One of the articles available to teachers outlines practical strategies that a teacher can use to address homophobic behavior in the classroom. Other resources for teachers include annotated bibliographies, guides on coming out, opening dialogue and creating safe spaces, and links to information about legislation affecting gay, lesbian, bisexual, and transgender students and families.

OVERTLY POLITICAL

Clearly the organizations listed in the previous two sections are also highly political in their mission and their activities as are all educational organizations, but we have reserved this section for those organizations who are overtly, explicitly and directly challenging the current conservative corporate and political agenda. The organizations listed next are activist organizations that are working for social, political, and economic justice for public school children.

National Center for Fair & Open Testing
(www.fairtest.org)

We begin our examination of overtly political organizations with the *National Center for Fair & Open Testing (FairTest)*. *FairTest* is "an advocacy organization working to end the abuses, misuses and flaws of standardized testing and ensure that evaluation of students and workers is fair, open, and educationally sound" (National Center for Fair & Open Testing, 2003). In addition to its Web site *FairTest* publishes a quarterly newsletter ($30 for a yearly subscription), a wide variety of fact sheets about standardized and alternative forms of testing, as well as a catalog of materials for parents, students, teachers, and researchers. Commercially published materials range from $15 to $50, but publications produced by the *Fair-Test* staff are reasonably priced between $5 and $15.

FairTest has a number of projects including promoting the optional use of test scores in college admissions, attacking the notion that test scores are equivalent to merit, and exposing the flaws in employment tests for hiring and promoting teachers, but perhaps, their biggest project is the Assessment Reform Network (ARN). On the ARN link educators will find information about antistandardized testing activities in states across the nation as well as information about how to start and sustain those activities in states that do not already have an ARN coordinator. The ARN Web site provides informational resources, media guides for working with local and national media sources, and critiques of local, district, state, and federal policy, particularly the No Child Left Behind Act. This Web site is an important first step for educators looking to connect with local organizations committed to resisting and repealing high stakes testing.

California Coalition for Authentic Reform in Education (www.calcare.org)

In addition to the ARN organization which provides a state by state listing of resources for activist working to eliminate or drastically reduce the use of standardized testing in public schools there are many other local and state antitesting organizations. The *California Coalition for Authentic Reform in Education* (*CalCare*) is one such group. We highlight it here as an example of the types of activities carried out at the local and state level. For example, *CalCare* has links to information about how standardized testing hurts children, how parents can opt out of having their child tested, what laws impact standardized testing, and suggestions for teachers, parents, and students interested in organizing local resistance to high stakes testing. *CalCare* also provides links to the activities of other state and national organizations involved in testing and education reform.

Teacher Union Reform Network (www.turnexchange.net)

The *Teacher Union Reform Network* (TURN) is an organization made up of members from the National Education Association and the American Federation of Teachers local unions. TURN members are making an effort to "restructure the nation's teachers unions to promote reforms that will ultimately lead to better learning and higher achievement for all students" (Teacher Union Reform Network, 2003). Specifically TURN seeks to involve more classroom teachers in the process of reform through Local Action Plans which promote "collaboration with other stakeholders; engagement of members and other partners; promoting union changes and increasing locals' capacity to implement these goals; and linking all reforms to improved student learning (Teacher Union Reform Network, 2003). Teachers who are interested in becoming politically active with local and national educational reform would find this site helpful.

No Child Left.com (www.nochildleft.com)

No Child Left.com is a Web site publication by Jamie McKenzie, Ed.D., and *From Now On* (FNO) press in Bellingham, Washington. McKenzie and this Web site are dedicated to repealing or amending the No Child Left Behind Act. McKenzie argues,

> After decades of both parties supporting a limited federal role in educational matters, we now face a broad-based assault on public education from the Beltway. State rights? Local control? This education law makes a mockery of those concepts as it imposes radical and often untested change strategies across all districts. (No Child Left.com, 2003a)

> High stakes testing by itself does not improve the lives of children and an undue emphasis on punishment, negative labels and threats can do great damage to schools and children. At the same time, experimentation with competitive, corporate management strategies is reckless and irresponsible. We have seen the marvels of corporate excess during the past decade and need not impose them on schools. (No Child Left.com, 2003b)

McKenzie's Web site is a wealth of information about the problematic and dangerous aspects of the No Child Left Behind Act. His list of 18 issues is compromised of topics ranging from the reckless nature of the Act to the invasion of corporate charters. In addition, McKenzie provides educators with a list of strategies in which they can engage to help change or repeal this law, including links to Senators and Representatives and a free subscription to the No Child Left.com newsletter.

Partners for Public Education
(www.everychildcounts.org)

The National Association for the Advancement of Colored People (NAACP) and the People For the American Way Foundation (PFAWF) created *Partners for Public Education* in 1997 bringing together the NAACP's 93 years of civil rights advocacy and the PFAWF's expertise on the Religious Right and civil liberties. On their joint Web site, the two organizations argue that,

> For years, the backers of school vouchers have told the public that our pub-
> lic schools are a bloated failure that could be improved only by competition.
> It is a message of despair, generated by critics who never much cared for
> public education anyway. (Partners for Public Education, 2003)

In addition to providing background information on why vouchers will
not work, the Web site also suggests 10 things a parent or educator can do
to help schools. And, of course, there are links to both the NAACP and
PFAWF Web sites which list ways in which educators can become politically active through either or both of the organizations including joining
the organizations and staying informed about the actions of the Religious
Right and the federal government.

CONCLUSION

As Carole Edelsky (chapter one) remarked at the beginning of this book
we are living in the best of times and the worst of times. Much of what is
"worst" has been delineated in the preceding chapters and it is bad, but it
is not without hope. What makes these the best of times are the everyday
teachers and teacher educators who are organizing and fighting and making a difference. As Paulo Freire (1996) once said, "you never get *there* by
starting from *there*, you get *there* by starting from *here*" (p. 58, emphasis
in the original). We hope this book has provided enough information
about where "here" is that you will join us in the struggle to reach a more
equitable, just, humane, and radically democratic "there."

REFERENCES.

Bigelow, B., & Peterson, B. (2001). *Rethinking globalization: Teaching for justice in an unjust world.* Milwaukee, WI: Rethinking Schools.
CorpWatch. (2003). "History & Mission" Web page. Retrieved on February 1, 2003 from
http://www.corpwatch.org/about/PAM.jsp.
EdResearch.info. (2003). "Home" Web page. Retrieved on February 1, 2003 from http://
www.edresearch.info.
Educators for Social Responsibility. (2003). "Home" Web page. Retrieved on February 1,
2003 from http://www.esrnational.org
Fairness & Accuracy In Reporting. (2003). "What's FAIR" Web page. Retrieved on February 1,
2003 from http://www.fair.org/whats-fair.html.
Freire, P. (1996). *Pedagogy of hope.* New York: Continuum.
GSLEN. (2003). "About" Web page. Retrieved on February 1, 2003 from http://www.glsen.
org/templates/about/index.html.
National Center for Fair & Open Testing. (2003). "Home" Web page. Retrieved on February
1, 2003 from http://www.fairtest.org.

No Child Left.com. (2003a). "Articles" Web page. Retrieved on February 1, 2003 from http://www.nochildleft.com/articles.html.

No Child Left.com. (2003b). "About No Child Left.com" Web page. Retrieved on February 1, 2003 from http://www.nochildleft.com/about.html.

Partners for Public Education. (2003). "More about our partnership" Web page. Retrieved on February 1, 2003 from http://www.everychildcounts.org.

Rethinking Schools. (2003a). "Who we are" Web page. Retrieved on February 1, 2003 from http://www.rethinkingschools.org/about/index.shtml.

Rethinking Schools. (2003b). "Publications" Web page. Retrieved on February 1, 2003 from http://www.rethinkingschools.org/publication/index.shtml.

Shor, I., & Pari, C. (1999). *Education is politics: Critical teaching across differences, K–12.* Portsmouth, NH: Heinemann.

Substance. (2003a). "Mission" Web page. Retrieved on February 1, 2003 from http://www.substancenews.com/mission.htm.

Substance. (2003b). "Update" Web page. Retrieved on February 1, 2003 from http://www.substancenews.com/update.htm.

Substance. (2003c). "Background" Web page. Retrieved on February 1, 2003 from http://www.substancenews.com/background.htm.

Teaching Tolerance. (2003a). "About Teaching Tolerance" Web page. Retrieved on February 1, 2003 from http://www.tolerance.org/teach/about/index.jsp.

Teaching Tolerance. (2003b). "Grant Application Guide" Web page. Retrieved on February 1, 2003 from http://www.tolerance.org/teach/expand/gra/guide.jsp.

Teacher Union Reform Network. (2003). "Why TURN" Web page. Retrieved on February 1, 2003 from http://www.turnexchange.net/about.htm.

Author Index

Note: Page numbers in *italic* refer to reference pages; those followed by "n" refer to footnotes.

A

Abanes, R., 99, *107*
A Beka Book, 95, *107*
Abell Foundation, 45, *47*
Adams, M. J., 34, *47*, 168, *183*
Alcoff, L., 129, *131*
Allington, R. L., 2, 4, *8*, 41, 42, 44, *47*, 56, 59, *61*, 88n, 90, *91*, 104, *107*, 168, *183*
Altwerger, B., 33, *47*, 57, *61*, 103, *107*
Alvarez, L., 136, *147*
American Educational Research Association, 137n, *147*
American Institutes for Research, 113
Anderson, G. E., 68, 69, 77
Apple, M. W., 14, *27*, 60, *61*
Appleby, R. S., 94n, *109*
Applegate, B., 136n, *149*
Armbruster, B. B., 44, *47*, *91*, *107*
Armstrong, K., 94n, 102, *108*
Asato, J., 161, *163*
Augustine, N., 37, *47*
Averill, L. J., 95, *108*

B

Baker, C., 153, *162*
Baker, D., 151, *162*
Baker, K., *162*
Baker, R., 12, 16, *27*
Balta, V., 59, *61*, 88n

Baquedano-López, P., 161, *163*
Baron, J., *131*
Bassett, K., *9*
Bebell, D., 68, *78*
Benen, S., 101, *108*
Berkowitz, B., 17, *27*
Berliner, D., 2, *8*, 14, *27*, 135n, 136n, 147, *147*, 154, *162*
Beykont, Z., 161, *162*
Biddle, B., 2, *8*, 14, *27*, 135n, 136n, 147, *147*, 154, *162*
Bigelow, B., 187, *195*
Bland, K., 144n, *147*
Blumenfeld, S. L., 96, 97, *108*
Bonfiglio, O., 93, *108*
Boruch, R., *131*
Bracey, G., 2, 5, *8*, 135n, 136n, *147*, *148*
Bridger, F., 99, *108*
Brinkley, E. H., 95, 100, 104, 107, *108*, *110*
Bulkley, K., 141, *148*
Burke, C. L., 68, *78*
Burns, M. S., 3, *9*, *48*, 55, *61*, 168, *183*
Business Roundable, 37, *47*, 71, 77

C

Caddy, B. B., 97, *108*
Camilli, G., 3, *8*, 141, *148*
Censorship Dateline, 99, *108*
Chapman, J., 95, *108*
Chastain, K., 153, *162*

197

Subject Index

Note: Page numbers in **boldface** refer to tables; those followed by "n" refer to footnotes.